MOSQUES IN AMERICA

A Guide to Accountable Permit Hearings and Continuing Citizen Oversight

2nd Edition

By Karen Lugo, Esq.

Constitutional Law Specialist
RLUIPA Analyst and Litigator

For more information about this book, visit
SECUREFREEDOM.ORG

Mosques in America is published in the United States
by the Center for Security Policy Press,
a division of the Center for Security Policy.

ISBN-13: 978-1540729170

ISBN-10: 1540729176

The Center for Security Policy
Washington, D.C.
Phone: 202-835-9077
Email: info@SecureFreedom.org
For more information, visit SecureFreedom.org

Book design by Bravura Books
Cover design by J.P. Zarruk

TABLE OF CONTENTS

FOREWORD

America has throughout its history been characterized as a "melting pot" in which immigrants from countries, cultures, religious backgrounds and ethnic communities around the world have created "E Pluribus, Unum" – out of many, one. While there have been times when the size of a particular influx has created backlashes towards the migrants, the United States' record, on the whole, is one of extraordinary tolerance and generosity.

On balance, the country has benefited greatly from the addition of those who have come, as the poet put it, "yearning to breathe free" and willing to assimilate, become part of the fabric of this country and make it a better place for newcomers and those who came before, alike.

Never in our national experience, however, have we faced the challenges associated with the arrival here of a large population that adheres, to varying degrees, to a totalitarian ideology that is utterly at odds with the foundational principles and constitutional freedoms of this Republic. Muslims who believe their faith requires them to respect Sharia dictates above American law seek neither to assimilate nor otherwise to support American values, norms or laws.

The danger posed by such Islamic supremacists to a pluralistic and open society like ours can be acute to the extent that they conceal as religious practice what are, in fact, fundamentally autocratic efforts by clerics and others aimed at, in the words of the Muslim Brotherhood, "destroying Western civilization from within...by [non-Muslims'] hands and the hands of the believers so that Allah's religion is made victorious over all other religions."

As this book documents, such Islamist ambitions are a threat to America's peaceable, tolerant and law-abiding Muslims – many of whom came here to get away from Sharia in their native lands – as well as to non-Muslim communities. Written by Karen Lugo, an attorney with extensive experience in First Amendment constitutional law and in helping those seeking to protect our freedoms against all enemies, foreign and domestic, *Mosques Under Scrutiny* is a how-to manual for patriotic Americans who are ready to counter the leading edge of Islamic supremacism: its infrastructure-building through the construction of Sharia-promoting mosques that serve to alienate and radicalize.

Ms. Lugo offers a model case study to illustrate how Islamist operatives may be using our laws and regulations designed to promote free and accessible religious practice to place isolationist and extremist mosques in

1

residential areas.   She both shows how scrutiny of the process and deliberative community input is critical to assuring outcomes that protect community interests while following federal law that governs religious land use. Of particular value are her insights and practical advice for activists on how to address the land use process, as well as challenge other Islamist assaults on the American way of life.

One element of Ms. Lugo's recommended approach bears special mention here: the crucial role that can be played by Muslims who reject Islamic supremacism. Those, like Dr. Zuhdi Jasser and the other signatories of the incalculably important "Muslim Reform Manifesto" – who recognize Sharia as "man-made law," not holy writ, and, therefore, reject its imposition in American mosques and American communities – are not just natural allies of freedom-loving non-Muslim Americans. They may be the single most effective force-multiplier to counter Islamists' demands for anti-constitutional accommodations.

It is our hope that this handbook will prove to be both an inspiration and an invaluable guide to our countrymen and women of all faiths in understanding – and effectively countering – the Muslim Brotherhood's civilization jihad.

Frank J. Gaffney, Jr.
President & CEO
Center for Security Policy
November 2016

2

Introduction

Americans have to face the fact that the cultural victories won by Islamists – as distinguished from reformist and compatible Muslims – are in no small measure due to American indifference.

To be sure, many elected representatives and judges are infected by "political correctness." But this is only because Americans have allowed these attitudes to shape official actions. Many missed opportunities at the local level, over as many years, have contributed to the victories that Islamists, often in alliance with the Left, have come to expect. This book is intended to help American citizens avoid such "unforced errors."

When schools offer up so-called "dominant culture" holidays like Christmas, Thanksgiving, and Valentine's Day to appease the diversity activists; when city councils and Human Relations Commissions move to censure the speech of citizens and other local officials; when the media endorse unverified "hate crimes" and peddle Muslim victimization; when schools assign projects based on overt Islamic religious dogma; when public officials appear with Islamist activists in one-sided townhalls; when church leaders invite unapologetic Islamists into the interfaith fold – all without remarkable objection – it should be no surprise that the cultural assaults gain steam and momentum.

In light of refugee resettlement and migration trends, it is more urgent than ever for communities to set constitutional cultural standards and assimilation expectations. Tensions have run high in places like Minnesota where Muslim immigrants, most from Somalia, have been settled in large numbers. Rather than hold Muslim groups accountable to reassure Minnesota residents with integration plans and anti-radicalization programs, Governor Mark Dayton and U.S. Attorney Andrew Lugar have used their official capacities to lecture citizens on Islamophobia and intolerance.[1]

When one contemplates that the city of Hamtramck in Michigan was ninety percent Polish in 1970, and in November of 2015, was the first American municipality to elect a Muslim majority city council, it shows that minor shifts in demographics and attitudes can accrue over years to a transformational pendulum swing. This 22,000-resident Detroit suburb

---

[1] Johnson, Scott W. "Islam and Minnesota: Can We Hear Some Straight Talk for a Change?" *Minneapolis Star Tribune* (23 Dec. 2015), http://www.startribune.com/islam-and-minnesota-can-we-hear-some-straight-talk-for-a-change/363426091/; *also see,* Ikeogu, Vidki. "Gov. Dayton Provides Harsh Criticism of Racial Tensions." *St. Cloud Times* (14 Oct. 2015), http://www.sctimes.com/story/news/local/2015/10/13/gov-dayton-provides-harsh-criticism-racial-tensions/73836696/.

became one the first in America to hear the Muslim call to prayer broadcast five times a day from several of a half dozen[2] mosques, starting at 6:00 in the morning. Schools and city government offices now close on Muslim holy days[3] and regulations prohibit the sale of alcohol within 500 feet of any of the city's mosques.[4]

Hamtramck is a textbook case from the European experience: concentrated Islamic immigrant settlements, piecemeal accommodation, and incremental cultural concessions. We may not know the extent of the radical tendencies of the mosques in Hamtramck – mostly Bosnian and Bangladeshi extraction[5] – but if they follow the trends across America, the tenets of Islamic supremacist doctrine known as Sharia likely taught there do not uphold American principles of free speech, freedom to choose or leave a religion, separation of mosque and state, and equal rights for women.

Other American towns and cities may choose a very different path. While the following account is based upon a different religious contest, it shows that Americans are capable of coming together in resounding defense of community values. When the Freedom From Religion Foundation organization in Pittsburgh, Wisconsin demanded that a post-9/11 "God Bless America" banner be removed from the town post office wall, fifteen hundred new "God Bless America" signs appeared all over town. Cars lined up for more than two blocks to pick up signs and banners but the supply was gone in forty-five minutes.[6] This community non-sectarian shout-out was irrefutable notice to any objector's attempt to suppress the town's show of cultural solidarity. This town may have lost the legal battle but it surely won the war of wills.

It is the responsibility of alert local citizens to plant the "land of the free; home of the brave" flag, and then fiercely hold the ground. Help is not coming from state or federal governments. Every time there is an impulse to apologize or concede a tradition, a reasoned and relentless counter-

---

[2] "Hamtramck, MI Mosques." *Yellowpages.com* (N.D). http://www.yellowpages.com/hamtramck-mi/mosques.

[3] Associated Press. "Hamtramck, A 12-Mosque Town in The Heart of America." *Daily Mail* (19 Jan. 2016). http://www.dailymail.co.uk/wires/afp/article-3406132/Hamtramck-12-mosque-town-heart-America.html..

[4] Bailey, Sarah P. "In The First Majority-Muslim U.S. City, Residents Tense About Its Future." *Daily Mail* (21 Nov. 2015). https://www.washingtonpost.com/national/for-the-first-majority-muslim-us-city-residents-tense-about-its-future/2015/11/21/45d0ea96-8a24-11e5-be39-0034bb576eee_story.html.

[5] *Ibid*. ("The city is about 23 percent Arabic, 19 percent Bangladeshi and 7 percent Bosnian.")

[6] Stavola, Michael. "Blessings - More Than 1,000 'God Bless America' Signs Given Away As Backlash Grows." *The Morning Sun*, Pittsburg, Kansas. (1 Feb. 2016), http://www.morningsun.net/news/20160129/blessings---more-than-1000-god-bless-america-signs-given-away-as-backlash-grows.

campaign is required. One lesson that should have been well-learned by now is that it is many times harder to regain ground lost – and then fortified – than it is to never let go in the first place.

It may be startling to consider but Islamists are entitled to exploit liberal free speech rights to advance their political and legal operations. Up to the point that they illegally subvert American law or plan specific violent acts, they are free to coerce thought leaders by threatening public officials with charges of bigotry and intolerance name-calling. Americans are equally free and certainly entitled to employ freedom of speech in counter-offensives to challenge this narrative and thwart excessive demands.

Islamists do get away with covertly teaching Sharia compliance in many mosques. Even though they advocate an alternate system of rules and loyalties, no Western countries or states have conducted serious investigations into how widespread is this practice. The few substantive investigations have been undertaken by journalists and think tanks as exemplified by an undercover expose from Denmark where a subject Muslim woman is counseled in several mosques that "[s]he must not take a job without her husband's permission, and even if her husband continues to beat her, she must not contact the police."[7] A similar BBC undercover project in Britain showed a Sharia judge responding to a wife who complained that her husband was hitting her. The Sharia arbiter advised her to "be courageous" enough to ask whether her husband was upset by her cooking, or was it happening because she sees her friends? He cautioned the woman to only go to the police as a "very last resort."[8]

The resulting communal allegiance to Sharia rules defeats interest in joining American culture but Islamists also go further by claiming victimhood to gain societal privileged status. Examples of success at curtailing free speech, demanding unreasonable employer concessions, requiring public halal food service, and imposing affirmative action-like curriculum bias are just first steps if America is to follow Europe's path.

Government officials and judges will not stop these influence operations and, in many cases, they have no constitutional authority to suppress the sophisticated public relations campaigns. Other minority groups have little interest in competing with the aggressive Islamist agendas. Thus, if American culture is to be preserved, these Islamist strategies must be

---

[7] Bergman, Judith. "Sharia in Denmark." *Gatestone Institute* (22 Mar. 2016), http://www.gatestoneinstitute.org/7648/denmark-sharia.

[8] "Panorama: Secrets of Britain's Sharia Councils, Part One, and Part Two." *YouTube/BBC* (22 Apr. 2013), https://www.youtube.com/watch?v=4gZCFdHkd4A, *and;* https://www.youtube.com/watch?v=tQ3PIhFHDdE.

challenged in the neighborhoods and communities that will marshal necessary moral resolve and political will.

Community interest in whether new migrants or resident Muslims intend to meaningfully integrate must start at the mosque. The mosque is the heart of Islamic religious life and, beyond offering religious teaching, most imams provide the rules that govern family, professional, political, and personal life. For adherent Muslims, the mosque is central to everything that touches life. As former Muslim and Sharia jurist, Sam Solomon has noted: "A mosque is a seat of government. A mosque is a school. A mosque is a court. A mosque is a training center. A mosque is a gathering place, or social center. It is not just a place of 'worship,' per se, as worship only."[9]

When Muslims deny the separation between mosque and state that must underlie a legislative societal compact, there will be an inevitable clash between strict religious authority and representative-created law. Compounding this challenge, Islamic Sharia rules deny the vital attributes of self-determination and equal standing that must bind a democratic society.

As America faces increasing Islamic assimilation and radicalization challenges, the mosque is the baseline for those concerned about the clash of cultures. Either mosques and imams will become part of the solution as promoters of integration and disruptors of radicalization, or they will be increasingly recognized as part of the problem.

Whether or not law enforcement's role in surveillance of suspicious mosque activity is further questioned and re-characterized, communities will always have a unique responsibility to ask defining questions of mosque leadership. If communities do not set the expectations for integration and engagement, countries in Europe and Great Britain have proven that the consequence will be separate settlements that breed victimization and hostility.

Similar to the religiously based groups that have confronted institutionalized scandals that also manifest as societal challenges, Muslim leaders must be held accountable. The Catholic Church and the Scientology organization provide recent example where the media, the public, and law enforcement forced internal issues out into the arena of general scrutiny and accountability. Any denominational religious organization in America that disrespects foundational human rights can expect pressure from outside forces. Why should Islamic groups be exempted? Was it any more "Cathlicophobic" to ask that church leaders confront sex sins than it is "Islamophobic" to ask Muslims to address dangerous radicalization advocacy?

---

[9] "Sam Solomon, What is a Mosque?" at the 1:10 mark, *MRCTV* (11 Dec. 2011), http://www.mrctv.org/videos/sam-solomon-what-mosque.

Engagement should start when plans are announced to site a new mosque in town. Most cities have zoning rules but federal and constitutional law requires that planning commissions treat religious assemblies generously. Even with these relatively new advantages, religious groups still must provide honest expectations of the burden to be borne by surrounding businesses and homes. They also are required to comply with officials' final approval terms.

Giving more demanding religious groups favored treatment, or relaxed enforcement, undermines the rule of law. Islamic applicants are very experienced at leveraging political pressure, legal tools, and Department of Justice intervention in search of protected status. But this is where equal standards and consistent enforcement are critical. The "broken windows"[10] enforcement doctrine generally stands for the proposition that when minor infractions are not corrected for the good of the public order (like allowing taxi drivers to double park during prayer hours[11]), those illicit practices will be accepted as norms, and even larger violations will follow.

When mosques are sited in residential neighborhoods, there is special sensitivity to their meeting schedules that are more frequent, different in purpose, and more heavily attended than numbers presented at land use permit hearings. Questions have arisen as to whether unique characteristics of Islamic practices should be fully described for more clear predictability during the initial permit process. There are legal and constitutional protections against religious discrimination and unequal treatment – as compared to other religious and to non-religious assemblies – of religious permit applications. Yet zoning authorities should be equipped to apply adequate restrictions on conditional uses that represent an intolerable burden on areas, like residential neighborhoods, that are zoned primarily for other than assembly purposes.

Concerned residents often do not understand the limits on city planners or the deference that must be shown to religious organizations. Federal law now requires that state and local authorities consider religious land use applications as similar to generic assembly uses: some examples might be restaurants, theaters, buildings with meeting areas, or organized groups like Rotary Club halls. Thus, the process of noting distinctions between one

---

[10] Mac Donald, Heather. "How Broken Windows Policing Puts Fewer Men in Prison." *Time Magazine* (17 Dec. 2014), http://time.com/3638183/eric-garner-nypd-broken-windows-policing/.

[11] Licea, Melkorka. "Hundred of Cabbies Ticketed While Praying in Mosque." *New York Post* (26 Jun. 2015), http://nypost.com/2015/06/26/hundreds-of-cabbies-ticketed-while-praying-in-mosque/, (Taxi driver cited for double parking near the Islamic Cultural Center on Riverside Drive near West 72nd Street in New York is quoted: "This is a special prayer time, a time for religion. We double-park here every Friday and they [allow it], but today they gave us all tickets, almost 100 cabs.")

and another kind of activity is complicated. Federal law also discourages municipal decisions that impose what the law considers to be a "substantial burden" on religious activity.

Based upon these issues, the public hearings for new mosques or expansions reflect frustration, uncertainty, and fear. Consequently, public comments are often confused and not focused on appropriate issues for official consideration.

In light of the consternation surrounding new mosque applications, this book is offered to provide an overview of applicable federal law, state regulatory power, and local zoning codes. It is also designed to suggest constructive roles for residents who will provide necessary oversight and scrutiny. Islamic applicants have the same rights as any other religious organization but they also have the same responsibilities to follow the rules: from filing of a detailed application to providing accurate responses to city queries. Importantly, city officials should not be either intimidated or overawed by the controversy that may attend these hearings. All permits, especially those that involve variances or conditional uses, must be based upon adequate research and a fully participatory public hearing.

This guide will also address the growing concern over radicalization activities in mosques, as an increasing number of people (according to one survey, fifty-two percent across nine Western nations) say they are very concerned about Islamic extremism.[12] There is confusion over what roles law enforcement, local land-use officials, and private citizens may perform in response to this trend. And there is controversy over what are the most effective approaches to combat extremism from legal and political tactics to organized local resident efforts.

Americans have a unique window of opportunity created by committed and courageous Muslim reformers. Enabled by constitutional speech liberties, these reformers seek to hold local imams accountable to the Muslim Reform Movement's declaration for secular governance, free speech including criticism of Islam, and freedom to leave a religion (or to express fidelity to no faith).[13] Concerned citizens should seize this offer to partner with like-minded Muslims in defense of foundational constitutional principles.

As a constitutional law attorney, this author has testified at many city and county hearings, has litigated religious land use cases, and has learned the

---

[12] Poushter, Jacob. "Extremism Concerns Growing in West Especially and Predominately Muslim Countries." *Pew Research Center* (16 Jul. 2015), http://www.pewglobal.org/2015/07/16/extremism-concerns-growing-in-west-and-predominantly-muslim-countries/.

[13] "Support Muslim Reform." *Change.org* (2015), https://www.change.org/p/muslims-and-neighbors-we-support-the-muslim-reform-movement.

inestimable value of being able to quote America's patriotic Muslim leaders, like Dr. Zuhdi Jasser of the American Islamic Foundation for Democracy (AIFD),[14] journalists Asra Nomani and Hala Arafa,[15] author Irshad Manji, physician and "non-Islamist Muslim," Dr. Qanta Ahmed,[16] author Dr. Tawfiq Hamid,[17] Ani Zonneveld of Muslims for Progressive Values (MPV)[18] and Shireen Qudosi of CounterJihad.[19] The words of reasoned and conscientious Muslims leaders make it is very difficult for elected officials to dismiss concerns over Islamist agendas that would defeat the very efforts of valiant Muslim reformers. These courageous activists are the vanguard that challenges Islamism from within the socio-religious construct while they fight to bring Islamic practices in line with American constitutional standards.

Each of these Muslim leaders has an individual and unique approach to a belief system generally called "Islam." How they interpret and contextualize the teachings is a personal matter. As long as anyone - of any faith - stands squarely and faithfully on constitutionally prescribed principles, rights, and foundational liberties as demonstrated by emphatic public declarations and consistent conduct, they are free to choose personal beliefs. Freedom of conscience guarantees all Americans this right. Freedom of speech then gives all Americans the opportunity to debate and discuss perspectives on religious and political matters.

Like the Ahmadi Muslim shopkeeper in Scotland[20] who was brutally murdered after posting on Easter of his love for his Christian nation, some

---

[14] American Islamic Forum for Democracy. http://aifdemocracy.org/.

[15] Nomani, Asra Q. and Arafa, Hala. "As Muslim Women, We Actually Ask You Not To Wear The Hijab in The Name of Interfaith Solidarity." The Washington Post (21 Dec. 2015), https://www.washingtonpost.com/news/acts-of-faith/wp/2015/12/21/as-muslim-women-we-actually-ask-you-not-to-wear-the-hijab-in-the-name-of-interfaith-solidarity/.

[16] Ahmed, Qanta. "Radical Islam Exists: Islamism IS The New Totalitarianism." *Investigative Project* (12 Feb. 2015), http://www.investigativeproject.org/4774/radical-islam-exists-islamism-is-the-new

> All Islamists are incontrovertibly Muslim. Even so, the most numerous subjugates of Islamism, including its violence, are Muslims. Islamism is connected to Islam while representing no aspect of Islam. Islamism is connected to Islam at Islam's expense. Without Islam, there would be no Islamism which steals both legitimacy and shelter from Islam. This parasitization is not to be blamed on Islam, but it is to be blamed on Muslims who are Islamists, and on Muslim patrons of Islamism.

[17] Dr. Tawfik Hamid, http://www.tawfikhamid.com/. ("I am a Muslim by faith ... Christian by the spirit ... a Jew by heart ... but above all, I am a human being.")

[18] Muslims for Progressive Values. http://www.mpvusa.org/ani-zonneveld/.

[19] Counter-Jihad. http://counterjihad.com/blackeid-youtube-censorship.

[20] Morgan, Tom. "Muslim Shopkeeper Murdered in Suspected Religiously Prejudice Attack After Posting Love for Christians." *Telegraph Newspaper,* London (26 Mar. 2016),

Muslims are happy to be part of Western societies. Some take great risks to declare for modernization as they courageously take on the cause of reform within their faith community. They may be the West's greatest hope in the campaign against Islamist hardliners. There is much that may be accomplished by uniting with them in defense of our neighborhoods and in the American cause of liberty, self-determination, and individual rights.

Some may turn to this book as concerned citizens and some may be municipal staff or zoning officials. In all cases, it may be a good idea to start by reviewing the Conclusion section for a survey of the content highlights and a summary of key points.

Karen Lugo, Esq.
November 2016

---

http://www.telegraph.co.uk/news/2016/03/26/muslim-shopkeeper-murdered-in-suspected-religiously-prejudiced-a/

1. CITY HALL AND MOSQUE BUILDING PROJECTS

State governments are vested with the power to regulate land use according to police powers, or what is commonly understood as the regulation of state policy to further health, safety, morals, and general welfare of inhabitants.[21] However, constitutional and federal law protections for religious assembly command higher status than these state powers and cities must recognize the supremacy of overarching federal laws. When politically savvy and financially capable organizations are prepared to appeal directly to the courts and federal agencies to gain the benefit of these protections, local agency proceedings will be scrutinized closely for balanced treatment and deliberative process. Dissatisfied minority-faith applicants and the Department of Justice Civil Rights Division may also initiate lawsuits over adverse land use decisions.

Although the overlapping legal layers appear daunting, there is a very important role for residents to play. And in order to provide oversight of the permitting process, concerned citizens do not need to be experts in zoning or religious land use law. Local residents must only invest the time necessary to monitor the process from start to finish, review the applicable zoning rules, and investigate the treatment of other similar applications. This simply involves research on the city or county website and attendance at hearings. Support projects may be organized according to individual interest and research may be assigned to volunteer committee members.

The real challenge for all involved in scrutinizing the zoning permitting process is to understand what role civil authorities are tasked to fulfill and what part community members may play both inside and outside of the hearing procedures. Understanding the limits on local officials on one hand, and the tendency for some to act outside those limits when pursuing a personal agenda or bias on the other, is vital to the indispensible citizen role in oversight and input.

As mosque sponsor organizations have acquired experience and learned to anticipate land use procedures and the corresponding political component, they have become increasingly sophisticated in presenting applications to local government land planners. They often organize their membership

---

[21] "Guide to Planning and Zoning Laws of New York State," *available at:* http://www.dos.ny.gov/lg/publications/Guide_to_planning_and_zoning_laws.pdf (e.g., New York state law provides, *inter alia:* "Such regulations shall be designed to promote the public health, safety and general welfare and shall be made with reasonable consideration, among other things, to the character of the district, its peculiar suitability for particular uses, the conservation of property values and the direction of building development, in accord with a well considered plan.")

along with subscribing interfaith community leaders to participate in a campaign that begins well before the application is filed. While this may be a legitimate part of the process, communities have begun to question whether officials always maintain proper objectivity. Of legal concern is whether officials apply the same inspection and verification rigors to these applications as they do the entire range of religious assembly applicants.

It is ironic that organized Muslim activists complain of disadvantaged treatment in the city planning process when many communities feel that officials seem predisposed to treat these applications favorably. Yet, the record shows that there is reason for both sides to have drawn these conclusions.

Some communities have staged highly emotional opposition to mosque applications without basing concerns in law and procedure. It is also true that some city officials have dismissed legitimate community input in what appears to be a rush to approve the mosque application. Confidence in these proceedings will suffer unless there is deliberation, transparency, full process, equal treatment, and reasoned dialogue.

All applicants for conditional – also called special or exceptional – land use permits bear responsibility to represent accurately the true nature, frequency, expected attendance and timing of activities planned. Otherwise, it is difficult to assess the appropriate restrictions and contractual conditions that formalize a permitted use. There is an important balance that local planners must find between accommodating a range of religious activities and allowing a very difficult mix of traffic, parking, and some cases of almost around-the-clock activity that burdens a surrounding community. It is important to anticipate the practical and real impact of the intended use and to provide code-based structure appropriate to the zoned area.

In short, mosque applicants lawfully should be treated in a manner that is equal to that applied to other religious organizations that are considered for permits to build or expand. Also of importance, Islamic applicants may not be given preferential treatment and regulatory processes should not be bypassed to avoid controversy.

While concerns over separatism and radicalization animate much of the focus on new mosque construction, *these issues are not within the purview of local officials*. These are very important cultural concerns and this manual will explain how they may be addressed in general at city hall and specifically in other community forums.

Concerned citizens must learn to express questions and reservations in a manner appropriate to the relevant civic forum's purpose. Land use officials act within a prescribed role that requires them to apply local ordinances according to state and federal statutory parameters. They are asked to interpret ordinances and engage deliberative reviews according to the goals of the municipality's Comprehensive Plan.

The following is an example from Portland, Oregon, of the broad goals of an overarching master plan:

> Portland's 2035 Comprehensive Plan guides how and where land is developed as well as where infrastructure projects are built to prepare for and respond to population and job growth. All cities and counties in Oregon are required to have a Comprehensive Plan. Portland's new Comprehensive Plan addresses future development and describes how and when community members will be involved in land use decisions. It helps coordinate policies and actions across City bureaus as well as with regional and state agencies.[22]

The comprehensive master plan calls for district plans that specify the goals and directives of zoned areas. The zoned areas provide for uses that share common features like commercial, agricultural, industrial and residential. Some uses are called out and may exist by right in these zones. Others may be permitted, as conditional uses, if they meet a set of requirements designed to minimize activity that conflicts with the host zone's purpose and character.

Conditional use applicants especially bear a significant burden to demonstrate that the exact details of the application will conform to the requirements that govern their exceptional presence in an area not directly designed for them. City planners must be able to measure the likelihood that the applicants' use will be compatible with the already established rightful users.

The process is often so technical that many applicants hire professional expeditors to deal with the challenging details and prolonged timelines.

Religious groups are not exempt from these requirements and they must declare with methodical reliability the full range of uses, occupancy, parking and activities. Current federal law does provide some special considerations for religious applicants, but minority religions are not granted an exemption from any part of this process.

---

[22] "City Council Proposed Comprehensive Plan Amendments Available For Review." *City of Portland* (2016), https://www.portlandoregon.gov/bps/article/569930.

2. UNIQUE MOSQUE APPLICATION CONTROVERSIES

Some city officials, including staff attorneys, come to the land use permitting process with little understanding of why community members may be concerned about the siting of a new mosque in town. When the land parcel intended for this religious use is in a residential zone, or near one, anxiety is often heightened.

There are land-planning officials who have bought into the meme that, where there is Muslim separateness and supremacism, it is a justified reaction to vocal critics. Thus, citizens who note anti-constitutional practices and challenge the insinuation of Sharia practices into American policy-making may be considered the problem. This mindset is important to consider since it may result in a conscious – or unconscious – effort to tip the scales in favor of Islamic applicants.

Communities must anticipate both the under-informed and the already agendized city official when approaching city hall. If residents come with fact-based and relevant presentations designed to inform the process, officials are obligated to give them a fair hearing. The key to effective advocacy is to know which issues are matters for city hall and how to express concerns properly.

Not all Muslims embrace Sharia socio-religious imam governance, but the numbers of "home grown" and immigrant Muslims that hold anti-constitutional views on such issues as freedom of conscience, women's rights, and free speech are very troubling. When Sharia-adherent mosques are central to Muslim life and culture, there are important concerns for American neighborhoods. As mosque-based life is communal to the degree that pious Muslims may be at the Islamic center most days of the week – sometimes for many hours in a day – and the lifestyle is cloistered to the point that participation is exclusive to Muslims, it is easy to see that integration trends will be heavily influenced by what is being taught in the mosque. Europe's example of separate and distinct cultures is a very troubling object lesson for Americans.

While the debate is joined as to whether the responsibility for balkanized Muslim communities lies with Western societies or with resistant Islamic Sharia subscribers, communities must deal with the practical challenges. Many local officials have no idea what to think about this conundrum and it is not their role to impose assimilation mandates. But they should understand when community concern is not based in bigotry but is a matter of residents attempting to promote awareness of the mosques that have been instrumental in perpetrating counter-American values. These residents also should be interested in hearing when any mosque leader proposes concrete, accountable, and trackable solutions.

The Muslim demographic that causes consternation is based in the twenty percent that responded to a Pew survey in 2011[23] by saying that Muslims should remain "distinct" from American society. This indicates resistance to integration and is reflective of those likely loyal to tribal custom, Islamic law, or Koranic doctrine rather than willing participation in secular civil society.[24] Just over half of American Muslims surveyed in this poll said that they supported assimilation into American society leaving the remaining twenty-five per cent somewhere in between acceptance of American culture and remaining "distinct." If Pew Research's 2016 estimate that 3.3 million Muslims live in the U.S. was accurate, as many as a million and a half Muslims might be indifferent to, if not actually hostile to, assimilation. Another troubling data point is the finding of a 2012 survey that some fifty-eight percent of Muslims said that the First Amendment *should not* protect speech critical of Islam.[25]

Although Islamist advocacy groups like the Council on American Relations (CAIR)[26] consistently assert that Muslims in general are experiencing bigoted treatment as have other immigrant groups like the Irish, no other immigrant wave has exhibited so much intransigence, rejecting American societal underpinnings.

Furthermore, CAIR's credibility in speaking for American Muslims has been called into question by CAIR's record of connections to Muslim Brotherhood origins, distortion tactics, and known misrepresentations. From court rulings that document CAIR's troubling ties, to CAIR's pedigree, to the FBI's denunciation of CAIR, the pronouncements issued from this organization should be roundly questioned.[27]

---

[23] Pew Research Center, U.S. Politics and Policy. "Muslim Americans: No Signs of Growth in Alienation or Support for Extremism" p.1 (30 Aug. 2011), http://www.people-press.org/2011/08/30/muslim-americans-no-signs-of-growth-in-alienation-or-support-for-extremism/.

[24] Lugo, Karen J. "American Family-Law and Sharia Compliant Marriages. *The Federalist Society* Vol 3, Issue 2 (19 Jun. 2012), http://www.fed-soc.org/publications/detail/american-family-law-and-sharia-compliant-marriages.

[25] Wenzel Strategies. WND Survey of Muslim Americans. (28 Oct. 2012), http://www.wnd.com/files/2012/10/WenzelMuslimsQ8.pdf.

[26] Council on American Islamic Relations. http://www.cair.com/.

[27] Powers, Richard C. "Letter to The Honorable John Kyl." *The Investigative Project* (28 Apr. 2009), http://www.investigativeproject.org/documents/misc/265.pdf. (Assistant Director of the FBI for Congressional Affairs Richard C. Powers explained the FBI's decision to end cooperation with CAIR in a letter to Senator Jon Kyl dated April 28, 2009. In the letter Powers wrote: "As you Know, CAIR was named as an unindicted co-conspirator of the Holy Land Foundation for Relief and Development in *United States v. Holy Land Foundation et*

Despite CAIR's pedigree, in 2016, the organization touted impressive numbers of consults with DC legislators and staff, as well as millions of dollars of earned media.[28]

Other Western countries are facing the same Muslim assimilation challenges, as well. For about half of Western European Muslims, and the number likely is higher for new refugees, attitudes are "somewhat" to "very hardened" against American and Western cultural foundations.[29] In parallel fashion, half of Britain's Muslims believe that homosexuality should be a crime.[30] This phenomenon is unique to the Islamic cohort that bases attitudes, politics, and practices in strict Sharia religious dogma. Sharia codes are especially uncompromising on matters of blasphemy (which conflicts with free speech guarantees that allow criticism of religion and religious figures) and apostasy (which conflicts with free choice of religion), including abandoning belief in Islam.

The challenge for American communities is to promote full assimilation that includes wholehearted embrace of key Western precepts like self-determination as expressed in the fundamental right to speak freely and the right to accept or reject any religion. Inquiring citizens should not be

---

al. (CR.No.3:04-240-P(N.D.TX.) During that trial, evidence was introduced that demonstrated a relationship between CAIR, individual CAIR founders (including its current President Emeritus and its Executive Director) and the Palestine Committee. Evidence was also introduced that demonstrated a relationship between the Palestine Committee and HAMAS, which was designated a terrorist organization in 1995. In light of that evidence, the FBI suspended all formal contracts between CAIR and the FBI."); *United States of America v. Holy Land Foundation for Relief and Development et al.* 3:04-cr-00240-P The United States District Court for Northern District of Texas, Dallas Division. *Judicial Watch* (01 Jul. 2009), https://www.judicialwatch.org/wp-content/uploads/2014/02/USA-v-HLF-Order-6282011.pdf. (Judge Jorge Solis grants in part a CAIR motion regarding its presence on an unindicted co-conspirator/ joint venture list, while noting: "The Government has produced ample evidence to establish the associations of CAIR, ISNA and NAIT with HLF, the Islamic Association for Palestine ("IAP"), and with Hamas. While the Court recognizes that the evidence produced by the Government largely predates the HLF designation date, the evidence is nonetheless sufficient to show the association of these entities with HLF, IAP, and Hamas."); In June of 2016, the D.C. Circuit Court of Appeals ruled that a case against CAIR's national office, brought by Muslims and non-Muslim plaintiffs, contained sufficient evidence of fraud that the lower court must investigate the record: http://www.americanfreedomlawcenter.org/wp-content/uploads/2016/06/Opinion-6-21-16.pdf; also see, Pipes, Daniel. "Is CAIR A Terror Group?" *National Review* (28 Nov. 2014), http://www.nationalreview.com/article/393614/cair-terror-group-daniel-pipes.

[28] "Watch: CAIR's Impact in Numbers." *Youtube.com*; *available at*: https://www.youtube.com/watch?v=4eaN0aUL384&feature=youtu.be.

[29] Koopmans, Ruud. "Fundamentalism and Out-group Hostility Muslim Immigrants and Christian Natives in Western Europe." *WZB Mitteilungen* (2013), https://www.wzb.eu/sites/default/files/u6/koopmans_englisch_ed.pdf.

[30] Perraudin, Frances. "Half of All British Muslims Think Homosexuality Should Be Illegal." *TheGuardian.com* (11 Apr. 2016), https://www.theguardian.com/uk-news/2016/apr/11/british-muslims-strong-sense-of-belonging-poll-homosexuality-sharia-law.

satisfied with vague platitudes about assimilation if there is no specific commitment to action. Americans cannot be shy about utilizing individual free speech protections to define the culture while framing discussions on the vital points of conflict with what former British Prime Minister Tony Blair calls "a problem within Islam."[31]

Constitutional law scholar and self-described liberal Prof. Jonathan Turley characterized the fundamental conflict between Islamism and the West as based in individual rights: "[P]unishing apostasy (when a Muslim renounces Islam) is a 'red line' that separates a person from the free world. It is the most vile form of majoritarian tyranny and oppression [because] the right to choose your faith and the right to free speech is a human right not [only] an American right."[32]

Based upon this cultural crisis, concerned citizens have shown up in impressive numbers to speak at mosque construction permit hearings. The escalating rate of isolation and radicalization[33] occurring in American mosques – or, at least, not discouraged in many – is naturally a concern to any community contemplating a new mosque or mosque expansion.

However, rather than expressing alarm as hysteria, speaking to local government officials and media requires a strategic response based upon reason, facts, precedent, and the law. To date, much of what has been said at city hall podiums by activists is not relevant to the hearing and it falls on

---

[31] Blair, Tony. "The Ideology Behind Lee Rigby's Murder is Profound and Dangerous. Why Don't We Admit It? Tony Blair Launches a Brave Assault on Muslim Extremism After Woolwich Attack." *The Daily Mail* (1 Jun. 2013), http://www.dailymail.co.uk/debate/article-2334560/The-ideology-Lee-Rigbys-murder-profound-dangerous-Why-dont-admit--Tony-Blair-launches-brave-assault-Muslim-extremism-Woolwich-attack.html.

[32] Turley, Jonathan. "Pew Poll Finds Overwhelming For Executing People For Apostasy in Afghanistan and Other Middle Eastern Nations." *JonathanTurley.org* (1 May, 2013), https://jonathanturley.org/2013/05/03/pew-poll-finds-overwhelming-support-for-executing-people-for-apostasy-in-afghanistan-and-other-muslim-nations/; *see also*, Fisher, Max. "Majorities of Muslims in Egypt and Pakistan support the death penalty for leaving Islam." *The Washington Post* (1 May 2013), https://www.washingtonpost.com/news/worldviews/wp/2013/05/01/64-percent-of-muslims-in-egypt-and-pakistan-support-the-death-penalty-for-leaving-islam/ ("[A]ccording to the 2013 Pew Research Center report, 88 percent of Muslims in Egypt and 62 percent of Muslims in Pakistan favor the death penalty for people who leave the Muslim religion. This is also the majority view among Muslims in Malaysia, Jordan and the Palestinian territories.)"

[33] Shea, Nina. "Saudi Publications on Hate Ideology Fill American Mosques." *Freedom House* (2005), https://freedomhouse.org/sites/default/files/inline_images/Saudi%20Publications%20on%20Hate%20Ideology%20Invade%20American%20Mosques.pdf; Kedar, Mordecai and David Yerulshalmi, "Mapping Sharia: Correlations Between Sharia Adherence and Violent Dogma in U.S. Mosques." *Perspectives on Terrorism* (2011), http://www.terrorismanalysts.com/pt/index.php/pot/article/view/sharia-adherence-mosque-survey/html; for abstract *also see*: http://mappingsharia.com/.

deaf ears. Even worse, some of what is said can be used to characterize the entire oversight effort as racially biased and ignorant.

It is true that the announcement of public hearings may provide opportunities for citizens to voice concerns but disconnected and off-point comments about Sharia, "jihad", and the Koran presented inside the hearing room can waste a valuable chance to hold officials to consistent application and enforcement of zoning rules. The history of these hearings in various communities shows that caustic comments, not focused on central and legitimate issues, only become fodder for the media and political Islamist groups to support accusations of bigotry and discrimination. Recent experience shows that the actions of injudicious activists who do not make this distinction will be used to fuel the impression with politicians, judges, and voters that Muslims are a persecuted group needing special privileges and protection.

With this caution in mind, there is a time and place, outside of "city hall," to voice reasonable community concerns about demonstrated radicalization trends, and assert community expectations regarding assimilation.

In reality, many mosques will be approved under liberal religious freedom laws and it is vital to recognize the congenial Muslim citizen who is not an Islamist, while identifying Islamist operators that advance radicalization. Most importantly, this is the time to seize opportunities to recognize the leadership of reformist Muslims that are working to recruit and train Muslims in the defense of the vital constitutional liberties essential to our civilization.

The audience at city hall is composed of two elements: the political decision-makers and the audience of interested citizens. When drama and theatrics overcome rational fact-finding and organized presentations, political instincts will prompt officials to default to withdrawal and detachment. Furthermore, legal obligations require officials to announce their objectivity when comments become overtly discriminatory.

The entire process – from application for a building permit to monitoring those mosques that are approved – benefits from oversight by a coordinated private citizen accountability group. Volunteer committees may be assigned to investigate all aspects of the regulatory process. These include: reviewing the zoning codes; researching and comparing prior approvals for similar treatment of other applicants; anticipating representations of event descriptions and activity levels; assessing safety concerns and impact issues; previewing comments to be presented at public hearings; and, preparing statements for other venues on radicalization countermeasures and assimilation concerns.

3. Path of Less Resistance for Mosques?

While Islamic groups may complain of community opposition, in some cases residents report that they encounter less bureaucratic resistance than other religious organizations seeking a worship site. It is true that there is often loud community opposition, but officials presiding over hearings and staff who prepare the recommendations sometimes are perceived as minimizing some regulatory processes.[34] This may also result from concern that the Department of Justice (DOJ) or the applicant may question adherence to regulatory rigors as the appearance of bias.

Islamic land use applicants often are prepared for the public relations part of the process and some have legal representation from early stages. As a minority group, Muslims are able to anticipate sympathetic intervention by the DOJ's Civil Rights Division for Religious Discrimination.[35] They are also adept at leveraging generous religious liberty legal protections that are available to all applicants, but not so assertively invoked by most.

A comparison of two recent cases, decided by essentially the same Minnesota mayor and city council, illustrates the potential for dramatically different results when a key federal religious land use statute is applied to benefit one case and ignored in the other. The first account details the application of Islamic Al-Farooq Youth and Family Center (AFYFC, also known as Dar al-Farooq) to use an existing school facility as a community center, school, and prayer space (mosque). The second profiled case describes the subsequent treatment of Resurrection Power Church, a black Nigerian Christian assembly, as this congregation applied to use a warehouse as a church.

It is critically important for any concerned citizen that is preparing to address a mosque land use application to read carefully these accounts.

---

[34] Pew Center's Forum on Religion and Public Life, "Controversies over Mosques and Islamic Centers Across the U.S." *Pewforum.org* (17 Sept. 2012), http://www.pewforum.org/files/2012/09/2012Mosque-Map.pdf (These profiles indicate community complaints addressing variance approvals for minarets, etc., conditional uses, insufficient environmental impact studies, and parking allowances. When reviewed, these issues generally survived judicial scrutiny but the complaints at hearings are often based in differential treatment as compared to other religious applications. These concerns usually do not become litigation actions unless the aggrieved party has the commitment, resources, and standing to file the complaint.)

[35] United States Department of Justice. "Religious Land Use and Institutionalized Persons Act." *The United States Department of Justice* (6 Aug. 2015), https://www.justice.gov/crt/religious-land-use-and-institutionalized-persons-act; *also see*: https://www.justice.gov/sites/default/files/crt/legacy/2010/12/15/rluipa_q_a_9-22-10_0.pdf.

These examples illuminate: how the process works; where there is need for oversight and accountability; how officials rely upon occupancy estimates from applicants to assess the burden on the surrounding homes or businesses; whether to restrict the occupancy permit for traffic, parking, and activity intensity; how the permitting agreement made between cities and applicants is expected to be binding; areas where enforcement should be anticipated; and, how elected city representatives ultimately must be able to rely on sound advice from staff attorneys, planning staff, and city managers.

In particular, the following profiles of religious land use permit applications should impress planning staff and officials with the vital need for: official training in religious land use law; insistence on detailed and accurate plans, renderings, and responses from the applicant; as well as, *enforceable* and explicit limitations as conditions on the use that will best provide for peaceful coexistence with surrounding community.

Naturally, the facts surrounding the following accounts of two religious sites differ in some particulars and the relevant zoning regulations vary in some aspects. But the public record videotape of the hearings, press accounts, and interviews with principal figures reveal a stunningly different approach by city officials as they considered the merits of the mosque and then the subsequent church applications. These case studies offer valuable insight into the institutional process, the political considerations and calculations, and the law that governs religious land use.

CASE ONE: AL FAROOQ YOUTH AND FAMILY CENTER

In March 2011, Islamic Al Farooq Youth and Family Center (AFYFC; later named Al-Jazeeri Academy; also called Dar al-Farooq, or DAF) applied for a land use permit to renew the existing conditional use on a "quasi-public" site in a residential zone (R-1). Residential homes and a park surround the site that previously had been occupied by a Lutheran high school and separate evangelical church. AFYFC's application described the intended use as similar to the prior religious education functions: an elementary – private primary school, day care, and place of assembly/community center.

This section may seem to be highly technical and comprehensive but the details provided may supply useful context for planning officials and residents when contemplating similar cases. Whether it is a matter of asking more questions, providing additional and structural limits, establishing a review period, or working toward a municipal "safe harbor" measure that may shift heavy assembly uses away from sensitive areas like residential zones, it is important to start with facts and end with a realistic permit.

Testimony and applicant exhibits (CUP hearings are defined as *quasi-judicial* proceedings in most states) reveal that AFYFC planned to schedule evening lectures, fitness programs, on-site medical clinic services, weekend school for children (like "Sunday School"), and one Friday prayer service. Ramadan observances were described as special evening prayers conducted between 9:00 p.m. and 10:00 p.m. nightly for the duration of the month-long observance.[36]

Even including the additional programs discussed with staff in early phases, there was little indication of the real range of activities planned, and the dramatically higher volume of participants that would immediately engage in the various AFYFC offerings. Readers will note that staff and planning officials based activity expectations, use limitations, and the final agreements on the testimony of AFYFC representatives. When accuracy in this part of the process failed, all regulations that followed were flawed.

Although some of the following statements are not included in the City of Bloomington "Synopsis" (some "City-approved minutes" of past meetings are no longer posted on the City website and a "synopsis" has replaced them) of the March 24, 2011 testimony by the AFYFC representative, the spokesperson for the institution emphatically stated that there were no major changes planned for the building "from what it used to be [in the past]." He said that the weekend school would be comparable to "Sunday School" and that the large gym will be used by the community at large although he demurred from offering a process for scheduling. The AFYFC spokesperson said that the large gym would be used by "50 – 100 members from 7:00 – 10:00 p.m. on weekends." He offered the community many assurances and addressed "Smith Park neighbors" to say that their interests would be included, an outreach committee would be established, and that the neighborhood would have access to the facilities, including a free weekend medical clinic (if approved by Planning Commission). He stated that leadership at the Center would "not tolerate any discomfort or inconvenience to [the Smith Park] neighbors" and he assured the community that AFYFC would promote good relations with them. At the conclusion, the spokesman apologized to local residents for overflow parking when the first "once in a blue moon" hospitality event drew "unanticipated" numbers of attendees and (reported 800-1000) cars.[37]

---

[36] "City of Bloomington Staff Report: Conditional Use Permit for a Private School, a Day Care, and a Place of Assembly/Community Center." p.16, *Bloomingtonmn.gov* (24 Mar. 2011), https://www.bloomingtonmn.gov/sites/default/files/media/08915A_11.pdf.

[37] "City of Bloomington City Council Meeting for Review of AFYFC Permit Application," *YouTube* (24 Mar. 2011), discussion begins at appx. 21 mins. on the marker, https://www.youtube.com/watch?v=wJ-9ci-gB3A&feature=youtu.be: *and*; "City of Bloomington Planning Commission Synopsis." p. 6, *Bloomingtonmn.gov* (24 Mar. 2011), https://www.bloomingtonmn.gov/sites/default/files/media/2507_032411pcs.pdf.

First, the application did not name the AFYFC assembly purpose as "mosque" use. Rather, this submission, consistent with most Islamic applications, described primarily community center and education purposes. The Friday prayer service was mentioned and appeared to be an incidental "chapel" interest. However, participation in Friday prayers has consistently been counted (per cars parked) at more than 500 attendees, rather than the maximum of 150 - 200 as submitted for the application record. Two consecutive prayer services were structured to relieve some of the parking overflow into residential streets.

The stated maximum of two hundred participants for High Holy Days (month-long Ramadan observances)[38], in reality, became attendance of well over a thousand at some services. These observances involved hundreds of cars coming and going *throughout the entire night* during the month of Ramadan. There have been heavily attended Eid ul-Fitr feasts, late night seminars, sports events, fundraisers, family festivals, and other widely promoted activities.

During the rest of the year, the site hosts ongoing regionally-promoted festivals and family gatherings, frequent seminars, coordinated – as well as unorganized – sports activities, a university administration office, university classes, concurrent weekend schools, and various other educational and social programs.

More accurate than the submitted AFYFC land use application, a YouTube video available for viewing during the hearing phase, promised "a full-time and hourly licensed Islamic Day Care Center, an Islamic Pre-School for Toddlers, an Islamic Weekend Academy, a Fitness Center for Muslim women, a state-of-the-art Multimedia Center, a Canteen, a full-time Islamic Elementary School, a Community Conference Room and a Prayer Room," as well as "educational lectures in multiple languages," and, "cultural, educational and athletic events and programs." Although the video was discovered as overuse problems grew at the facility, AFYFC management denied any intent to use the facility beyond what was described at the CUP hearing.[39]

Even AFYFC's own website advertised that it would be open "for all five daily prayers, Jumah prayers and evening lectures on Monday, Tuesday, Wednesday and Friday evenings after Salatul Isha."[40] In addition to

---

[38] *Id.* at 14–16.

[39] "Al-Farooq Youth and Family Center." *YouTube.com* (29 Jun. 2011) https://www.youtube.com/watch?v=TwF7tRcjZv0.

[40] "Al-Farooq Youth and Family Center is Now Open." *daralfarooq.org* (2011), http://daralfarooq.org/index.php?option=com_content&view=frontpage; http://mosquesinamerica.org/wp-content/uploads/2016/10/40_AFYFC.pdf

religious prayer services and school sessions, the organization advertised regional adult education classes, sports leagues, family nights, area-wide tutoring,[41] and widely advertised all-day Saturday family events.[42]

Although parking restrictions included in the staff report, and affirmed by the final CUP Resolution, predicated the permit upon "strict adherence to conditions that would control any off-site or on-street parking on local residential streets,"[43] there has been consistent overflow use of residential street parking and double-parking in the lot. During Ramadan, residents report that street parking some days and evenings has extended for blocks in all directions. Some linked activities run through the night.

Of the hardships on the neighborhood, some of the worst are late night sessions, an example of which is a 10:30 p.m. fundraiser advertised during Ramadan in 2013. This meeting was planned and publicized to conclude at 2:30 a.m.[44]

The neighborhood park shares parking spaces and a field with AFYFC per a joint use agreement that was originally created to coordinate neighborhood and Lutheran school activities. On, or before, September 1, 2011, AFYFC was required to update the prior agreement to reflect new use patterns. This agreement, in part, coordinates annual sports field schedules and assures city residents access to the fields and parking space. When AFYFC instead deliberated and negotiated the joint use terms for years, neighbors reported that all spaces in the parking lot were taken when the AFYFC facility was in use, and the field use was not scheduled by the first-of-year deadline frustrating community planning for the fields. By 2016, residents were reportedly told by police that they were excluded from "Muslims only" areas at times that the agreement was invoked by AFYFC. These areas included the *public* parking lot.

---

[41] Al-Farooq Family and Youth Center. "After School Tutoring Program." *campaign-archive1.com* (2016). http://us6.campaign-archive1.com/?u=197ada357663d650727a8e00c&id=1f0018d6a4; http://mosquesinamerica.org/wp-content/uploads/2016/10/41_AFYFC_After_School.pdf

[42] Al-Farooq Youth and Family Center. "Shaykh Samiral-Nass Weekend Courses." *campaign-archive2.com* (23 August, 2013). http://us6.campaign-archive2.com/?u=197ada357663d650727a8e00c&id=0d250624f8; http://mosquesinamerica.org/wp-content/uploads/2016/10/42_AFYFC_Weekend_Courses.pdf

[43] City of Bloomington AFYFC Staff Report, *supra* note 36 at p. 4; *also see*, "City of Bloomington Planning Commission Synopsis." *Bloomingtonmn.gov* (24 Mar. 2011), https://www.bloomingtonmn.gov/sites/default/files/media/2507_032411pcs.pdf at Pp. 6-11; City Council Hearing Video, (24 Mar. 2011), item 3: https://www.youtube.com/watch?v=wJ-9ci-gB3A&feature=youtu.be.

[44] AFYFC fundraiser flyer. http://mosquesinamerica.org/wp-content/uploads/2016/10/44_AFYFC_Fundraiser_Flyer.pdf

One of the most egregious unauthorized uses of the property has been the addition of a university administration office and class meetings.

In the intervening years, residents have complained that the mosque was generating heavy and dangerous traffic, overlapping activities, call to prayer broadcasts at close of Ramadan, residential street parking, buses and semi trucks parked on street and idling for hours, double- and triple-parking, parking in fire-lanes, intruders into neighborhood yards at night, cars blocking driveways, family picnics in neighborhood yards, heavy litter issues, consistent overflowing garbage preventing door to storage area from closing, rodent infestations, inadequate portable toilets, negligent grounds and retention pond maintenance, visitors coming and going when buildings and parking lots are dark – and some nights, lights on late-and-all-night, regional weekend events without required permits, dumping of concrete and debris into berm on property shared with the city, improper disposal of asbestos, non-compliance with food service requirements, operation of an unlicensed restaurant, reckless (some due to taxis) driving, increasing police visits for burning of outhouses, etc., and frequent late-night-to-early-morning car and patron noise.[45]

WHAT WENT WRONG?

This permitting process began as most do with the City of Bloomington planning department. Planning staff is tasked with reviewing applications and accompanying statements that answer questions about property use and occupancy. In this case, city staff applied the provisions of the Comprehensive Plan, the District Plan, and City Code for the specific zoned area, and staff then reported that the "proposed use will not create an excessive burden on parks, schools, streets, and other public facilities...; and that the proposed use was "consistent with other uses in similar locations and buildings throughout the City." Finally, "subject to Conditions of Approval, the proposed use will not be injurious to the surrounding neighborhood or otherwise harm the public, health, safety and welfare of the community."[46] Staff recommended approval of the application with conditions – or what could also be considered restrictions.[47] City staff reported during the council meeting session that they relied upon the applicant's statements indicating "200 expected maximum occupancy" to calculate the required parking provisions and to identify the venues and activities that were conditionally approved for the site.

---

[45] Many complaints, along with a record of City responses, have been chronicled on a resident blog: http://5yearsofcollectingdata.weebly.com/blog/about-the-restaurant.

[46] City of Bloomington Staff Report for AFYFC Application, Mar. 24, 2011, *supra* note 36 at p. 7.

[47] *Id.* at p. 6.

The City Council, in turn, relied upon this set of staff recommendations when the members adopted all the research and recommendations to issue a final Resolution expressing the terms of approval for the CUP.[48] At the hearing, councilmembers noted in the presence of mosque representatives that AFYFC was in agreement with the final terms and conditions. The hearing video recording shows that the AFYFC spokesman affirmatively confirmed the projected attendance and parking numbers for the mosque and school conditional permit.[49]

The CUP effectively created a contract with City enforcement power behind it. Thus, if the contract was breached or conditions violated, the City had the power to revoke the CUP. The very meaning of "conditional" in popular and legal use is that one thing is "subject to" the other; one action or inaction triggers another. All of this appeared to be a straightforward city hall transaction.

In this case though, there was another important contract that would also control the terms of the City of Bloomington's – and, possibly more intimately, the neighborhood's – relationship with AFYFC: a Joint Use Agreement (JUA) for shared city park athletic fields and a parking lot. The agreement pre-existed the AFYFC conditional permit and it was in place at the time that the CUP was granted to AFYFC. The CUP conditioned permission to operate at the site, and to share City facilities, on adherence to a September, 2011 deadline to update the JUA. However, the dramatically altered, re-negotiated, JUA was not signed until March, 2015 – three and one half years after the deadline.

These structural safeguards failed while neighbors report that they suffered inconsistent and lax enforcement of the CUP requirements as well as city ordinances. There was opportunity for some corrective language in the renewed JUA that would continue to govern the shared spaces in the athletic fields and parking lots, but the final contract, instead of updating the prior agreement, provided exceptionally lenient terms. Residents felt excluded from this process as it negotiated conditional late-night and all-night use, fluid terms governing field use, and serial warning and discussion phases instead of compliance measures.[50]

---

[48] "Bloomington City Council C.U.P. Resolution No. 2011-62." p. 3 (2 May 2011), http://mosquesinamerica.org/wp-content/uploads/2016/10/48_Bloomington_CUP_2011-62.pdf

[49] City of Bloomington City Council Meeting video, Mar. 24, 2011, *supra* note 43, at 21 minutes on the marker.

[50] "Agreement Between The City of Bloomington And Dar Al-Farooq: Re: Smith Park and Dar Al-Farooq Property Improvements, Leases, Easements, Maintenance, and Use." (formally executed by both signatories on 3 Mar. 2015) (also known as Joint Use Agreement (JUA)) p. 7, http://mosquesinamerica.org/wp-content/uploads/2016/10/50_AFYFC_JUA_3-2-2015.pdf

During the intervening five years, tensions have mounted, the facility went into foreclosure proceedings (although ultimately other Islamic investors purchased the property), and city staff speculated that the gas service had been turned off for non-payment. The new investors at the AFYFC campus did not indicate that closer attention would be paid to regulations or CUP requirements, and it was discouraging that some staff members that held positions of authority under the prior management kept the same or similar roles. Worst was the City's betrayal of resident trust and civic duty when the CUP was not enforced.

→ The month of Ramadan 2016 (all years have generated similar complaints) brought *all-night* noise that came with *all-night* cars and patrons coming and going, constant sessions, and days of activity with parking on the streets. For Eid ul Fitr, attendance at one service was estimated between 1500 and 2500, based upon the resident count of upwards of 550 cars that were parked for five blocks around the mosque. Trash overflowed the storage area. Residents resorted to calling the police for cars illegally parked near driveways or fire hydrants. The call to prayer was broadcast into the neighborhood just before 7:30 a.m. One night during Ramadan, a resident confronted several youths after midnight. The boys had set up a driving course around city garbage cans on the shared parking lot. Police responded, and residents report that they were told they could not enter the parking lot when the public space was "for mosque members only" (according to the times that the JUA was activated by the use of certain facilities). Yet nothing in the JUA says that the public is excluded from public spaces, unless the question involves the contractually reserved athletic fields.

→ A City staffer noted in an email exchange that there were sixty-seven drafts of the Joint Use Agreement before it was finalized.[51] Although the CUP codified a hard deadline of September 1, 2011 for the updated use agreement governing terms of the shared parking and fields, the agreement was not finalized until early 2015, three and a half years late. [52] The protracted negotiations yielded permissive terms, incorporating all-night use of the shared facilities, to include lighting, as

---

[51] City of Bloomington staff email: "67 Versions of Joint Use Agreement." (10 Dec. 2014) http://mosquesinamerica.org/wp-content/uploads/2016/10/51_versions_of_Joint_Use_Agreement.jpg

[52] "Bloomington City Council C.U.P. Resolution No. 2011-62." p. 3 (2 May 2011), *available at* http://mosquesinamerica.org/wp-content/uploads/2016/10/52a_AFYFC_CUP_Resolution_2011-62.pdf; *and:* "City of Bloomington Study Meeting #42." City Approved Minutes, p. 7 (20 Aug. 2012), *available at*: http://mosquesinamerica.org/wp-content/uploads/2016/10/52b_2012-8-20_study_meeting.pdf

long as "permitted" (with no limit on number of permits). This updated JUA installed a protracted five-step – potentially more than a 120-day process – for addressing non-compliance. Even after a series of warnings (including "verbal"), negotiations, and penalty markers, the final steps leading to termination of the JUA for non-compliance were ordered such that corrective measures may be interpreted as conditional.[53]

A request was submitted for copies of any permit applications and authorizations for the subsequent Ramadan – and other – all-night activities, recreation, and sessions. Arguably, the compliance measures that control the combined use of these public spaces all hinge on the veracity the threshold verbal warning. If this initial step fails, the subsequent mechanisms may all be called into question.

→ AFYFC advertised a Sudan-accredited Islamic university administrative center [54] (also called in various publications a "help desk" and "headquarters") and class offerings at AFYFC, some dismissing at 10:00 p.m. The 2013 spring class schedule shows seventeen classes scheduled at the AFYFC facility in clear violation of CUP terms.[55] A May 2016 course in "Modern Hadith" was scheduled to dismiss at 10:15 p.m.[56] The website declares that "IUM is locally registered with the Minnesota Secretary of State as well the Minnesota Department of Higher Education as a degree granting institution"[57] but the Minnesota Department of Higher Education reports that this statement is inaccurate due to IUMN's "strictly religious" course content.[58] Of great concern to the community, the leadership at IUMN and some

---

[53] Agreement Between The City of Bloomington And Dar Al-Farooq (JUA), Pp. 12,13, *supra* at note 50.

[54] "Islamic University of Minnesota." Administration Page, *available at*: http://iuminnesota.com/administration/; see also in Appendix: "Islamic University of Minnesota Spring 2013 Semester Schedule." Note that 17 classes are offered at the AFYFC/DAF Bloomington campus in Rooms #101 – #105. (The City sent a letter to AFYFC in October 2013 stating that use of the site for a university was a violation of the CUP, yet an office, as well as various classes, some co-sponsored with AFYFC, continued to be sited at the facility.)

[55] "Islamic History Seminar." Also see, samples of notices for IUMN seminars offered at AFYFC facility in 2016: 8201 Park Ave., South, Bloomington, MN. *See* http://mosquesinamerica.org/wp-content/uploads/2016/10/55_IUMI_Spring_2013_Semester_Schedule.pdf

[56] "A Scientific Session in Modern Hadith." *See* http://mosquesinamerica.org/wp-content/uploads/2016/10/56_Scientific_Session_in_Modern_Hadith.pdf

[57] "Islamic University of Minnesota" accreditation page. *Available at*: http://iuminnesota.com/accreditation/.

[58] E-mail from Minnesota Department of Higher Education (27 May 2016), *See* http://mosquesinamerica.org/wp-content/uploads/2016/10/58_Email_from_MN_Dept_of_Higher_Ed_27May2016.pdf

instructors have been reported to openly teach from Sharia-based curriculum[59] and some have been described as extremist.[60]

→ Double parking: During prayer and meeting times, the parking lot has been stacked with double-parked and triple-parked cars that unlawfully block emergency access.[61] The City acted to change City Code regarding double-parking while the controversies at AFYFC were ongoing to generally permit double-parking citywide.[62]

→ Class III vehicles: Shuttle and school busses, delivery trucks and vans, semis, and auto transports, have parked at the facility and on the street although this is against City ordinances. Police responded that even warnings for this "violation" would not be a priority as the regulation was "intended" to address blight due to oversized homeowner vehicles.[63]

→ Parking and Traffic: Over more than four years, overflow curbside parking has been reduced to an average of a dozen cars on "routine" Fridays. Police have responded to complaint calls and have cited some cars parked on the street. But during the thirty days of Ramadan, festivals days, and regionally promoted events, parking limits have been exceeded with heavy street parking.

→ Public nuisance: In response to complaints, the City has presented a number of corrective notices to AFYFC on a variety of the issues that have plagued the neighborhood: trash in the holding/storm pond, trash and debris (e.g., PVC pipes, rusted goal posts, area rug, lumber, discarded fencing, snow fences) around the site – including the City

---

[59] Dr. Hatem Ahaj M.D., Ph.D: http://www.amjaonline.org/en/dr-hatem-ahaj; http://www.thebuildingblocks.org/about-us/board-of-trustees.html; https://vimeo.com/channels/90830.

[60] Rossomando, John, "Islamic University of Minnesota a Hotbed of Extremism." *Investigative Project on Terrorism* (8 Apr. 2016), http://www.investigativeproject.org/5288/islamic-university-of-minnesota-a-hotbed#; "Islamic University of Minnesota." *Facebook.com* (N.D). https://www.facebook.com/Islamic-University-of-Minnesota-1591998911033844/timeline; "Organization Page of Dar-Al-Sarooq." (*sic.*) *Razoo.com,* (N.D), https://www.razoo.com/us/story/Dar-Al-Sarooq.

[61] Photos from AFYFC parking lot: http://5yearsofcollectingdata.weebly.com/blog/archives/02-2016.

[62] Double-parking was a violation per City of Bloomington Code Section 8.155 and comments in the June 6, 2011 City of Bloomington Study Meeting Approved Minutes (see Appendix for p. 8). Yet, in April 2013, the City Code was revised per Code Section 8.08, *available at*: http://library.amlegal.com/nxt/gateway.dll/Minnesota/bloomington_mn/bloomingtonminne sotacodeofordinances?f=templates$fn=default.htm$3.0$vid=amlegal:bloomington_mn.

[63] October 26, 2015 Memorandum from Bloomington Police Department on low priority for Class III vehicle parking on residential streets. *See* http://mosquesinamerica.org/wp-content/uploads/2016/10/63_October-26-2015_Police_Memo_on_low_priority_parking.jpg

Park – trash area metal doors left open, trash outside the holding area, ongoing lighting issues (property in use with no lighting, lights burned out, and lights on late into the night – and all night), and temporary signage that has remained months after the codified limits.[64] AFYFC has been fined for lighting violations only but no record of payment has been provided in response to records requests. There is no indication that penalties or fines were added for delinquency.

→ Property invasions: Police have been called for night-time intrusions into neighborhood back yards and other areas of private property.

→ Reckless traffic and bullying at playground: these anecdotal reports go to the heart of neighborhood concerns. One neighbor was involved in a traffic accident when a taxi darted around another vehicle and there have been many pedestrian near-misses reported. Parents complain that they cannot take their children to the playground after they have been shoved off of playground equipment and threatened.

→ Dumping: Large chunks of concrete and debris were dumped and buried in a shared athletic field creating an unpermitted berm in the shared athletic field. The City performed at least surface clean-up on the berm so that the grass could be mowed.[65] There is no record that the City investigated the depth of the refuse site and no record that AFYFC was charged for the partial remediation.

→ The City Council also discussed changing City Code to allow parking in public lots past 10:00 p.m. (or 11:00 p.m. an athletic facility/field is in use), but the effort was unsuccessful. However, the 2015 updated JUA allowed AFYFC to have parking lot lights on, for the shared City lot, into the night "when permitted." The AFYFC facility has been given license to have lights on at the facility and the related AFYFC parking lots whenever the buildings are in use.[66]

---

[64] City staff emails related to public nuisance, trash in holding pond, debris including goal posts, and discussion regarding the possibility that the City will remove goal posts: *available at:* Citizen Oversight Blog: "5 Years Later",
http://5yearsofcollectingdata.weebly.com/blog/previous/2, see posts dated May 19, 2016 and August 5, 2016, down to about three-fourths marker on page.

[65] *Id.* See photos of the berm here: http://5yearsofcollectingdata.weebly.com/.

[66] Agreement Between The City of Bloomington And Dar Al-Farooq (JUA), p. 4, *supra* at note 50. (The 2015 Joint Use Agreement between the City of Bloomington and Dar al-Farooq allows extended night use (past 10:00 p.m., and no further limitation on end time) and permits overflow into the City parking lot when a permit is obtained. Although, City regulations warn that cars remaining in public park lots past 10:00 p.m. will be towed. A document request was pending at the time this manuscript was published to learn if any such permit had been requested by AFYFC or granted by the City.)

→ There have been resident reports of concurrent use of the gym for AFYFC community events while the school and fields were also occupied in violation of CUP terms. One example was gym use for weekend school while a different academy session was offered elsewhere on the campus, as well as a simultaneous carnival event held on the field.[67] There has also been a general failure to schedule the field and publish a calendar at the beginning of each year to coordinate field use with the neighborhood.

→ Renting and profiting from the City fields has been a recurring issue (apparently without required liability insurance). AFYFC was instructed to not rent the athletic fields and yet continued to charge various teams and leagues fees, according to athletic coordinators. This has exacerbated the activity level issues and has also limited Bloomington resident use of the field. The summer of 2016 field calendar revealed that AFYFC had scheduled the shared field for near full-time use. The field was subdivided to allow more teams to use the venue, although there are careful provisions protecting the fields from overuse. To make matters worse, despite repeated requests, it was years before the City obtained evidence that AFYFC had purchased the JUA-*required* liability insurance for the field. The first evidence of insurance provided by AFYFC showed coverage beginning October 31, 2015 but, even then, AFYFC failed to include the City of Bloomington as "also insured." This violates the spirit of the Joint Use Agreement as well as City prohibitions against profiting from rental of public park space.

Neighbors have also reported that City staff has cleaned up the AFYFC parking lot and mowed the grass. One email from the City to AFYFC states that if an issue was not corrected that the City would provide a contractor to do the work. There was no mention of billing procedures to reimburse City costs.[68]

In July of 2016, a local attorney presented a petition of resident grievances to the City Council detailing the long list of community complaints for non-enforcement of the CUP limits, re-negotiation of the weak JUA terms, and

---

[67] Flyers announced a March 6, 2016 AFYFC Grand Opening beginning at 2:00 p.m. (https://www.facebook.com/events/533984560106329/) when an Al-Jazari Academy (separate from Dar al-Farooq Academy, DAFA) carnival began at noon, in apparent violation of the CUP prohibition against concurrent use of the gym and school facilities. Residents reported many hours of overlapping participation; also see photos of the festival bounce houses installed by truck on the City field, apparently without the required permit, and in violation of field preservation interests. *See* http://mosquesinamerica.org/wp-content/uploads/2016/10/67_Grand_Open_House_Event.png

[68] See City staff e-mail discussion on cleaning up AFYFC grounds at citizen oversight blog, *supra* at note 64.

advantaging AFYFC as compared to other religious organizations in Bloomington.[69] The neighborhood turned out and filled the hearing room. The conversation between the attorney and the residents continued with a question and answer session after the Council dismissed.

A proverbial line was drawn and Friends of Smith Park have demanded accountability. Although councilmembers did not comment immediately on the petition complaints, it will be up to the community to press relentlessly these serious concerns. Among the most egregious, was the demand for accurate and available minutes of City meetings. It is a foundational requirement in state and local law that original records must be archived and made available to the public, within a specified time period. Most cities and counties are required to take special care with records related to hearings, like a CUP proceeding. This is because there is important *testimony* and official *findings* that must be recorded and preserved.

Finally, and this is not a matter that connects to City Hall, the AFYFC mosque has been connected to cases where at least nine Muslims radicalized to join ISIS. A lawyer and legal commentator who attended trial proceedings made these startling observations about the young Somali Minnesotans:

> Growing up Muslim, receiving religious education and attending local mosques – the Al-Farooq Youth and Family Center in Bloomington was mentioned frequently – the defendants appear to have needed little more than the videos supplied by ISIL to recruit them.... They had social lives centered on local mosques. They supplemented their education with Islamic studies. They are ungrateful for the good lives and conventional opportunities afforded them in Minnesota. They are all observant Muslims. They wanted to live under the caliphate declared by ISIL. They yearned to wage jihad and to die as Islamic martyrs. They hate the U.S.[70]

This mosque is in the Twin Cities area that consistently is mentioned when commentators list the most radical centers in America. While not generally a matter for consideration at city hall – the focus on this institution as a

---

[69] "City of Bloomington City Council Meeting Video." (25 Jul. 2016). *See* public comment section at approximately 11:42 on the timer, and after two residents are denied the procedural step of yielding their time), http://bloomingtonmn.granicus.com/MediaPlayer.php?publish_id=8d3fe848-52d8-11e6-8170-f04da2064c47 and Hanks, Mike "Neighborhood Formalizes Complaints." *Sun Current* (Jul. 2106).

[70] Johnson, Scott W. "Somali-Minnesota Terror Recruitment: What I Saw at The Trial." *Star Tribune* (14 Jun. 2106), http://www.startribune.com/somali-minnesota-terror-recruitment-what-i-saw-at-the-trial/383038331/.

negative socialization factor does speak to the City of Bloomington's imperative duty to enforce fully CUP terms, city regulations, and state law – and the racialization fears that do weigh heavily on the community.

The difficult city hall process is chronicled below with a summary of comments that represent the exchanges between residents and city officials – and city officials and attorneys. This section is important to review for learning the critical need to confirm details in the application and the imperative concern for providing clear enforcement terms. (Some remarks were paraphrased to provide context. The footnotes provide sourcing to the city council or study meeting minutes, video or audio tapes, *Powerpoint* presentations, photos, emails, and news articles.):

RESIDENTS' POINTS OF VIEW

A few residents appeared at the City Council meetings to comment regularly so what follows is a synopsis that serves to establish the continuity of the complaints heard from residents of the AFYFC neighborhood.

In response to many complaints about AFYFC, including issues like "hundreds of people come and go at all hours from the old high school building at Park Avenue and 82nd Street and that residential streets are clogged with parked cars ... too much noise and too much traffic,[71] the Bloomington City Council convened a public study session on September 1, 2012. This was one year past the deadline to have executed a contract with AFYFC for terms of the shared athletic fields and city parking lot.

Then, when the 2012 study session resolved little, this exchange shows that a year and a half later, the same complaints continued (there still was no agreement with AFYFC on the expired Joint Use Agreement (JUA)). Similar comments were made at most meetings between the dates shown below. These are merely samples:

April 21, 2014, City Council Meeting

RESIDENT ONE (summarized): Overflow parking in park lot and on streets is constant. City attorney says that basketball is legally protected [religious] outreach, but in the middle of the night? **The City does not have to allow basketball in the middle of the night!** Do we not expect all the other businesses in Bloomington to follow what they proposed? The CUP requires "sufficient off-street parking" but now City Attorney says there must be a

---

[71] Smetanka, Mary Jane. "Cities Tread Warily on Holy Ground: Bloomington and Other Metro-Area Cities Have Found That Restricting Religious Groups Is Dicey." *Star Tribune* (1 Sep. 2012), http://www.startribune.com/metro-area-cities-tread-warily-on-holy-ground/168230826/.

trigger before City enforces. Now AFYFC wants to use the park lot for 40 – 50 late nights or all nights per year?[72]

RESIDENT TWO (summarized): AFYFC uses many blocks for street parking during Ramadan and attendees say 2000 participate. Ramadan parking is through the night until 4:30 a.m. on some nights. All parks' parking lots in the City should close at the same time. (No comment from City Council members or staff to either RESIDENT.)[73]

Editorial Comment: Almost three years after AFYFC took possession of the property, and continuous during the entire period, the activity, parking, and traffic complaints were of the same nature. In 2016, the concerns continued as reflected in the one sample below:

January 25, 2016

RESIDENT ONE – During Council meeting comment session, a resident presented data (repeat attempt as concerns had not been addressed) on dangers to park users when AFYFC practices double-parking and potentially blocks emergency vehicles serving the public park, and showed how AFYFC dumping in the public athletic field diminished the park. The mayor and city manager admonished any speaker who would present repetitive concerns and the mayor informed this speaker that she would only receive a copy of previous responses.[74]

ANALYSIS:

Residents have had the same complaints for years. Over time, some councilmembers, the mayor, city manager and attorney became highly critical of citizen comments made at Council sessions. Some officials complained that the concerns were repetitive, giving rise to warnings that residents would not be allowed to speak on issues presented at prior sessions. On the other hand, some councilmembers were also on record noting the absence of religious animus in presentations of neighbor frustrations.

---

[72] "City of Bloomington City Council Meeting." (21 Apr. 2014), See appx. 29 mins and later at 42:30 on the marker,
http://bloomingtonmn.granicus.com/MediaPlayer.php?publish_id=729dd983-1b18-1032-bfdc-23d7cb73de00.

[73] Id.

[74] "City of Bloomington City Council Meeting Video." See marker at 25:00 to 32:00 mins. (25 Jan. 2016),
http://bloomingtonmn.granicus.com/MediaPlayer.php?publish_id=5b6ba654-c3e3-11e5-8170-f04da2064c47.

8/20/2012 City Study Meeting

At the August 2012 public study meeting two councilmembers voiced concern: "If they're not going to obey the conditions, I'm ready to vote to pull the conditional-use permit," and "We're letting the neighbors down."[75]

COUNCILMEMBER ONE: **The City Council based parking limits on [AFYFC] numbers. [This is like] taking out a permit to build a bedroom addition that turned out to be a 10-room addition.** Then it is like saying, "Oops, I guess I lied. I guess I misrepresented what I was doing." Tough enough to make these decisions without the misrepresentations that were made. No one on the Council (including City attorney) would appreciate that kind of activity that is occurring at AFYFC across from their home.[76] Can I, as a homeowner, set up a hockey rink in my backyard with flood lights and bounce hockey pucks off the boards until midnight?[77] We said, 'welcome to the neighborhood' but he broke the needle off in our backside.[78]

COUNCILMEMBER TWO: **We were assured time and time again that we had protections in the permit to stop this from happening.** What's concerning me is code violations. This weekend AFYFC visitors had picnics on neighbors' front lawns and residents who wanted to use the park were told they were not allowed to use the parking lot [by AFYFC members]. This community has a Neighborhood Watch program but hard to monitor activity when park is dark and people are sleeping in cars overnight [in AFYFC parking lot]. Today, there were all sorts of hand-painted signs put up on private property telling people where to park. If I put up campaign signs without permission, you would tear them down. I could go on and on … [79]

---

[75] Hanks, Mike. "Late Nights, Parking at Muslim Community Center Anger Bloomington Neighbors." *Sun Current* (15 Aug. 2012), http://current.mnsun.com/2012/08/15/late-nights-parking-at-muslim-community-center-anger-bloomington-neighbors/.

[76] City Council Study Meeting Minutes, Aug. 20, 2012, p. 4, *supra* at note 52. Comments not found in the Minutes may be located on the audio recording of the Aug. 20, 2012 study meeting at 1:14 on the timer: (URL here) http://mosquesinamerica.org/wp-content/uploads/2016/10/76_08-20-12sm1.mp3

[77] *Id.* at p.8.

[78] *Id.; also see*: "Bloomington City Council Study Meeting Audio Recording" Part One (20 Aug. 2012), at approximately 1:15 on timer. (This statement would have appeared on page 4 of the Council-approved minutes, but it was not included in the final version of the minutes). http://mosquesinamerica.org/wp-content/uploads/2016/10/78_08-20-12sm1.mp3

[79] *Id. see* audio recording for Aug. 20, 2012 study meeting pt. 1, at appx. 1:24 on the marker. (This statement does not appear in the approved version of the minutes). http://mosquesinamerica.org/wp-content/uploads/2016/10/79_08-20-12sm1.mp3

MAYOR: It sounds like RLUIPA [federal law] has gone completely in one direction (against city zoning authority). (And, on the question of whether AFYFC was being unresponsive): It's interesting they're too busy to deal with the problems they're creating.[80]

10/22/2012 City Council Meeting

COUNCILMEMBER ONE: It is unrealistic to compare a one-day festival (addressing a typical church practice) with events such as Ramadan (lasting 30 days with festivals at ends). Facility (mosque) on Cedar Avenue violated its CUP but the City did nothing and it hasn't done anything about AFYFC. It hasn't and it won't and the City can't do much if it involves a church. When the City grants [CUPs like these], it gives away all of its authority to enforce conditions.[81]

MAYOR: We have been told that when there is excessive use or overflow problems, the City doesn't have the ability to discontinue or revoke the permit.[82]

ATTORNEY Response: City has the right to consider a CUP revocation when there is verified violation. But AFYFC parking issues [only] trigger need to provide more proof of parking [off streets].[83]

9/23/13 City Study Meeting and discussion about CUP for Mt. Hope Church

COUNCILMEMBER: "I see us punishing, probably a good church because we are all so paranoid at least I know I am. I look at these things and I say, 'Oh my God, here comes another one.'" (This recognizes the restrictions imposed on other religious institutions in light of AFYFC abuses.)[84]

MAYOR: "If we go forward with this church they're going to be able to have services but they can't have day care and they can't do this and can't do that. My God, what did he (planning department) do, put the Al Farooq thing in the copy machine, and say here's the conditions?"[85]

---

[80] City Council Study Meeting Minutes, Aug. 20, 2012, p. 5, supra at note 52.

[81] "Bloomington City Council Approved Minutes." Pp. 6-7. (22 Oct. 2012).

[82] *Id.* at 7.

[83] *Id.*

[84] "City of Bloomington City Council Meeting Video." (23 Sep. 2013), at appx. 4:31 on the marker, http://bloomingtonmn.granicus.com/MediaPlayer.php?publish_id=deed4eb7-7681-1031-bf4f-32d5966f69c1. (Year indicated under video is incorrect; see Agenda date on opposing page.)

[85] *Id.*

10/14/2013 Study Session

COUNCILMEMBER ONE: I remember spokesman telling us that if assembly exceeded 200 per assembly meeting, he would turn them away or would seek to find a way to shuttle members. I think that some parking estimates from police and City are grossly understated. When I observed in August (Eid, during Ramadan), there were cars were parked in all directions for blocks. (Answer from City Manager: This is no different than area churches and Holy Week, etc.; Response from City Attorney: **Mosque spokesperson's [attendance representations at the CUP hearing] were his "best estimate."**) They have far exceeded 500 in the gym.[86]

MAYOR: When is a special event a special event, or when is it a regular event? Is it 2, 4, 6, 8, 10 -- 20 times? That's where we have found ourselves in the unknown. Could we have anticipated this up front? Could we have defined it? Appears to be a fairly large number of special events regularly.[87]

COUNCILMEMBER TWO: When does a miscalculation become a misrepresentation? **This was brought in to us as a grade school, an elementary school, with a small prayer room. At the same time it was being presented to us as that, they were advertising on their website that this was going to be the largest mosque in the state of MN.** I mean, that's a flat out lie. You can call it a miscalculation; it's a misrepresentation. It's a lie. To say that we have no authority to back up our own CUP just tells me that you just wasted 20 years of my life – and that infuriates me, frankly. (Attorney: You have no authority to amend [the CUP] at this point. We have learned a lot over the two-year-plus history working with this group. There are no violations of the CUP at this point. In every case, they have complied with City orders. There isn't a history of being a scofflaw.)[88]

7/28/2014 City Study Meeting

COUNCILMEMBER ONE: During discussion on whether to consult an outside attorney: There is an item on the [AFYFC] CUP that has been unfulfilled for three years.[89]

---

[86] "City of Bloomington Study Session Audio." (14 Oct. 2013), at appx. 3:00 – 3:10 on the timer. http://mosquesinamerica.org/wp-content/uploads/86_10-14-13ccsm.MP3
[87] *Id.* at 3:10.
[88] *Id.* at 3:12:30 – 3:20:00. (Mayor comments that his notes on protracted JUA negotiations are "shame on us.")
[89] "City of Bloomington City Council Study Meeting Approved Minutes." p. 14 (28 Jul. 2014), *available at*: http://meetings.bloomingtonmn.gov:8080/agenda/cityofbloomington/286/UHJpdmF0ZSBNa W51dGVzIERvY3VtZW50/10/n/3912.doc.

COUNCILMEMBER TWO: The Council is being asked to put some teeth in the enforcement process. It would be helpful to have more openness regarding how the facility is being used, as there is no practical leverage for the City to exert.[90]

COUNCILMEMBER THREE: The City needs to be able to respond to the needs of the community. There is no guarantee the JUA will be followed. What happens when a condition isn't being followed? How did the original CUP happen?[91]

10/21/2014 City Study Meeting

COUNCILMEMBER ONE: The number of users at AFYFC is considerably more than what they were three years ago when the agreement was made with them.[92]

MAYOR: Many people have expressed frustration with DAF; its structure and its management. There are [AFYFC] events listed on the internet that have not been reported by [one of the AFYFC officials] such as a restaurant with a menu and dollar amounts.[93]

ANALYSIS:

Several new councilmembers have replaced departing members on the council since this saga began. Generally, the frustration level with this matter has remained high: some members were exasperated with AFYFC's misrepresentations and lack of compliance with the law and other members eventually were annoyed that the same residents kept appearing at council sessions to enumerate the problems.

As with many intractable conflicts, the discrete harms were incremental; some were not significant if considered alone. But once multiple wrongs are allowed to accrue as here, the impact on the community is much the same as if the city had issued variances to allow the exceptional uses.

A number of neighbors, besides the few that consistently spoke at the podium, felt that the response to this series of challenges was an equal series of concessions, especially at these critical junctures: when City Code on double parking was conveniently changed to make it acceptable city-

---

[90] *Id.* at 10.

[91] *Id.* at 11.

[92] "City of Bloomington City Council Study Meeting Approved Minutes." p. 8 (21 Oct. 2014), *available at*:
http://meetings.bloomingtonmn.gov:8080/agenda/cityofbloomington/314/UHJpdmF0ZSBNa
W51dGVzIERvY3VtZW50/10/n/8231.doc.

[93] *Id.*

wide; when this group essentially was exempted from the *residential* norm that noisy group activity is concluded by 10:00 p.m. (with the understanding that traffic/parking, lights, and related noise ends by 11:00 p.m.); when consistent street parking was tolerated; when the frequency of, and attendance at, large events was well beyond what was anticipated; when neighbors reported that events during Ramadan stretch virtually through the night with perpetual in-and-out, residents felt that local government had failed to protect their family and property interests. First, the applicant had not accurately represented levels and scope of activities and then lacked commitment to comply with City and CUP regulations. Second, the City failed to uphold the agreements and regulations and, instead, adjusted the rules, norms, and agreements to accommodate the users.

Observers should also consider what would be the likelihood that other religious organizations would get a pass *for years* while officials tried to find solutions and engaged in protracted negotiations that resulted in a weakened oversight agreement.

The city attorneys, city manager, and parks director have provided context to show that some churches in Bloomington have also conducted large events and that there are annual well-attended civic festivals. But these comparisons do not represent the same kind of consistent heavy traffic, late hours, parking chaos, and periodic takeover of city park facilities that the AFYFC neighborhood experiences. The next section will demonstrate that the city attorney and manager are largely responsible for the confusion, delays and political paralysis.

CITY ATTORNEY AND CITY MANAGER POINTS OF VIEW

The city attorney is expected to provide legal guidance on the issues that elected city officials confront. This relationship vests a great deal of trust in the city attorney as well as a duty to provide reasoned advice before final action is taken by the Council.

The city manager is like a business manager and he or she also relies upon attorney guidance to inform decisions and to conduct management duties.

In this case, the city attorney has taken a risk-averse perspective to the AFYFC controversies. Arguably, her approach has privileged AFYFC compared to other religious applicants and institutions in Bloomington. When the City Council considered a subsequent church application, and a Councilman that had reached such a level of frustration that he opined that the Council was "punishing, probably a good church because we are all so paranoid," the attorney responded that the Council had learned not to rely on applicant statements, although "almost all" other applicants did honor what they said they were going to do.[94]

The advice provided and cases selected for justifying guidance to the Council did not represent adequately the full range of federal rulings, even in the federal Circuit jurisdiction for Minnesota. It is true that geographical regions are subject to appellate court rulings in the respective Circuit court district – unless the Supreme Court settles an issue – but federal caselaw on the Religious Land Use and Institutionalized Persons Act (RLUIPA)[95] is notoriously confused and specious rulings can be found to buttress almost any position.

It is always politically and financially safe to steer clear of Department of Justice inquiries and to avoid costly litigation. But city officials still have a fundamental duty to uphold local ordinances and permit conditions in a consistent manner.

A full discussion of federal law – chiefly RLUIPA – along with practical insight as to what elected officials and citizens may do to avoid government investigation or the litigation danger zone will follow in a later chapter. It is important here to note that in some instances the attorney appears to say that this federal law applies to permit violations and enforcement response, when the law's text and the subsequent rulings show that the law was written to protect religious groups during the highly discretionary *permitting* stage. Once a permit issued, municipality authority to enforce the terms evenly is not questioned.

During the August 2012 Bloomington City Council Study Session, the city attorney provided a *Powerpoint* briefing on the applicable provisions of RLUIPA and warned councilmembers of personal liability and civil rights penalties if city officials were found to have discriminated against AFYFC (even during *enforcement* actions). The following are bullet points extracted from a copy of the slides (the substance is paraphrased if not in quotation marks):

- "Elected officials are often sued in their individual capacities. Costs could wipe out (municipal) insurance reserves." – and City insurance may not cover individual defense expenses if there is a

---

[94] Bloomington City Council Meeting Video Recording, Sep. 23, 2013, *supra*, at note 84; find discussion at approximately 4:15 on the marker; city attorney dire warnings on RLUIPA at 4:28. (Minutes have not been made available and the City-provided date of 23 Sep. 2012 under the video is apparently in error.), *available at:*
http://bloomingtonmn.granicus.com/MediaPlayer.php?publish_id=deed4eb7-7681-1031-bf4f-32d5966f69c1..

[95] 42 U.S. Code Chapter 21C – "Protection Of Religious Exercise In Land Use And By Institutionalized Persons," Legal Information Institute, Cornell University Law School, *available at:* https://www.law.cornell.edu/uscode/text/42/chapter-21C.

known violation of RLUIPA. If insurance does kick in, premiums will rise.[96]

- "Decision-makers must disassociate themselves from opponents of the property use who are motivated by dislike of the religion."

- "Courts can impute the *discriminatory intent* of opponents to the decision makers." (Emphasis in original.) "This is particularly true if the land use approval is returned to the local board."

- "Never negatively comment on the religion's belief, practices, celebrations, national origin, manner of dress, or any other characteristic.

- For religious uses occupancy limits are set by the Fire Code safety limits. The limits are not enforced pro-actively – just in response to a safety concern for building occupants. The current occupancy limits only relate to parking capacity."

- "City code has no limit on hours of operation for any assembly. Some religious observances continue for days."

- "Adding conditions (to the CUP) ... may violate RLUIPA."

- "Although night-time parking in other parks is not allowed – it is allowed [for AFYFC] because of the joint use agreements. Prohibiting night-time use of the shared parking lots would violate the City's agreements for joint use. Therefore, nighttime use of these lots is allowed by the users of AFYFC."

- "A local law restricting the hours of operation for all places of assembly may violate the (RLUIPA) 'substantial burden' test."

- "Requiring on-site parking capacity for peak periods during special seasons would pose a substantial burden (on a religious assembly and could trigger lawsuit)."

ATTORNEY: Representations of an applicant [documents and data submitted at formal CUP hearing to provide attendance, functions, and hours of use] are not enforceable. Unless a limitation (on activity levels,

---

[96] Bloomington City Council Study Session Audio, and Approved Minutes, Aug. 20, 2012, *supra* at note 76 (audio) and 52 (minutes) respectively. *Find* this audio discussion at approximately 58 mins. on the marker.

traffic, or parking) is in the CUP, what applicant said during Council deliberations is legally irrelevant.[97]

ATTORNEY: Under the terms of the pre-existing JUA, night use of the facilities are completely legal and there can be no prohibition.[98]

September 23, 2013 City Council Meeting

ATTORNEY: **Just remember with the RLUIPA lawsuit, here's what happens: They get punitive damages, they get attorney's fees, and they get whatever they want. This is probably your highest value lawsuit. And because the attorney's fees are paid for, there are attorneys fishing for these cases . . . because they are guaranteed to get paid. This is huge risk. The cases out there are truly frightening."[99]**

Editorial Comment:

The city attorney stressed the risk of a personal lawsuit for officials who deny a religious land use decision. Court cases just do not support this emphasis. When city officials act outside their designated authority, there is potential personal liability, but it is very rare that courts will penetrate the protections afforded public servants who are trying to perform their proper roles. The facts of the AFYFC saga do not provide reasonable support for this unqualified warning.

Additionally, there was little reason for the City to restrict night activities under the agreement with the Lutheran high school, and then Concordia High School, since night activities were minimal and only incidentally burdensome on neighborhood. And, the premise that night use must remain unrestricted per the terms of the original agreement was undermined by the many other altered terms of the negotiated 2015 AFYFC Joint Use Agreement. Also, according to interpretations of RLUIPA, if AFYFC is permitted all-night use and unrestricted "night use" is "completely legal", other assembly applicants may demand the same treatment.

---

[97] *Id.* at 57 mins. However, the March 24, 2011 AFYFC CUP Staff Report, *supra* at note 36, provides AFYFC documents that clearly show applicant-submitted data, including attendance and activity numbers, that became the basis for issuing the staff approval recommendations, as well as the conditions for the issuance of the final conditional use permit.
http://mosquesinamerica.org/wp-content/uploads/2016/10/97_AFYFC-Staff-Report.pdf

[98] *Id.* at 52 mins. (Night activities, past 10:00 p.m. (or 11:00 p.m. final clear-the-parking-lot regulation), under the prior Lutheran/Concordia High School and Church use were extremely rare and comparatively much lower levels of participation.) http://mosquesinamerica.org/wp-content/uploads/2016/10/98_08-20-12sm1.mp3

[99] Bloomington City Council Meeting, Sep. 23, 2013, *supra* at note 84. *See* 4:28:30 on the marker.

The Bloomington attorney stressed some extreme and unlikely hazards of disregarding RLUIPA terms, but she did not emphasize the fact that the limits in the CUP were responsive to AFYFC's own detailed application and testimony. Again, a CUP hearing is a *quasi-judicial* proceeding that includes both *testimony* and *findings of fact*. These formal processes should not be rendered sham spectacles by applicants that shirk factual presentations and answers.

Finally, when the city attorney attempted to justify overriding the CUP limits (e.g., the large gym may only be used by students during the times that there are school/day care activities, and only students may use the large gym and cafeteria when there are other on-site assemblies), as accepted at the CUP hearing by AFYFC, the applicant could reasonably conclude that much of the CUP was nullified by the much greater fire code attendance allowance that the attorney began to impose.

7/28/2014 City Study Meeting

CITY MANAGER: AFYFC can have their parking [lot] lights on all night if they want when they're in use. The question is if City refuses use of parking lot for overflow then they can legally park in the street (editorial: but this is in violation of the CUP).[100]

The reason that [legal opinions on the CUP] have been strung out are because there are neighbors that don't want the AFYFC in their neighborhood and staff has answered their questions over and over again.[101]

10/21/2014 City Study Meeting

ATTORNEY: Occupancy cannot be limited for a religious land use unless there is a health, life, safety hazard (editorial: although the CUP does provide limits through parking restrictions and occupancy of gym at 500). Neither can the City restrict nighttime use of a religious facility. Occupancy can only be limited by Fire Code and [the city attorney] had never heard of a Fire Marshall counting people as they entered a religious place of assembly.[102] Traffic, parking, and intensity of use are not compelling government interests.[103]

---

[100] *Id.* at 13. http://mosquesinamerica.org/wp-content/uploads/2016/10/100_2012-Jy-to-Dc.pdf; http://mosquesinamerica.org/wp-content/uploads/2016/10/100_08-20-12sm2.mp3

[101] *Id.* at 14. (This is indicative of City Council reprimands of resident comments at Council meetings as warnings were issued that repetitive concerns would not be heard.)

[102] City of Bloomington City Council Study Meeting Approved Minutes, Oct. 21, 2014, p. 6, *supra* at note 92.

[103] *Id.* p. 7.

Editorial Comment: This conclusion on the part of the city attorney implies that a religious group has successfully demonstrated with factual evidence that the government has imposed a substantial burden on it. However, this "burden" is subject to legal tests and is not based upon perceptions or complaints alone. And, this specific RLUIPA legal test applies at the time of the applicant's hearing; generally speaking, the test does not apply during the enforcement phase of a settled CUP.

The attorney stated that fire code limits are the only restriction that may be placed on a religious assembly (and also general assembly) use, but then she said that there is no procedure (other than a safety inspection) that would measure compliance and, therefore, trigger enforcement.

CITY MANAGER: The City has video and audio of the same people coming to the podium to complain about AFYFC, which puts the City in a bad position.[104] The CUP condition of having a new JUA in place by a certain date is moot.[105]

ANALYSIS:

What has occurred over time is that the City has accepted the city attorney's instruction that there may be no other limits on AFYFC occupancy of the large gym other than Fire Code (maximum) allowances of 1900 persons.[106] Thus, the CUP restriction on gym occupancy, and other spaces, was nullified. Parking findings in the staff report were modified accordingly to require acquisition of additional parking provisions to match occupancy. No official mention was made of traffic volume and impact on residential streets and homes. As these CUP rules were modified, did it not occur to officials that the core of the CUP had been hollowed out, and a revised or amended CUP, including legal notice and a hearing for neighbors, should replace it?

In the AFYFC case, the neighborhood never had opportunity to consider and respond to the adjusted CUP terms and negotiated rules provided to regulate the athletic field use and park parking lots. After all, neighbors were told from the beginning, by AFYFC and by the City, that the usage of the property would continue as before. No changes. The neighbors were satisfied with this. AFYFC was required to report to the City on attendance, hours of events, and kind of events. AFYFC's data, submitted to a *fact-finding* body, became the basis for staff assessments of frequency and

---

[104] *Id.* at p. 6.

[105] *Id.* at p. 7.

[106] *Id.* (The City Manager noted here that the CUP was tied to fire code capacity for the bleachers in the gym of 500, although full limits for the gym was 1900 occupants.)

impact of the submitted reports. The neighbors trusted that these predictions would be accurate, and accepted them. The City used this data to formulate permit conditions and restrictions on use. The neighbors felt secure.

All subsequent regulatory modifications to accommodate AFYFC's dramatically higher activity have been City pronouncements that have functioned like City allowances. The neighbors have complained but they have had no meaningful input. In the final analysis, the planning staff's recommendations – as adopted by the City Council – for the approval of AFYFC's conditional permit, based upon "area, hours of use or operation, and limits[107]" were rendered meaningless.

The de facto "full fire code" rule turned land use staff planning procedures on their head. Predictably, religious applicants, according to this Bloomington "full fire code occupancy" land use standard, will be held to meet parking capacity potential *as if they consistently* run full maximum capacity of the building. Using this logic, a religious organization applying to use a property that is rated for two hundred per fire code, but that has fifty attendees on average, with one hundred and fifty on Christmas and Easter, may be expected to qualify for potential parking space – even though not yet "triggered" – as if attendance is rated as two hundred.

It may be said that, as the City found a way to come to terms with AFYFC levels of activity and occupancy under fire code allowances, the same standard then had to be applied to all assembly uses going forward. Therefore, arguably, all applicants would have to qualify for what the City Council members described as "the worst case scenario." This conceivably limited options for religious organizations that desire to use a portion of a building and who cannot provide sufficient assurance that proof of additional parking will be available, or affordable, for maximum fire code occupancy limits.

In 2013, the City codified limitations on trips over residential streets such that new or *increased* institutional use (including religious use) of more than 300 additional trips per day or 100 additional trips per hour during peak times (at least once a week) – or the total of over 1000 trips per day – would be presumed incompatible with "residential livability and pedestrian and motorist safety" and only allowed with a City finding of sufficient mitigation.[108] With the declared opening of a university on the AFYFC campus, and if participation became the advertised one thousand students (in recognition of the attendant increased traffic burden), these standards

---

[107] City of Bloomington Staff Report regarding AFYFC, *supra* at note 36, p. 4.

[108] Bloomington Code Sec. 21.302.06, *available at*:
https://www.bloomingtonmn.gov/clerk/city-charter-and-code-ordinances.

arguably should have been considered. As stated in the AFYFC CUP, changes in "occupancy or building use" require City Council review and, if approved, an amendment to the CUP. At the point of this review, trip count rules might have been applied.

Incidentally, the City did send notice to AFYFC stating that use of the facilities for a university was not authorized. However, the office and various classes continued to be advertised as sited at AFYFC after the warning was issued.

Also, by allowing AFYFC the potential for so many burdensome events with so few restrictions, the AFYFC model provides legal precedent, under RLUIPA, for other assembly uses to expect the same kinds of rule changes and allowances that benefited AFYFC. The fire code ceiling on participants and frequency also solidified this precedent by affording all subsequent assembly uses the same mechanism. This is a cycle that is not easily broken once the applicant's own testimony detailing the type and intensity of use is delinked from the City-approved CUP license to operate.

Also, in theory, the full fire code "religious use" occupancy allowance overrides the 2013 trip count policy that the City of Bloomington attempted to implement restricting daily or hours-per-day entrances and exits in traffic-sensitive areas like residential zones. This policy also serves to limit the number of cars that may stack into a left-hand turn lane. But, how may a city limit the number of cars in and out of a driveway during a period of time when the fire-rated maximum occupancy guarantees approval for the building's maximum fire occupancy? To carry this rationale further, why even discuss attendance projections at a religious land use hearing when the decision makers may just proceed directly to fire code limits, as long as promised future parking spaces are assured?

If religious occupant non-compliance can be excused, why bother to conduct a CUP hearing and why have staff perform the studies examining the burden on streets, and injury to the surrounding neighborhood?

The attorney further instructed via a *Powerpoint* presentation that there could be no "proactive" fire code occupancy inspections and that the City would not count attendees at the door. She provided that occupancy might only be inspected in response to a safety complaint or concern.[109] One must then wonder how the limits are to be enforced, especially when an organization like AFYFC has papered over the facility's glass doors and entry area windows. It also is notable that Bloomington's Community Development Director advised planning officials that fire code occupancy varies according to the use of the room. Therefore, removal of walls (as

---

[109] Bloomington City Study Session Minutes, Aug. 20, 2012, *supra* at note 52, p. 3 of *Powerpoint* slide attachment.

neighbors suspected AFYFC had done) or an altered dedicated purpose for part of a facility ostensibly should trigger revision of the occupancy.[110]

A subsequent discussion will note that code-based zoning rules and enforcement may have been relaxed for AFYFC but they were in full force when the application for Resurrection Power Church was considered, and denied.

The city attorney also warned several times that defending and losing a religious land use lawsuit could mean responsibility for city legal costs in addition to paying the prevailing side's attorney fees and [punitive] damages, while insurance coverage would be in question. This was accompanied by the warning that elected officials are *often* sued in their individual capacities (but, almost as often, suits against officials in their individual capacities are removed from these cases).[111] This is a grave risk to present to political representatives who must account to voters. And, it may be overstated without proper context. In this case, the staff legal advice also strongly implied that city officials may not have normal immunity protections from lawsuit costs and damage payments to the complainant.

But the courts have not construed provisions of RLUIPA to mean that cities should refrain from enforcing generally applicable ordinances and reasonable permit conditions once the use permit was issued according to RLUIPA guidelines. There is no constitutional protection from the consequential force of law as long as constitutionally proper regulations are enforced in a lawful manner.

For the many attempts by councilmembers to suggest that a permit condition should be enforced, the city attorney had a legal reason to excuse infractions, many times based upon the opportunity for AFYFC to claim that imposing a "substantial burden" upon this religious organization would be legally indefensible.

As the Bloomington residents and city council members grew more frustrated with AFYFC's disregard for CUP requirements, the city attorney continued to advise deference to the group warning that "anti-Islamic comments" could be attributed to official hostility. However, a review of the record does not reveal anti-Islamic comments but only concern, and sometimes anger, over misrepresentations and violations of city code and

---

[110] Bloomington City Study Session Minutes, Oct. 21, 2014, p.6, *supra* at note 92.

[111] City of Bloomington Study Meeting Minutes, Aug. 20, 2012, p.5, *supra* at note 52.

the permit. In fact, City Council members on several occasions noted the lack of religious or racial animus behind comments.[112]

Furthermore, it is the responsibility of city planners to put comments that are not germane to the civic land use process into context. City planners are expected to affirm their commitment to assess an applicant's qualifications, objectively and according to proper procedure. When public comments reflect personal opinion regarding the applicant's beliefs or practices, government officials should restate their focus on regulations and required procedures. They may remind commenters that productive statements are those relevant to the hearing business. But to suggest that comments should be restricted or censored runs dangerously close to violating First Amendment free speech rights.

Some judges have inquired when there is a notable record of community hostility surrounding a mosque permit hearing as to whether land planners were influenced by the atmospheric animus. When there is unusual delay or a denial, this question may arise. This does not mean that legitimate concerns should be muted, but it is important that speakers at the podium and in the audience bear in mind the defined purposes and limits of these hearings.

A resident who is irate over the unanticipated congestion and disturbance caused by many hundreds to over a thousand people flowing into and out of the neighborhood on a routine basis may simply be upset about the nuisance factors of noise and congestion. This is also the case with mega-churches. Complainers may not be expressing hostility to a group, but may just be upset that the community was not afforded opportunity to assess this eventuality. When a city is failing to enforce appropriate zoning regulations, exasperation may be aimed at city officials. The entire idea behind conditional use is defeated when the provisions for tailoring that use to the character of already established zone, and intended character of the area, are ignored.

Should the city impute "discriminatory intent" to a mosque "opponent" when the resident is just demanding that the city enforce explicit use and parking restrictions upon which the conditional use was originally granted? Is a frustrated resident out of order when questioning extravagant breaches of the conditional user's own projections provided for application purposes? Or, should resident outrage at the intentional planning of activities not even scheduled to dismiss until well after 10:00 p.m. be imputed to discriminatory animus?

---

[112] Bloomington City Council Meeting Video Recording, Sep. 23, 2013, *supra* at note 84. Discussion begins at appx. 4:29 on the marker. (This is an example of several discussions regarding whether there is animus behind citizen comments.)

The task of discerning how much of a speaker's angst may be attributed to frustration with unchecked exploitation of a use permit and whether any of it stems from pre-existing animosity towards the general group responsible for the overuse is formidable. This is the reason that the Constitution allows for robust free speech on matters of public concern.

At this point, it is important to understand that this area of Minnesota has long had a growing Muslim population and many neighborhood children grew up with – and befriended – Muslim children. Some that are most disturbed today report that they were not at all concerned upon learning that the vacant school property would be occupied by an Islamic group. Residents remember being assured that the use would be much like it had been before, and there was only one resident who registered a written concern with AFYFC's original application. Repeated and excused breaches of the assurances, and the sharply contrasting treatment of another religious institution, understandably have undermined confidence in Bloomington land use governance.

CASE TWO: RESURRECTION POWER CHURCH

About two years after the AFYFC CUP approval, on May 9, 2013, essentially the same city officials summarily denied the CUP application of Resurrection Power Church.[113] This forty-congregant non-denominational church was represented at the hearings by Pastor Eddy Udeh. The selected site was zoned as "industrial," but "assembly" use was allowed if conditional code requirements were met (CUP). Although the church had negotiated an agreement with the owner of the parcel, met with city staff to answer concerns, and worked to address the issues on the city planner's checklist, the city staff's answer was first a qualified yes, and then -- while the applicant was meeting staff demands in good faith -- officials reversed and declined the application.

Bear in mind, that this case is one of several religious land use applications considered in the years after AFYFC. This one was the first, and it provides clear contrast. There are others that also demonstrate the City's unusual treatment of AFYFC as compared to any religious case that was presented in the several intervening years.

For Resurrection Power Church, there was only perfunctory, if any, public mention by the city council or the city attorney of the RLUIPA obligations that government decision-makers must consider when evaluating a religious use application. Nor did anyone mention that the unique hardship

---

[113] "City of Bloomington City Council Meeting Video." (20 May 2013) See appx. 1:00 on the video marker, *available at*:
http://bloomingtonmn.granicus.com/MediaPlayer.php?publish_id=fd65ee4d-1310-1031-8b21-673bf20d68e3.

50

this congregation suffered during an extended and confusing process – including the bewildering reversal from a qualified approval to a denial – may well qualify as "substantial" for the purposes of RLUIPA's concerns about uncertainly and delay. It did not appear that the pastor had an attorney present to raise these issues.

Just six months before the council voted to deny, permit approval was officially recommended for Pastor Udeh and his congregation. The owner of the larger parcel who intended to lease a warehouse to the church had assured the pastor that the warehouse had already received a 3-year termed approval for what was considered an assembly use (by a youth soccer organization). All appeared to be going smoothly when the first city planning staff report, as presented to council on December 6, 2012, recommended approval for Resurrection Power Church. This approval was subject to normal conditions like a shared parking agreement and limitations on the use of excess warehouse space that was not needed for services.[114]

Not one, but two, staff reports recommended approval for the Resurrection Power Church application. The amended staff report provided on February 25, 2013 increased the number of conditions that the church would have to meet but Pastor Udeh was willing to address all concerns. He noted at the Council meeting that it would take 30 years for his congregation, at past rates of growth, to fill up parking spaces!

Yet on May 20, 2013, city council members gave "thumbs down" to the project citing myriad and speculative "what ifs": involving truck traffic (for an adjacent battery business warehouse even though the recorded agreement limited activity to hours different from the church), parking concerns, maintenance of an access point, and potential development of a freeway. Most of these issues were addressed in Pastor Udeh's proposal, including shared parking with back-up plans for additional overflow lots.[115]

---

[114] "City of Bloomington Staff Report: Conditional Use Permit for a Place of Assembly in an Existing Warehouse Building." (29 Nov. 2012) and (25 Feb. 2013), *available at* https://www.pdffiller.com/24000056-10654A12pdf-Case-10654A-12---City-of-Bloomington-Various-Fillable-Forms; http://mosquesinamerica.org/wp-content/uploads/2016/10/114_Conditional_Use_Permit_Warehouse.pdf

[115] The Bloomington City Attorney risked legal jeopardy when causing legally qualified "delay, uncertainty, and expense" as mentioned in several presentations to the Bloomington City Council when discussing enforcement of the AFYFC CUP terms, but disregarded clear signs that "delay, uncertainty, and expense" may have constituted a indefensible "substantial burden" in the case of Resurrection Power Church. For example, the Seventh Circuit Court of Appeal found that the City of New Berlin caused a substantial burden when imposing "delay, uncertainty, and expense" by forcing the church either to sell its land and find another parcel or to restart the permitting process on the same parcel. *Sts Constantine and Helen Greek Orthodox Church Inc v. City of New Berlin*, 396 F. 3d 895 (7th Cir. 2005).

Safety concerns, like co-existing with a neighbor tenant's delivery patterns, are similar to others that have been negotiated in various shared parking lot arrangements around the country. And any final questions about use of the warehouse space should have been satisfied when Pastor Udeh waived rights to use that space. Yet, the City still worried that a future user would revive the warehouse sectional use. If this concern were not simply a pretext to decline the CUP, a provision might have been included in the CUP terms for review, if, or when, the warehouse option was reconsidered.

One Councilmember surmised, "somebody else (i.e., a subsequent owner of the building) could totally abuse that site." The mayor added that "this kind of use has proven to be unpredictable."[116] As this CUP did not have a term limit, councilmembers engaged in seemingly endless anticipation of worst-case scenarios. Rather than make a decision with clear terms that would be subject to review for non-compliance, the City effectively denied the application by declaring that this applicant or some future potential occupant – even if there was a revocable CUP in force – would not honor the contract with the City and local residents.

When the Councilmembers discussed a term-limited CUP as had existed for the soccer organization that was the previous conditional permit-holder on this property, the attorney ruled out the option as no longer available.[117] While a religious organization would expect a longer term than the three-year permit given the soccer group, Pastor Udeh likely would have considered a reasonable termed permit.

The Resurrection Power Church appears to have been punished for a prior applicant's (AFYFC) inaccuracy, insincerity, and eventual non-compliance when submitting plans and describing the scope of activities for a religious land use. Rather than give Pastor Udeh an opportunity to respect the terms of a CUP, the council just said no.

The City of Bloomington was on risky legal ground when projecting its distrust of AFYFC and the series of broken commitments onto Resurrection Power Church. Under RLUIPA, land planners may not discriminate between religious organizations. All come to the application process on equal footing. Presenting more hurdles to one group than another, like the

---

[116] City of Bloomington Approved Minutes, Feb. 25, 2013, p.13 (These minutes were removed from the City website during a system change and have not been replaced. A data request has been submitted and the minutes will be posted when provided.)

[117] The City of Bloomington later offered a "CUP subject to six months review" to a religious applicant called Father's House in 2016, declaring that "if harm to neighborhood safety or welfare," the CUP would be revoked. "Bloomington City Council Meeting." (25 Jan. 2016), at appx. 57:00 on the marker, http://bloomingtonmn.granicus.com/MediaPlayer.php?publish_id=4fd18265-1bd2-11e6-8170-f04da2064c47.

requirement discussed for Resurrection of official traffic and site studies (not listed for AFYFC), also adds to a court's view that local government has acted in a "capricious" manner. Most importantly, speculating about how one group may violate CUP terms based upon the history of another group calls into question the warning in RLUIPA against making these procedural decisions in an arbitrary manner.[118]

This speculation was in apparent contradiction to a constant reminder given the council members by their attorney that applicants often cannot accurately predict usage, and even if applicant lies, there is no recourse. Thus, in one case, if an applicant misrepresents or underestimates the number of attendees, number of cars, or intended activity level, the city will not hold the group accountable. But, in another case, the permit may be denied on sheer speculation that *somebody*, *someday* may *do something* not expressly permitted. One councilman summed up the City's decision to deny Resurrection Power Church's application when he declared that "the *potential* for problems was just too great" in this case.[119] (Emphasis added.)

Finally, as the city planner summed up his presentation as to why the church should be denied, he mentioned complaints against Resurrection Power Church's proposed use of the property but then only produced a single, vague, and uninformed penned note that expressed concern about parking if the church experienced "dramatic growth." This concern was overriding – even though this congregation had attendance numbers of thirty members on average for years!

Again, this worst-case scenario standard is not defensible and this church should not have been held hostage to the overuse of AFYFC. This unequal treatment and hostility to religious use is exactly what RLUIPA was designed to counter. Rather than choose the procedural and legal method of

---

[110] "City of Bloomington Council Meeting Video." (20 May 2013), discussion at approximately 1:08 on the video timer; *available at*: http://bloomingtonmn.granicus.com/MediaPlayer.php?publish_id=fd65ee4d-1310-1031-8b21-673bf20d68e3. One of the most significant congressional interests in RLUIPA was to prevent arbitrary local government decisions in religious land use cases. As in the Fortress Bible Church case where Second Circuit Court of Appeal found "that arbitrary and capricious application of land use regulation 'bolstered' a substantial burden claim," the unfounded "what if, and worst case scenario" speculation that supported the seemingly pretextual Bloomington City Council denial of Resurrection Power Church's application calls into question several RLUIPA protections; chiefly the question of "substantial burden," but also potentially implicating RLUIPA's nondiscrimination and equal terms provisions. *Fortress Bible Church v. Feiner*, 694 F.3d 208, 219 (2nd Cir. 2012); *Chabad Lubavitch of Litchfield County, Inc. v. Borough of Litchfield*, 2014 WL 4652510 (2nd Cir. 2014).

[119] "City of Bloomington City Council Meeting Approved Minutes." p.8 (4 Mar. 2013), *available at*: (These minutes were removed from the City website during a system change and have not been replaced. A data request has been submitted and the minutes will be posted when provided.) http://mosquesinamerica.org/wp-content/uploads/2016/10/119_March-4-2013_Bloomington_Council_Minutes.pdf

asking an applicant to detail the use wanted and then test that use against the zone setting and applicable General and District Plans and finally draft an agreement where the City agrees to the conditional use if the applicant accepts the reasonable restrictions, the AFYFC experience took the City of Bloomington off the rails and into the don't-even-bother-to-apply territory of worst-case-conjecture denials.

The City's overriding concern for safety also appears pretextual based upon the fact that the prior permit holder at the site was a youth soccer organization with predicted numbers of children moving through the parking lot. Furthermore, Pastor Udeh had agreed to a contractual provision for keeping separate hours from the nearby business to restrict traffic overlap. Additionally, the church had agreed to provide parking lot divisions if required.

The City officials and attorney ultimately relied upon parking lot safety reasons to deny the Resurrection Power Church case but the attorney did not engage the important discussion as to the difficult RLUIPA legal tests that must be satisfied to defend this rationale. It is also interesting to consider that AFYFC was permitted to allow double-parking in the lots, arguably, a highly unsafe condition in an emergency.

This very situation illustrates why uses that are "allowed" in a zone not specifically designed for them may be permitted as *conditional* uses. The RLUIPA was passed to say that religious uses should be permitted on the same basis that secular uses are permitted. The array of zoning restrictions, conditions, and code requirements accompany permits to address the concerns of future abuse of permit terms. These restrictions and conditions serve to define what is allowed, what is not allowed, and stipulate that deviations from the terms require amendment or corrective action.

Under RLUIPA, when a city denies a religious use the city must take care to use the "least restrictive means" and courts have looked for good faith efforts on the part of cities to help religious organizations find suitable alternative locations if the city is inclined to deny the desired site. Yet, in the case of Resurrection Power church when the city planner was asked if alternate sites were available, he suggested that Resurrection Power Church consult the Realtor Multiple Listing Services to locate other options. He also advised that the church might consider sharing time with some existing school.

Finally, it is interesting to note in light of the evolution of this application from "likely to approve" to a flat denial, that another of the city attorney's slides at the August 2012 study meeting regarding the AFYFC infractions warned the council that "adding conditions and delaying the approval process may violate RLUIPA." This apparently was not a concern when Resurrection Power Church was the applicant.

To use the mayor's own words, it seemed that RLUIPA has gone "completely nuts" (but apparently only for the benefit of select congregations) – and, also in "one direction" (clearly not for all religious permit applicants).[120] In many cases, the federal RLUIPA law is ignored until invoked by either worried city attorneys or savvy applicants that have the resources and demonstrate will to fight.

In fact, RLUIPA was passed unanimously and signed by President Clinton for the very purpose of curbing what courts call "unfettered discretion." This term describes the tendency of local government officials to apply regulations unequally or to make a decision based, at least in part, on personal bias. In order to prevent the political impulse of acting on whim or evidencing economic preference for non-religious land uses, Congress passed the RLUIPA for the very cases where local politician's "individualized assessments" are the basis for granting or denying applicants' religious rights.[121]

It may be that Pastor Udeh did not know of the powerful arguments that RLUIPA provides against discretionary local zoning decisions. On the evening of the official denial, Pastor Udeh spoke passionately from the podium. He told of how often he thanked God for the council and how he prayed for members every day. He spoke of "justice for all" and said he was puzzled by the inconsistent treatment. Understandably frustrated after months of working to clear changing hurdles, he was not even given

---

[120] "Metro-Area Cities Tread Warily on Holy Ground," *supra* at note 71. (This article also contains a quote attributed to the City Attorney warning that "one of the most litigiously risky actions a city can do" is to "reverse a prior proposal, particularly in light of public protest ..." This admonition implies that official action would be responsive to public protest but it fails to qualify the aspects of public complaints that concerned violations of CUP terms and the City's duty to enforce those.)

[121] As President Clinton stated as he signed RLUIPA into law, it was needed to "protect the exercise of religion ... where State and local governments seek to impose or implement a zoning or landmark law in a manner that imposes a substantial burden on religious exercise." Statement on Signing the Religious Land Use and Institutionalized Persons Act of 2000. *Department of Justice* (22 Sep. 2000), https://www.justice.gov/sites/default/files/jmd/legacy/2014/04/28/presidentialstatement-09-22-00.pdf.; The Second Circuit Court of Appeal said that RLUIPA applies when local government performs "a 'case-by-case evaluation' of a land use application, carrying as it does 'the concomitant risk of idiosyncratic application' of land use standards that may permit (and conceal) 'potentially discriminatory' denials." *Chabad Lubavitch of Litchfield County, Inc. v. Borough of Litchfield*, 2014 WL 4652510 (2nd Cir. 2014).

uninterrupted time to express his disappointment. Instead, the mayor cut in three times to admonish Pastor Udeh to "get to the point."[122]

The irony present in the treatment of these two cases is inescapable when one considers that Christians at the time were under severe persecution in Nigeria by the Islamist Boko Haram. Pastor Udeh's heavy accent indicates that he has not lived in the United States for very long, and he must be aware of the high price that his Christian brethren in Nigeria paid to practice their faith. What a devastating blow it must have been to receive this dismissive treatment after spending sums of money and quantities of time to meet City of Bloomington demands.

Some religious groups just consider these defeats to be a manifestation of "God's will," and others who would fight often have depleted staff time and financial resources to the degree that a legal appeal is not an option. In contrast to the Islamic groups who bring attorneys to city meetings and who seek DOJ intervention, some other religious applicants seem to be unaware of the need for legal advice, whether the case qualifies for DOJ interest, or the possibility of pro-bono legal help.

All religious organizations must seriously consider that if one group is garnering disproportionate attention and that this may afford local concessions: what is the net effect across the nation? If other religious groups are timid or reluctant to avail themselves of the legal and institutional help available, one group may be consistently advantaged. If all religious organizations began to assert the rights and protections offered by the First Amendment and RLUIPA in zoning settings, local governments would have to confront the realities of legal equal treatment requirements and would learn that preferential consideration given any group means that all other comers should obtain the same considerations.

No religious organization should expect to operate outside the legal limits placed on use terms so that there is "excessive burden on parks, schools, streets, and other public facilities," nor should the use be "injurious to the surrounding neighborhood or otherwise harm the public health, safety, and welfare." [123] It is important that area residents are able to predict

---

[122] City of Bloomington Council Meeting Video, May 20, 2013, *supra* at note 118, discussion at appx. 1:09:30 on the marker; *available at*:
http://bloomingtonmn.granicus.com/MediaPlayer.php?publish_id=fd65ee4d-1310-1031-8b21-673bf20d68e3.

[123] Most municipalities apply similar language to the City of Bloomington Code Section 21.501.04(e) where each Conditional Use Permit must meet the following affirmative findings: The following findings must be made prior to the approval of a conditional use permit: (1) The proposed use is not in conflict with the Comprehensive Plan; (2) The proposed use is not in conflict with any adopted District Plan for the area; (3) The proposed use is not in conflict with City Code provisions; (4) The proposed use will not create an excessive burden on parks, schools, streets, and other public facilities and utilities which serve or are proposed to serve

government action if code terms are breached. The entire rationale for zoning is based upon providing communities some degree of predictable order, intra-zone standards that protect conditions favorable to the anchor use, and preservation of the right to peaceful enjoyment of one's property.

the planned development; and, (5) The proposed use will not be injurious to the surrounding neighborhood or otherwise harm the public health, safety and welfare. See the AFYFC City of Bloomington Conditional Use Permit Staff Report, *supra* at note 36. p.7, https://www.bloomingtonmn.gov/sites/default/files/media/08915A_11.pdf.

4. UNDERSTANDING ZONING AUTHORITY

For almost one hundred years, American cities and counties have worked to organize residents and businesses by grouping the most compatible uses of property into districts, or zones. The goal has been to preserve the character of these areas by keeping similar uses closely situated. Business, agricultural, industrial and residential zones then have their own categorical distinctions and technical guidelines.

Subsets of rules regulate potential annoyances like noise and pets as well as safety concerns like parking and traffic.

Under constitutional state police powers, state statutes provide the authority for cities and counties to regulate privately owned land and structures. Underlying the ability to regulate is the constitutional notion that a property owner should have notice and benefit of a public hearing when a decision that may affect his use and enjoyment of his property is proposed.

Land use decisions have become a time-consuming process and interested developers often pay substantial sums of money for expert assistance with bureaucratic demands and shifting timelines.

Many communities have established local planning boards that perform the first level of review. That board makes a recommendation to the city or county and then the staff begins an intensive process of checking off requirements as they are met, partially met, or noting those that fail. The planning staff subsequently issues a report to the city planners advising whether the use is appropriate for the zone requested. After one or more public hearings, there is often a vote taken of the appointed planning officials and in some cases a final vote by the elected city council or county official board of supervisors.

If a particular zone does not list the desired use as approved, applicants may apply to have "conditional" use considered. This process accommodates uses that are not recognized as approved per the zoning but thought to be compatible, if regulated, with area traffic flow and typical use and enjoyment of property.

In these cases, conditional uses may be approved for a few years to an indefinite period as negotiated and as per state guidelines. Most court rulings say that the permit stays with the property in the event of a change in ownership. Courts have also said that there is some level of property interest in predictable renewal of a short-term (e.g., two to ten years, or a term in between) conditional permit, unless substantive failure to comply with the permit limits is demonstrated. In all cases, a change in conditions and use may trigger a re-evaluation of the CUP.

In some cases a use not listed as permitted (as of right) or allowed (by conditional permit) may require a full variance or exception to the zoning code. Many churches, temples, and mosques find no available sites in zoned areas since master development plans often do not place a high priority on religious facilities. Consequently these uses usually must apply for a zoning variance or a conditional, sometimes called "special," use permit.

Islamic, as well as other religious, groups have drawn attention for siting worship space in residential areas by obtaining an outright variance from zoning rules. Sometimes this variance application has been submitted after a private party purchased the home, stating intent to occupy, and then later an application was filed to convert the property.[124]

---

[124] Following is a sampling of controversies that involve mosques in residential areas: St. Cloud, Minnesota: Collins, Jon. "Mosque Proposal in St. Cloud Tabled After Hearing." *MPR News*, (14 Aug. 2013). http://www.mprnews.org/story/2013/08/14/news/islamic-center-st-cloud: West Chester, Pennsylvania: http://www.isccpa.org/uploads/1/0/6/7/10678234/iscc_brochure.pdf; Sheepshead Bay, New York: http://www.sheepsheadbites.com/tag/2812-voorhies-ave/; DuPage County, Illinois: Sabella, Jen. "Dupage County Debates Ban on New Religious Facilities." *Huffington Post Chicago* (27 Aug. 2010), http://www.huffingtonpost.com/2010/08/27/dupage-county-debates-ban_n_697290.html; Chino, California: Tasci, Canan. "Mosque Supporters Claim Chino Neighborhood Is Anti-Muslim." *Daily Bulletin* (17 Jun. 2013), http://www.dailybulletin.com/general-news/20130617/mosque-supporters-claim-chino-neighborhood-is-anti-muslim: Basking Ridge, New Jersey: Sadlouskos, Linda. "Mosque Traffic Expert Presents Case for Fewer Spaces." *Patch.com*, (6 Feb. 2013), http://patch.com/new-jersey/baskingridge/mosque-traffic-expert-presents-case-for-fewer-spaces; Edmond, Oklahoma:

"Expansion of Edmond Mosque Causing Controversy." *KOCO 5 News* (12 May 2016), http://www.koco.com/news/oklahomanews/Expansion-of-Edmond-Mosque-causing-controversy/15659760; Lomita, California: Green, Nick. "Lomita Mosque Files Religious Discrimination Suit Against the City." *Daily Breeze News* (21 Mar. 2012), http://www.dailybreeze.com/news/ci_20227062/lomita-mosque-files-discrimination-suit-against-city-nixing (Lomita, California, was zoned low-density residential then re-zoned to commercial-retail but still bordered on residential area); Temecula, California: Willon, Phil. "Temecula Approves Mosque after Contentious 8-hour Hearing." *L.A. Times* (12 May 2016) http://latimesblogs.latimes.com/lanow/2011/01/temecula-approves-mosque-after-contentious-8-hour-hearing.html; Sterling Heights, Michigan:

Martindale, Mike. "Residents Protest Planned Mosque in Sterling Heights." *Detroit News* (12 May 2016). http://www.detroitnews.com/story/news/local/macomb-county/2015/08/29/residents-protest-planned-mosque-sterling-heights/71380634/ (this mosque proposal generated additional controversy due to the Islamic organization's plan to locate in a predominantly Iraqi-Christian community); Lexington, Kentucky:

Wymer, Garret. "Project Leaders Respond to Concern over Proposed Islamic Center in Lexington." *WKYT* (12 May 2016), http://www.wkyt.com/home/headlines/Neighbors-concerned-over-proposed-Islamic-center-in-Lexington-288463121.html. (The project's architect told neighbors that there will be no changes to the house at the front of the property

A New Jersey residential single-family home purchase serves as a case in point. When the private purchase of a home in the Basking Ridge neighborhood of Bernards Township was transacted, residents were not alarmed. But as neighbors learned that this Church Street home in the Liberty Corner district was to be razed and a full-service mosque (five daily prayers) was planned for the site, they organized to investigate the process. This area is one of special sensitivity due to a 9-11 memorial constructed at the fire station to commemorate the 343 firefighters who died on 9-11. The township council ultimately denied the proposal for reasons of non-compliance with code requirements almost three years – and many hearings – later. In response, the Islamic applicants sued, and the DOJ investigated. Neither proceeding had concluded at the time this book was published.[125]

---

at this time, but the plan does leave open the possibility for construction of a mosque on the property in the future."); Afton, Minnesota: Divine, Mary. "Afton City Council Signs Off on Plans for Mosque in City." Twin Cities Pioneer Press (19 Apr. 2016), http://www.twincities.com/2016/04/19/afton-city-council-signs-off-on-plans-for-mosque-in-city/; Yonkers, New York: Maciaszek, Amy. "Yonkers Mayor Agrees To Landmark Status For Building Housing Mosque." Yonkers Daily Voice (31 Mar. 2016), http://yonkers.dailyvoice.com/politics/yonkers-mayor-agrees-to-landmark-status-for-building-housing-mosque/663379/; Kerr, Zak."Community Meeting Addresses Mosque." Windemere Observer (25 Mar. 2016), http://www.orangeobserver.com/article/community-meeting-addresses-mosque; Champion, Allison Brophy. "Freeze on Permanent Pump & Haul in Culpeper County." Star Exponent (16 Jul. 2016), http://m.dailyprogress.com/starexponent/news/freeze-on-permanent-pump-haul-in-culpeper-county/article_735b0868-4b83-11e6-93a6-ffa2860f16db.html?mode=jqm.

[125] Perry, Jacob. "Numerous Documents Sought in Basking Ridge Mosque Case." The Bernardsville News (15 Jul. 2016), http://www.newjerseyhills.com/bernardsville_news/news/numerous-documents-sought-in-basking-ridge-mosque-case/article_42c29ef2-fdbb-575d-a655-07719cbf8592.html.

5. Is RLUIPA Always a Trump Card?

As "smart growth" goals began to drive local planners, allocation of land for religious use became a low priority. Because religious buildings and worshippers do not produce either jobs or taxes – while creating traffic, congestion, and parking concerns – it was easy to just leave them off of the grid.

Responsive to complaints that houses of worship were being squeezed out of residential and commercial areas, a federal law was enacted in 2000. This statute, the Religious Land Use And Institutionalized Persons Act (RLUIPA) prohibits outright exclusion of religious worship sites from a municipality. And the law provides that government shall not "impose or implement a land use regulation in a manner that imposes a substantial burden on the religious exercise of a person, including a religious assembly or institution."[126]

Government may overcome RLUIPA provisions if it can demonstrate that the "imposition of the burden on that person, assembly, or institution is in furtherance of a compelling governmental interest." As courts have only rarely recognized a governmental interest so compelling that it overrides individual constitutional rights this is a formidable threshold to meet. Examples of recognized governmental interests that survive this test would involve national security or police power duties. Complaints of heavier traffic, congestion or parking often do not qualify as so compelling that the choice of a worship site can be foreclosed by a city planning analysis or zoning ordinance.

If government does impose a substantial burden on a religious institution, courts will ask that the government body justify the hardship by proving that it had a vital reason for the regulation, and that the rule was refined to the most essential expression; in other words, the burden on the religious practice must be as light as possible while government maintains its core duties. In legal speak this is called "narrow tailoring."

As interpreted by many courts, RLUIPA also prohibits discrimination among religions and it instructs against selection of a religious use in a given zone for different treatment than one not religious. An easy example to consider is that a zoned district that permits theaters, social membership

---

[126] "Religious Land Use and Institutionalized Person Act." *Thebecketfund.org* (2016), http://www.becketfund.org/rluipa/; and: "ACLJ Memorandum: An Overview of Religious Land Use and Institutionalized Persons Act –RLUIPA." *AmericancenterforlawandJustice.com* (2004), http://aclj.org/us-constitution/aclj-memorandum-an-overview-of-the-religious-land-use-and-institutionalized-persons-act-rluipa-2004.

clubs or recreation halls as a general assembly use usually means that a religious use should be considered on a similar basis.

RLUIPA was constructed with broad terms that are responsible for some of the difficulties in interpreting and applying the law. The vague standards meant to pave the way for religious worship sites have also opened the door to potential manipulation by applicants, land planners, and their advisors.

It is very important to know enough about the law to be able to recognize when planning departments are preparing to give so many allowances to an applicant that the very structure of the zoned area is at risk. If attorneys, commissioners, or land use staffers appear to be presenting RLUIPA as if it were meant to overcome zoning authority or remove accountability from the religious applicant, it may be a good idea to invite a lawyer with RLUIPA background to analyze the official pronouncements, and possibly make a presentation. Some commissioners have been tutored on RLUIPA while others have not. There are few experts on RLUIPA, even in the general lawyer community. In many cases, officials have appreciated a second opinion on the complex law.

When families come to a residential zone, they can expect that the zone was designed for quiet and safety as reflected in the comprehensive and district plans. Churches and other houses of worship should be allowed as long as there is a plan, usually with conditions attached to the use permit, to protect the overall residential use and enjoyment priorities.

Only a small percentage of judges have construed RLUIPA to mean that religious applicants should have almost any kind of use and level of activity as long as comparable to any other loosely-defined assembly use similarly situated in the zone. Conversely, most judges have tried to strike a balance under RLUIPA, one that allows planners to customize permits, while incorporating religious use, but not entitling the religious institution to function like a nuisance-bearing activity center.

One aspect of RLUIPA that has been particularly challenging for cities is the definition that Congress provided for "religious exercise." Using a very broad brush, the law says that "any exercise of religion, whether or not compelled by, or central to, a system of religious belief" is protected. In other words, depending on the judge, even social activities, sports, secular education, communal eating, etc., may be considered "religious exercise" for purpose of challenging zoning restrictions.

Localities should also consider what is called "safe harbor" policy by allowing for assembly (clubs, community centers, meeting halls, theatres, auditoriums, recreational facilities, etc.) and religious use with relaxed restrictions in the areas most hospitable to the activity and traffic.[127] Cities would then have more latitude to restrict additional religious use in zones like residential without appearing to generally exclude religious sites. These provisions should be considered as a matter of normal routine for updating district plans since any such activity during a religious application hearing may be construed as targeting a particular applicant.

In cases where there is concern about the predictability of the use, the accuracy of the application, or overall compatibility with the surrounding area, cities sometimes grant a shorter-term conditional use permit for a period of initial years. At this juncture, it is important just to learn that many religious applicants have received initial CUPs for seven or ten-year terms and then have applied for renewals upon demonstrating an effort to comply with the regulations and conducting their affairs in a manner that is compatible with the occupants for which the zone was created.

Some courts have ruled that there is a legally protected property interest in an extension of the term-limited use permit but violations of the terms and demonstrated disregard for the conditions would allow for challenge of this property interest. This approach is described in more detail later but it is an important tool to have available when searching for constructive approaches that may still meet RLUIPA provisions.

All of this is somewhat complicated and requires education and official training. This is the reason that the DOJ requires that entire city planning departments participate in RLUIPA training as part of some legal settlements. Accordingly, it is best to have training and any safe harbor plans in place before an applicant presents a legal challenge that leaves a municipality with only difficult options. Finally, it bears repeating that these strategies may not be inserted in the middle of an application process in light of potential discrimination complaints.

---

[127] Seeman, Evan J. "Finding Salvation in Religious Law's Safe Harbor: Municipal Governments Can Take Steps to Mitigate RLUIPA Claims." *Connecticut Law Tribune* (23 Mar. 2015), https://rluipa.robinsoncoleblogs.com/wp-content/uploads/sites/9/2015/04/Reprint_Seeman_032315.pdf; *also see* this article describing Minnesota federal case where judge recognized RLUIPA safe harbor practice: https://www.rluipa-defense.com/2016/09/rluipa-case-of-the-year-minnesota-municipality-uses-rluipas-safe-harbor-provision-to-avoid-liability/?utm_source=RLUIPA+Defense&utm_medium=email&utm_campaign=f73dfc0e2f-RSS_EMAIL_CAMPAIGN&utm_term=0_baf0b0c430-f73dfc0e2f-172974469.

6. WHAT COURTS HAVE SAID ABOUT RLUIPA

This basic overview, highlighting the range of judicial opinions on what RLUIPA terms mean, is very important for the concerned resident, as well as for municipal land planning staff. Religiously based permit decisions will be governed by local ordinances, and local interpretation of the governing state, federal, and constitutional law. Many city attorneys and managers who argued in the past that the protections for religious land use could be overcome by zoning priorities are now understanding that religious organizations are increasingly likely to complain about RLUIPA-defined declines or delays. As frustrated religious groups have learned of RLUIPA's generous protections, they have effectively used the leverage of even threats of lawsuits and Department of Justice inquiries.

What municipalities have had to learn is that essentially a religious applicant should be treated the same as an applicant that brings jobs and tax revenue. And, cities must create and apply all regulations so that they do not target a religion or religious use generally.

Municipalities most often grapple first with the RLUIPA provision that declares: "No government shall impose or implement a land use regulation in a manner that imposes a substantial burden on the religious exercise of a person, including a religious assembly." It has proven to be a very difficult task for local governments to interpret Congress's intent when applying the "substantial burden" term.

Also, although the statute prohibits discrimination "against any assembly or institution on the basis of religion or religious denomination" history shows that there is much room for interpretation as to how rules are applied and when exceptions are made. What would be called discrimination when a waiver that was given to one party is declined for another is typically justified according to the circumstances that provide context. In other words, discretionary power – or wide latitude to make and waive the rules – will stand, *unless* the wronged party has the resources to appeal.

The RLUIPA contains an "equal terms" section requiring that religious assemblies and institutions must be treated at least as well as non-religious assemblies and institutions. As interpreted by the courts, this provision generally means that religious organizations should be treated like any other broadly defined assembly use for permit consideration purposes. Thus, standards that apply to a variety of buildings where meeting use is incidental have been used comparatively as a basis for considering church, temple or mosque applications.

It is not surprising that there have been fundamental conflicts in court rulings on the standards that local officials should regard when applying the RLUIPA burden and discrimination terms. The various judicial interpretations may be clarified by the U.S. Supreme Court at some time in the future. But in the interim, it is not likely that Congress will provide needed clarifying language to resolve the confusion as to what is a "substantial burden" and what standards should measure "unequal treatment."[128]

Should municipalities consider pushing the lines that may trigger a substantial burden or discrimination complaint, moreover, how do courts say that land planners might defend their decisions as overriding "compelling governmental interests"?[129]

RLUIPA AND SUBSTANTIAL BURDEN

As one might imagine, legally defining a substantial burden has been problematic. This author was part of a litigation team that won a major RLUIPA case. In that federal court case, the substantial burden inquiry was very fact intensive. In this instance, the church had to prove that the local planning department should accommodate this religious worship application to locate in an industrial zone. This involved addressing a series of questions: First, was the church really growing out of the existing facility; did it really need to move? Second, was any other appropriate site available? Third, would the church's budget allow it to site the new worship facility at an alternate location? Fourth, what distance did most congregants drive; would it substantially burden the parishioners if the church were to be asked to consider an alternate site?

These inquiries play out in RLUIPA cases all over the country. The following cases show the ways that courts have defined substantial burden before they then inquired as to whether facts proved that the burden was really substantial.

The Fifth Circuit Court of Appeal (circuit courts are one level below the Supreme Court), for purposes of applying RLUIPA in the jurisdiction,

---

[128] For the larger legal RLUIPA discussion, this article details many of the cases and conflicts: Alden, Bram. "Reconsidering RULIPA: Do Religious Land Use Protections Really Benefit Religious Land Users?" *UCLA Law Review* (2010); *available* at:
http://www.uclalawreview.org/pdf/57-6-4.pdf

[129] Following is a substantive RLUIPA aid offered by Albemarle County, Virginia, and organized by tables to show the range of legal cases for every element of RLUIPA: The Albemarle County Land Use Law Handbook. "The Religious Land Use and Institutionalized Persons Act of 2000: An Introduction." *Albemarle.org* (2015), *available at*:
http://www.albemarle.org/upload/images/Forms_Center/Departments/County_Attorney/Fo
rms/LUchapter34-RLUIPA.pdf.

decided that "substantial burden" was legally defined as "government action or regulation [that] truly pressures the adherent to significantly modify his religious behavior and significantly violate his religious beliefs." To arrive at this conclusion the Fifth Circuit opinion noted the level of disagreement on the definition in the various circuit courts while listing the range of other appellate determinations as follows:[130]

> The RLUIPA does not contain a definition of "substantial burden," and the courts that have assayed it are not in agreement. Despite the RLUIPA's eschewing the requirement of centrality in the definition of religious exercise, the Eighth Circuit adopted the same definition that it had employed in RFRA cases, requiring the burdensome practice to affect a "central tenet" or fundamental aspect of the religious belief[131] The Seventh Circuit, in contrast, abandoned the definition of "substantial burden" that it had used in RFRA cases, holding instead that, "in the context of the RLUIPA's broad definition of religious exercise, a ... regulation that imposes a substantial burden on religious exercise is one that necessarily bears direct, primary, and fundamental responsibility for rendering religious exercise ... effectively impracticable." [132] Neither did the Ninth Circuit retain the definition of "substantial burden" that it had employed in RFRA cases, which required interference with a central religious tenet or belief. Turning to Black's Law Dictionary and Merriam-Webster's Collegiate Dictionary, the Ninth Circuit defined a "substantial burden" as one that imposes "a significantly great restriction or onus upon such exercise." [133] The most recent appellate interpretation of the term under the RLUIPA is that of the Eleventh Circuit, which declined to adopt the Seventh Circuit's definition, holding instead that a "substantial burden" is one that results "from pressure that tends to force adherents to forego religious precepts or from pressure that mandates religious conduct." [134] (Some citations omitted, underscore emphasis added.)

---

[130] *Adkins v. Kaspar*, 393 F.3d 559 (5th Cir. 2004), *available at*: http://caselaw.findlaw.com/us-5th-circuit/1059426.html

[131] *Murphy v. Missouri Dept. Of Corr.*, 372 F.3d 979, 988 (8th Cir. 2004).

[132] *Civil Liberties for Urban Believers v. City of Chicago*, 342 F.3d 752, 761 (7th Cir. 2003).

[133] *San Jose Christian Coll. v. City of Morgan Hill*, 360 F.3d 1024, 1034 (9th Cir. 2004).

[134] *Midrash Sephardi v. Town of Surfside*, 366 F.3d 1214, 1227 (11th Cir. 2004).

The Ninth Circuit appellate court has also reasoned that "for a land use regulation to impose a 'substantial burden,' it must be 'oppressive' to a 'significantly great' extent."[135]

As referenced at the end of the block quote above, the Eleventh Circuit definition from *Midrash Sephardi v. Town of Sephardi* has emerged as something of a "rule of thumb." It is often applied when religious applicants claim that an intended site is more convenient or is better suited to the group's purposes than alternative locations. In 2014, the Middle District Court in Florida used the test when ruling that "convenience" (often distance that parishioners have to travel) would not satisfy a substantial burden finding as the Court affirmed that "a 'substantial burden' must place more than an inconvenience on religious exercise;" instead, it must exert the kind of "pressure that tends to force adherents to forego religious precepts . . . or mandates religious conduct."[136]

This Eleventh Circuit *Midrash* test, in addition to the whole range of substantial burden appellate court tests, was designed for use during discretionary deliberations where government officials may be tempted to pick religious winners and losers. Surely, the City of Bloomington at least could have argued that there was defensible ground to stand on when asserting authority against activities in a residential area like activities planned for hours past midnight. Furthermore, cities stand on very different legal ground when the question concerns equitable enforcement rather than discretionary permitting processes.

Whether AFYFC members may have been burdened by regulations to a degree that adherents were forced to forego religious precepts (that would then require the City of Bloomington to prove a compelling government interest) would be a valid question during the application phase. But that is the point: AFYFC was happy with all the conditions at the permit hearing. There was no question then about the terms and AFYFC had not undergone such significant growth that conditions should have been re-evaluated to reflect a change in attendance. Activity levels and all attendant compatibility issues were immediately dramatically higher than the levels presented in the proposal.

Rather than challenge, for example, the late-night activity in a residential area, or limit the gym use to 500 occupants as per the CUP, or enforce the prohibition against concurrent use of the gym and other assembly facilities,

---

[135] *Guru Nanak Sikh Society v. County of Sutter*, 456 F.3d 978 (9th Cir. 2006); *available* at: http://caselaw.findlaw.com/us-9th-circuit/1363129.html.

[136] *Church of Our Savior v. City of Jacksonville*, 26 (M.D. FL 2014), quoting *Midrash*, 366 F.3d at 1227; *available* at: http://www.becketfund.org/wp-content/uploads/2015/10/2015.05.19-District-Court-Final-Judgment.pdf.

city officials appeared to accept the presumption that potential enforcement measures would likely impose an indefensible substantial burden under RLUIPA on this organization. They failed to make the distinction between the discretionary permit application process – where RLUIPA does apply – and the later period when the applicant has agreed, as a conditional user of property in an area that is not designed for his particular use, to live by the rules codified in the permit.

Court rulings on substantial burden have also been stern with municipalities that issue "arbitrary and capricious" decisions and courts have found a substantial burden when processes cause the applicant undue or significant delay.[137] These are likely complaints that Resurrection Power Church could have considered when an approval recommendation became a denial with no change in Resurrection Power Church's permit proposal. Pastor Udeh had executed a five-year lease contract and he had testified that he was prepared to meet the suggested conditions for approval at the time of the reversal.[138] The City of Bloomington essentially canceled this lease contract without offering Pastor Udeh any alternative sites. Also, when the City denied the application months into the staff findings that recommended approval, both parties lost the "opportunity time" to consider other options during that period.

Courts review RLUIPA compliance through a filter of good faith. If regulations allow religious institutions in some zones with reasonable conditions, there may be a presumption that the city is not hostile to religious land use. If an applicant's permit is denied, yet the denial is issued with opportunity to address concerns and then return for re-consideration, or if suitable alternative sites are offered to the applicant in the case of an initial denial, courts sometimes do not find the process to be substantially burdensome.

RLUIPA AND EQUAL TERMS AND NON-DISCRIMINATION

It is important to recognize that the Constitution has been interpreted to say that land use policies when implicating religious practice must be neutral and generally applicable. As noted previously, local government may not target religion in general, or religious sects in particular, for

---

[137] *Fortress Bible Church v. Feiner,* 694 F.3d 208 (2d Cir.2012), *available at:* http://law.justia.com/cases/federal/appellate-courts/ca2/10-3634/10-3634-2012-09-24.html. ("Accordingly, we conclude that the Town lacked a rational basis for delaying and denying the Church's project and therefore violated the Church's Free Exercise rights.")

[138] *Guru Nanak Sikh Society of Yuba City v. County of Sutter,* No. 03-17343 (9th Cir. 2006) ("[T]he Board of Supervisors neither related why any of such mitigation conditions were inadequate nor suggested additional conditions that would render satisfactory Guru Nanak's application.")

discriminatory treatment. The motivation for the regulation as well as the application must heed these requirements.

The RLUIPA equal terms provision, where it provides that "[n]o government shall impose or implement a land use regulation in a manner that treats a religious assembly or institution on less than equal terms with a nonreligious assembly or institution,"[139] demands generally that localities apply the same standards to religious land use applications as would be used to consider secular assembly uses.

The Supreme Court has not ruled on the religious land use provisions of RLUIPA and each appellate circuit court has its own record of applying the statute. The "equal terms" section is especially confusing as several circuits have offered varying tests for determining unequal treatment of religious land use applications.

Appellate circuit court reasoning is exemplified by tests used in the Eleventh Circuit and the Seventh Circuit Courts of Appeal. The Eleventh Circuit inquiry takes a definitional approach and asks whether the religious use "fall[s] under the umbrella of "assembly or institution"[140] and the Seventh Circuit considers how the secular assembly use is *similarly situated* to the religious assembly with regard to "accepted zoning criteria."[141]

In other words, the first test looks for whether any other legally comparable assembly has located in the same or a similarly zoned district. If so, planners should also consider locating a religious assembly there on the same basis. There is potential that the "general assembly" comparators may be as unexpected as bus terminals, air raid shelters, restaurants that have private dining rooms in which a book club or professional association might meet, sports stadiums or hospital operating theaters.[142]

---

[139] A sample presentation of RLUIPA substantial burden provisions found *here*: https://www.law.cornell.edu/uscode/text/42/2000cc; and collection of articles relating to RLUIPA's equal terms provisions found *here*: RLUIPA-Defense Archives: Equal Terms, https://www.rluipa-defense.com/category/equal-terms/.

[140] *Midrash Sephardi, Inc. v. Town of Surfside*, 366 F.3d 1214, 1230-31 (11th Cir. 2004).

[141] *River of Life Kingdom Ministries v. Vill. of Hazel Crest*, 611 F.3d 367 (7th Cir. 2010).

[142] Seeman, Evan and Merriam, Dwight. "City Wins When Federal Court Applies Narrow Apples to Apples Analysis to Identify 'Comparators.'" *RLUIPA-Defense* (22 Apr. 2014), https://www.rluipa-defense.com/2014/04/city-wins-when-federal-court-applies-narrow-apples-to-apples-analysis-to-identify-comparators/. ("[The court] used an "apples to apples" comparison to determine a comparator and found that a non-religious school was the only proper comparator to the religious school. It rejected the School's contention that other permitted uses, such as banks, barber shops, beauty parlors, daycare centers, coffee shops, hotels/motels, and hospitals were also comparators. The court's approach appears to restrict the types of uses that may be considered a proper comparator rather than permitting a comparison with all other secular assembly uses.")

For the second test, the Seventh Circuit focuses more on preserving municipality zoning authority by looking to the text of a zoning ordinance for establishing common characteristics and zoning intentions for the existing assembly, and applied-for religious, use.

Planning officials struggle with this level of nuance, especially if staff attorneys as in the AFYFC case imply that comparators may be located anywhere in the city, failing to note that there is also an expectation of "similar situation." Practically speaking, not just any far-flung assembly example will do to measure equal treatment. Commercial zones have different rules than industrial zones or residential zones – as well as subsets of each – since all are designed to accommodate different levels of noise, traffic, and hours of use.

And importantly, the RLUIPA Equal Terms test was designed for the city planning department application phase. It does not govern post-CUP enforcement policy as implied in the AFYFC City Council deliberations.

There is also a RLUIPA directive against discrimination that looks at religious comparators to learn if one sect or religion has been treated less favorably than another. This element of the law seeks to prevent purposeful discrimination by planning officials on the basis of religious denomination.[143]

One indicator of potential discrimination is hostility to the group as evidenced by indicators like biased official comments. There is a difference between discriminatory comments about a group based upon religious belief or practices and inquiries into how the property will be used. In a Church of Scientology case, a Georgia federal district court judge reasoned that "[o]nly the most blatant remarks, the intent of which could be nothing other than to discriminate on the basis of some impermissible factor constitute direct evidence of discrimination."[144] The court also said that discriminatory intent was not necessarily present when a religious organization merely experienced disparate treatment based upon a parking calculation or square footage allocation while there was no other evidence of discrimination. However, in this case, the court did withhold final judgment on the matter until there was a full trial of the facts and record.[145]

When the Islamic Society of Ridge sued Bernards Township for denying the organization's application to site a mosque on a residential lot, the federal judge ruled that the Township violated RLUIPA's non-discrimination provision by applying a parking standard differently to churches than to

---

[143] *Bethel World Outreach Ministries v. Montgomery County Council*, 706 F.3d 548 (4th Cir. 2013)

[144] *Church of Scientology v. City of Sandy Springs*, 843 F.Supp.2d 1328 (2012).

[145] *Id.*

mosques. He opined that proof of hostility toward Muslims was not required. He also reasoned, deviating from appellate precedent, that the discrimination determination need not be supported by comparable examples.[146] This ruling is an outlier as it pushes interpretive legal limits in several areas but there was no decision to appeal at this time of this writing.

When cities deliberate the merits of a religious land use they must be careful to follow sound reasoning and all prescribed processes. Courts have noted that the more arbitrary or inscrutable the decision, the more likely that discrimination is involved. (The baffling reversal in the Resurrection Power Church case when no new facts were presented comes to mind). Therefore, it may be useful to keep a record of findings and note the reasons that the determinations do not arise from bias.

Some charges of bias may be based in circumstantial evidence where there is no direct link between racist or discriminatory speech and official actions. A later section will deal with official conduct and local resident speech. But it is sufficient to say here that courts look first for a connection between biased expressions and government decisions. Therefore, it may be advisable for an official who has made a definitively discriminatory remark to recuse from the final vote so that the entire decision is not called into question. There will be a deeper discussion of how the courts view resident-private, resident-public, and official communications in the later section on public hearings.

RLUIPA AND GOVERNMENTAL COMPELLING INTEREST

A very brief discussion of the legal "compelling interest" is important for the reason that city attorneys who are not trained in RLUIPA sometimes give advice that directs government authority in a manner that is either too cautious or too confident. Sometimes attorneys support municipal authority too much by justifying zoning authority to deny religious use when the government interest is insufficient (e.g., cities usually will not succeed in defending an assertion of zoning authority for reasons like preserving aesthetic character of the neighborhood). Or, they may advise that municipalities have almost no authority. For example, they may say that it is virtually impossible for a city to prove an interest in denial that meets the legal definition of "compelling." Yet, localities should defend zoning criteria when a serious safety or nuisance concern is presented. Whether these decisions survive judicial review also largely depends upon what hard

---

[146] *Islamic Society of Basking Ridge v. Township of Bernards.* 3:16-cv-01369-MAS-LHG (Dec. 31, 2016) New Jersey District Court, *available at:*
http://www.yumpu.com/en/document/view/56618529/islamic-society-nj-20161231/28.

evidence of safety or health concern that the city is able to provide in defense its authority.

The bottom line is that the Supreme Court did set a high bar when saying that local government land planning may only interfere with religious exercise when its concern is of "the highest order."

For example, when courts have considered a locality's interest in expressions of zoning authority under RLUIPA, the Second Circuit Court of Appeal noted that a city (or village) may have a justifiable compelling interest in protecting traffic flow administration. However, the issue was not adjudicated at the appellate court and was sent back to the trial court for consideration.[147]

When zoning authority was considered generally by the Seventh Circuit, the Court decided when denying the RLUIPA claims of a Christian group that wanted to build a camp facility that there was no substantial burden imposed by city zoning regulations behind the city denial (additionally, the city had offered what appeared to be appropriate alternative sites).[148] And a federal court in Massachusetts ruled that traffic concerns are not "generally compelling" interests against a RLUIPA claim of substantial burden but the court would not rule out that some specific traffic concerns may be compelling.[149]

These decisions show that municipalities have to work hard to make the case to defend zoning authority against a substantial burden claim, and must provide a thorough record. In New York, a federal court instructed that "the [locality] must demonstrate that the enforcement in those zoning laws is compelling *in this particular instance*, not in the general scheme of things." (Emphasis added.)[150]

While court rulings provide confusing standards for RLUIPA deliberations, Islamic groups are often turning directly to the Department of Justice for

---

[147] *Day School v. Village of Mamaroneck*, 386 F.3d 183, (2d Cir. 2004) (We know of no controlling authority, either in the Supreme Court or any circuit holding that traffic problems are incapable of being deemed compelling. It is true that one circuit opinion in the Eighth Circuit recited that "interests in traffic safety and aesthetics ... have never been held to be compelling." *Whitton v. City of Gladstone*, 54 F.3d 1400, 1408 (8th Cir.1995). However, the fact that the case reports do not reveal any case in which a court has found traffic concerns compelling does not support the proposition that traffic concerns by nature cannot be compelling. . . . In fact, there are very few rulings discussing the question, and none that we know arising under RLUIPA.) (Adam block indent?)

[148] *Eagle Cove Camp and Conference Center Inc. v. Town of Woodboro, Wisconsin*, 3:10-cv-00118 (7th Cir. 2013); for summary, *also see*: https://rluipa.robinsoncoleblogs.com/wp-content/uploads/sites/9/2015/01/7th-Cir1.pdf.

[149] *Mintz v. Roman Catholic Bishop*, 424 F. Supp. 2d 309 (D. Mass. 2006).

[150] *Cholim, Inc. v. Village of Suffern*, 664 F. Supp. 2d 267 (S.D. N.Y. 2009).

assistance in winning permit approvals. Just the mention that the DOJ will be called upon to invoke civil rights protections and generous RLUIPA interpretations may have tipped the scales for a number of Islamic permit applications. Few cities will hazard an expensive investigation by the DOJ or a costly trial with the DOJ in opposition.

7. WHAT ZONING LAWS MAY SURVIVE RLUIPA TESTS?

Although the RLUIPA limits a municipality's defenses against a religious land use complaint, the law cannot mean that communities are doomed to suffer frequent traffic gridlock, overburdened utility infrastructure, and nuisance disturbances. Any of these issues may implicate property interest or public safety concerns to the point that a phased conditional permit is contemplated, or more suitable alternatives may be proposed.

In other words, just because a municipality may not summarily deny a religious application does not mean that the scales should tip dramatically the other direction. Permits should still be carefully structured with all forethought to peaceful co-existence with surrounding established uses and to enforcement mechanisms if this fails.

Additionally, in those cases where the proposed site proves unsuitable, municipalities still may show the "good faith" expected by RLUIPA when working with the applicant to find solutions, including the step of searching for appropriate alternative options.

Most Islamic center uses include an array of activities. AFYFC is an example where the site is used for services and it is also used for a school, day care, counseling, meal service, adult education, university classes, regional events, and family festivals. In fact, in this case, the application showed the prayer component of the overall use to be incidental. Also, this application, as many others, did not use the term mosque or *masjid*. A mosque proposed for the Windermere community in Florida was simply called the Windermere Religious Center. Applications are often submitted in the name of a cultural center or community center.

Any religious organization should be prepared to describe the full range of activities, participation levels, and hours of use at the time of application.

The surrounding commercial or residential neighborhood, in the case of an Islamic land uses, should prepare for much larger attendance and higher activity levels for the month of Ramadan/Eid. Some other ceremonial events and festivals also generate weekend-long crowds. Also, mosques sometimes host regional programs as advertised on internal websites. Some mosque-community center complexes offer education opportunities, workshops, and seminars. When large events exceed a specified attendance limit, permitted hours, or involve food service, a special permit is usually required. There is also typically a limit to the number of times per year that an organization may exceed the permit restrictions.

It is predictable that churches, mosques and temples will host intermittent events that draw larger crowds but frequency is the key to how much the community can tolerate. Knowing peak attendance days and times, as well as accurate participation levels, is foundational to realistic permit terms. Clear limits for hours of programming, parking, and traffic volume should also be accompanied by specific instructions as to when a special event permit will be required and what are standards for approval.

Additionally, infrastructure issues including environmental review, sewer capacity, soil permeability, left hand turn lanes, and water availability can be pressing questions, especially in residential areas. Online research and request for documents will reveal the history of permits for the zone in question as applied to past applications, testing, results, and requirements.

Importantly, code-based objections to mosque planning that predict high volume activities will only be taken seriously if there is a professional study that is compelling to the point of triggering a city inquiry. The presentation of personal pictures of peak-hour traffic mounted on poster boards, or ad hoc counting of cars to illustrate parking concerns, is not compelling and does not require an official response. When parking and traffic fears are described as vague complaints based upon experiences of other communities, the concerns may be dismissed as anecdotal stories. Without professional reports and credible case histories that include the record of under-estimation as it occurred in places like Bloomington, Minnesota, the concerns may not be addressed.[151]

Density: Occupancy allowances are fairly standard and usually require seven square feet of space per person when there is non-fixed seating.[152] Some mosques expect to qualify for a standing occupant rating since there are no seats – fixed or non-fixed – which may allot one person per five square feet. Churches often plan for seventeen square feet per person, if seated in pews, due to allocation of space for platform and choir.[153] City planners should be careful to consider that a standard church use for a 5000 square foot building would be 294 persons while an Islamic assembly could potentially be 1,000 persons. Islamic groups may plan to accommodate three times as many attendees in a space as would a conventional church assembly use. In the final analysis, fire code

---

[151] Schwartz, John. "Zoning Law Aside, Mosque Projects Face Battle." *New York Times* (3 Sep. 2003),
http://www.nytimes.com/2010/09/04/us/politics/04build.html?pagewanted=all&_r=1.

[152] See this chart for examples of worship space allocations used in major U.S. cities:
International Code Council. "Number by Table 1004.1.2" *publicecodes.cyberregs.com* (2016),
http://publicecodes.cyberregs.com/st/ny/ci-nyc/b200v08/st_ny_ci-nyc_b200v08_10_sec004_par002.htm.

[153] "Church Building 101." *Churchconstruction.com* (2016),
http://www.churchconstruction.com/article-churchbuilding101.php.

determines the *outer limits* of occupancy based upon exits and access to those exits, but the ability to anticipate attendance for the variety of regularly scheduled Islamic center activities will enable planners to prepare permit limits and to structure enforcement thresholds.

Also, there likely will be areas dedicated to one or more Friday prayer services, including a designated space for women. It may be useful to ask the mosque organizers for a specific designation of the space that will be rated for either "standing assembly" or "non-fixed seating assembly."

Prayer sessions are not only observed on Friday *when attendance at a mosque is highest,* but mosques may be open for other daily prayer sessions as well. At the informational hearing for the proposed Windermere (Florida) Worship Center, a mosque-goer told a reporter that since he travels to the mosque five times a day for prayer, it would be much easier to have a mosque located closer to his home.[154] When the Kennesaw (Georgia) mosque was approved, two weeks after an initial vote to deny triggered a DOJ inquiry, a member of the Islamic community said much the same in a PBS interview:

> Muslims try to make it five times a day to the mosque and in this day and age, it's a little difficult to be there five times a day. But usually, if you are close enough — five, ten minutes' drive — you can go there early in the morning prayers, in the evening prayers at least.[155]

While religious applicants may not be treated differently, at least these standards may forecast more accurately the actual activity levels for purpose of all religious permit construction and enforcement.

Parking: Parking code regulations vary per area, per type of use, and according to municipal formulas, but the typical calculation for assembly use, based upon average patterns, is one car per three people. Regulations that address parking and fire code occupancy should be verified and reviewed for historical application to similar situations. In both cases, variances may be requested and the community should consider the impact on surrounding neighborhoods when exceptions are considered.

In 2016, Bernards Township (New Jersey) denied the Islamic Society of Ridge's application for a religious use permit in a residential area. The applicants then sued the Township for unlawful discrimination, among

---

154 "Proposed Mosque Has Some Windermere Residents Concerned." *ABC WFTV* (16 Mar. 2016), http://www.wftv.com/news/local/some-windermere-residents-raise-concern-over-proposed-mosque/165185097.

155 Brangham, William. "Freedom of Religion? Mosque Debate in Georgia Town Reveals Sharp Divide." *PBS Newshour* (20 Dec. 2014), http://www.pbs.org/newshour/bb/freedom-religion-mosque-debate-georgia-town-reveals-sharp-divide/.

other complaints, when the township applied a different parking formula to the applicants' unique patterns than it would have used for a church.[156] A federal judge ruled on parts of the case (an appeal had not been filed at the time of this writing) and he determined that the Township's ordinance where it provided a "3 person for each car" rating to determine the number of parking spaces for "churches" was automatically discriminatory if the Township would not apply the formula to mosque parking.[157] The township had presented a study showing that Islamic peak Friday service(s) are frequented by attendees coming from places of employment and driving solo. This pattern differs from Sunday morning church attendance that often represents family unit attendance.

Interestingly, a news report on the travails of the Bernards Township mosque applicants discussed attendance at an exemplary Friday prayer meeting and the reporter noted that "the turnout at Friday's prayer was consistent with [the Township's] testimony" as the participants were overwhelmingly single males.[158]

Judges make their legal determinations based upon facts and records in these cases and ordinances should be flexible enough to consider a variety of religious attendance patterns. The record of Township deliberations would provide insight into whether the ordinance was applied in a discriminatory fashion as would past treatment of other religious applications but the judge in the Bernards Township case found that the mechanical application of the ordinance alone was proof of discrimination.

As long as generally applied to all religious applicants and not adopted during the religious land use deliberations, religious applicant use patterns may be matched with formulas that logically reveal the expected activity and occupancy levels. These calculations also might be used for quantification of trip count data and realistic occupancy rates according to fire code *maximum limits*. This information can be useful especially for the formulation of final permit conditions and triggers for remedial actions.

While conducting a fact-finding process according to a quasi-judicial (as described in most states) framework, it is important to understand actual

---

[156] "Bernard Township Answer to ISBR Complaint." (Basking Ridge is an unincorporated area within Bernard Township.).

[157] *Islamic Society of Basking Ridge v. Township of Bernards.* 3:16-cv-01369-MAS-LHG (Dec. 31, 2016) New Jersey District Court, *available at:*
http://www.yumpu.com/en/document/view/56618529/islamic-society-nj-20161231/28.

[158] W. Jacob Perry. "Local Muslims: 'Dark Forces Unleashed' by Immigration Ban." *The Bernardsville News* (8 Feb. 2017),
http://www.newjerseyhills.com/bernardsville_news/news/local-muslims-dark-forces-unleashed-by-immigration-ban/article_30c877c5-5c84-54bd-840f-99faa340297f.html.

expected levels of activity and occupancy. This is especially true for peak attendance services within the context of established schedules like schools that pre-exist the applicants' competing activity. Probing questions should be asked of *all assembly applicants* who plan to site busy multipurpose facilities in a residential area.

Traffic: Many municipalities now evaluate traffic levels for land use applications in light of average "daily trip counts" or "periodic trip counts" for cars entering and leaving the property during certain hours. This is key in situations where the use should be defined by the nature and frequency of actual events and not on the basis of generalized and vague plans. The codes detailing trip count regulations are shown on municipal websites and often require an authoritative assessment. In some cases, there is no published code but trip count standards may have been applied to prior applications in residential areas. Trip count data has proven to be a useful tool when there is indication that use of a facility will entail massive visits per day or heavy use both coming and going as events overlap.

Noise: Noise is a serious concern when many Islamic practices end late in the evening, continue through the night, or begin in the early morning. When these practices occur at times that are outside of city "quiet use and enjoyment" tolerances, an exception to local ordinances may be requested. For example, a permitted mosque in Raritan Township, New Jersey, was preliminarily approved to "begin operation" one and one half hours before sunrise. [159] And, as mentioned in the introductory section for this monograph, the Hamtramck (Michigan) mosque issues the call to prayer over a public address system five times per day with the first broadcast set ostensibly at sunrise. Before reaching a decision, communities should define exactly what this kind of proposal means in terms of burden on the surrounding area, traffic activity, frequency of gatherings and anticipated disturbance factors.

The standard rule is that nuisance noises like loud parties should not disturb residents after 10:00 p.m. and noisy activities like construction should not begin before 7:00 a.m. Generally, there are other regulations about noise above particular decibel levels and noise that is heard over a certain distance. In the case of a religious use, these codes do not strictly apply. However, the spirit of the law should not be disregarded. There may be reasons that very late – or extremely early – activities conducted in a residential area should be held in a different space. Or, if it is important to schedule such events on a routine basis, a suitable non-residential alternative site for the mosque might be suggested. Noise disturbances

---

[159] Sievers, John. "Raritan Township Planning Board Approves Mosque." *Lehighvalleylive.com* (26 Jul. 2013), http://www.lehighvalleylive.com/hunterdon-county/express-times/index.ssf/2013/07/raritan_township_planning_boar.html.

should be considered carefully at the permit hearing before there are conflicts and resulting animosity over unrealistic expectations.

Any substantive concerns on these issues should be thoughtfully presented at the permit hearing. Citizen monitors and interested neighbors may consider organizing as accountability committees under several articulate spokespersons for "tag-team" serial presentations, rather than presenting concerns in a series of disjointed and repetitive comments. This entails understanding the process, providing cogent analysis, and organizing checklists for holding city staff responsible.

A dedicated team should be assigned to evaluate prior assembly permit approvals and the attached conditions. Previous decisions dictate many of the limitations that bind officials if they intend to be in compliance with RLUIPA and other equal protection concerns.

The objective should be to address all of the regulatory concerns that apply while also being prepared to offer factual data as to how religious groups may differ in use levels, occupancy rates, and noise factors. Accountability groups should require that full fire marshal, environmental, flood, soil, drainage, parking, traffic, and other applicable tests required by code, and as applied to other applicants, apply equally to mosque applicants. Just because RLUIPA protects minority religious assembly does not mean that generally applicable zoning regulations should be not be taken seriously.

8. THE DEPARTMENT OF JUSTICE, RLUIPA, AND MOSQUES

Under RLUIPA, the Department of Justice is authorized to intervene, as well as sue, on behalf of aggrieved groups. This DOJ has been especially active in investigating Islamic zoning complaints through the Civil Rights Division. Under former Attorney General Eric Holder, the Department of Justice Civil Rights Division declared a special partnership between the Equal Employment and Opportunities Commission (EEOC), and the Islamic community.[160]

In 2012, Eric Treene, Special Counsel for the Justice Department's Civil Rights Division, reported that the Justice Department "ha[d] opened twenty-seven RLUIPA matters involving mosques and Muslim schools since RLUIPA passed. Of these, seventeen ha[d] been opened since May of 2010."[161] By 2016, the DOJ reported that the percentage of RLUIPA investigations involving mosques or Islamic schools had risen from 15% in the 2000 to 2010 period, to 38% during the 2010 to 2016 period.[162] The AP reported in 2016 that a DOJ review revealed data showing that mosque and Islamic school complaints grew to twenty-five percent of the Civil Rights Division's caseload from 2011 to 2015.[163] If so, it is apparent that the pace and extent of intervention is accelerating.

The DOJ also injected an enhanced warning for city halls into the July 2016 report when advising that it will press discrimination charges in mosque and Islamic school cases, even when the cases do not involve "anti-Muslim animus," but just because of the "sharp increase" in complaints.[164] The DOJ is following a legal theory that says there is discrimination if the results show a disproportionate "adverse impact" on a protected group. This legal

---

[160] "Justice Department Settles Discrimination Lawsuit Against Berkeley School District in Illinois." *United States Department of Justice* (13 Oct. 2011), https://www.justice.gov/opa/pr/justice-department-settles-religious-discrimination-lawsuit-against-berkeley-school-district.

[161] Amici Curiae brief for Muslim Advocates, et al: *Al Falah Center, v. Town of Bridgewater*, No. 13-4267 p. 6 (3rd Cir. 2014); *available at*: http://d3n8a8pro7vhmx.cloudfront.net/muslimadvocates/pages/216/attachments/original/1393544536/Amici_Brief_Al_Falah.pdf?1393544536.

[162] Seeman, Evan, et al. "U.S. Department of Justice Issues RLUIPA Report." RLUIPA Defense (27 Jul. 2016), https://www.rluipa-defense.com/2016/07/u-s-department-of-justice-issues-rluipa-report/.

[163] Hajela, Deepti. "Muslims See Anti-Mosque Bias in Landmarking Decision." *Bismarck Tribune* (11 Jun. 2016), http://bismarcktribune.com/muslims-see-anti-mosque-bias-in-landmarking-decision/article_ba7864fc-b2ed-5b95-87b8-e12140ae33ed.html.

[164] Department of Justice. "Update on RLUIPA Enforcement." p.6, *Justice.gov* (Jul 2016), https://www.justice.gov/crt/religious-land-use-and-institutionalized-persons-act; and, https://www.justice.gov/crt/file/877931/download.

approach is based upon cases that come from housing and employment law, and it does not require a finding that discrimination was intended or animus was present. This application of disparate impact legal theory has not been tested in the courts at this time.

In 2015 and 2016, city leaders began to report that DOJ case numbers were assigned at first reports of opposition to a mosque, and in Kennesaw, Georgia, even before the decision-makers held the first public meeting to consider the merits of the application. The Bernards Township (New Jersey) Planning Board's 2016 legal pleadings disclosed that the Islamic Society of Basking Ridge attorneys threated RLUIPA discrimination legal action at the very first hearing session.[165] In 2016, the DOJ filed a lawsuit against the Pennsylvania township of Bensalem, independent of the complaining Islamic organization's pre-existing and parallel litigation.[166]

Although the DOJ "RLUIPA" information webpage does not cite to appellate court rulings as authority, the nation's highest legal office provides a very generous explanation of what may constitute an unjustifiable burden on a religious group seeking a use permit: "Whether a particular restriction or set of restrictions will be a substantial burden on a complainant's religious exercise will vary based on context, such as the size and resources of the burdened party, the actual religious needs of an individual or religious congregation, the level of current or imminent space constraints, whether alternative properties are reasonably available, the history of a complainant's efforts to locate within a community, *the absence of good faith* by the zoning authorities, and many other factors.[167] (Emphasis added.)

These generalized guidelines are summarized from court cases and some would be useful if more definition had been provided. Without appellate law context, legal rules of thumb can be confusing. One especially problematic standard that needs further definition is what the DOJ calls the "absence of good faith."

---

[165] Bernards Township Answer to ISBR Complaint, available at: http://mosquesinamerica.org/wp-content/uploads/2016/10/162_Bernards_Answer_Complaint.pdf

[166] McDaniel, Justine. "Justice Department: Bensalem Discriminates Against Muslims" *Philly.com* (23 Jul. 2016), http://articles.philly.com/2016-07-23/news/74648404_1_township-officials-zoning-hearing-board-joseph-pizzo. (The lawsuits may be combined by the court or the parties at a future date but, it is unusual for the DOJ to file a separate lawsuit.)

[167] "Statement of the Department of Justice on the Provisions of the Religious Land Use and Institutionalized Persons Act of 2000." *United States Department of Justice* (22 Sept. 2010), https://www.justice.gov/sites/default/files/crt/legacy/2010/12/15/rluipa_q_a_9-22-10_0.pdf

Local government officials are expected to do their jobs according to state law that defines their purpose, federal law that provides protection for individual and group rights, and local zoning regulations. Committing the "absence of good faith" error - a subjective and vague standard - may occur when too much discretion is applied to either slight or favor an individual or a class of persons. Officials are most likely to commit these errors when not following settled procedure and zoning precedent.

While courts do pursue this "good faith" legal inquiry in religious land use cases as discretion crosses into actual bias, it is important for government officials to understand that "good faith" really just means doing their jobs regardless of the pressures. Good faith means keeping a record of procedural steps that do not reflect bias, arbitrariness, or favoritism. What it does not mean is bending over backwards to accommodate one group, thus advantaging this group over others, as a means of inoculating the city or county against a complaint of discrimination.

Local governments usually rely upon one staff attorney to advise them. Some city attorneys have attended a workshop on RLUIPA and may understand the details of the statute but the competing court interpretations complicate the application of the law to any set of local facts. In light of the challenges, it may be valuable to enlist supplemental legal advice from sources that have litigated RLUIPA cases.

In the DOJ's own words, RLUIPA investigations have sent a powerful message. And localities have responded predictably with a risk-management emphasis. Former Assistant Attorney General for the DOJ Civil Rights Division Tom Perez revealed that the many DOJ investigations had "served to educate local officials about their obligations under RLUIPA, and have led to changed policies without litigation becoming necessary."[168] When cities are coerced and intimidated by even early notices of an investigation, officials are tempted "cry uncle" without mounting a defense of zoning rationale, local resident interests may not be considered.

In fact, litigation is often not necessary because few municipalities will undertake an expensive and time-consuming legal defense. The DOJ has the deepest of pockets and an army of RLUIPA-wielding attorneys. In theory, this could be a boon to religious liberty in America. But, investigations are triggered by complaints and complaints seem to come disproportionately from one group. At least, the investigative responses are largely in the interest of one group: Islamic institutions.

---

[168] "Assistant Attorney for the Civil Rights Division Thomas E. Perez Speaks at the American Constitution Society for Law and Policy's RLUIPA Event." *United States Department of Justice,* (21 Sept. 2010), https://www.justice.gov/opa/speech/assistant-attorney-general-civil-rights-division-thomas-e-perez-speaks-american

In light of the size and capability of DOJ resources, it is important to bear in mind that some local government officials are volunteers, and many are part-time. They just did not sign up for intensive and politically complicated inquiries, especially given the staying power of the DOJ and the all-but-inevitable result.[169] As a consequence, there is reason for concern that these early settlements advantage the complaining group by short-cutting local zoning prerogatives, land-use procedures, public comment, and important judicial review.

It is easy to understand then that the mere prospect of a looming federal investigation may cause local governments to be extremely cautious – and potentially more accommodating than in other cases – when considering a minority group religious use application. Defending against a federal inquiry, not to mention the implied next step of litigation, is costly; not just in terms of city resources but also political accountability to taxpayers. It is not surprising that many taxpayers would interpret the interest of federal investigators in local affairs as evidence that their elected city or county officials were in error. Still there is a solemn duty required of local lawmakers to formulate law, apply law, and enforce the law in a diligent manner that equally respects applicants and other interested parties. That is especially the case when the Department of Justice appears to be increasingly intervening on behalf of one religious community, as compared to – even other minority – faith organizations.

WHEN GOVERNMENT AGENCIES USE DUBIOUS HATE CRIMES TO DRIVE LAW AND POLICY

The DOJ is tracking what it calls "backlash" hate crimes, as exemplified by retaliatory incidents against Muslims that are said to follow after Islamist threats and jihadist terror attacks. The "special backlash crime task force" is centered in the DOJ's Civil Rights Division and is staffed with some of the most experienced federal prosecutors within the federal system.[170] Where this backlash operation works with DOJ attorneys in the states, it documents threats of violence and refers cases of actual violence for prosecution. The backlash unit acts as a clearinghouse for documenting complaints of threats of violence and actual violence, conducting investigations, referring cases to state and local prosecutors where

---

[169] Deak, Mike. "Bridgewater, Mosque Settlement Reaches $7.75 Million." *myCentralJersey.com* (2 Dec. 2014), http://www.mycentraljersey.com/story/news/local/somerset-county/2014/12/02/bridgewater-mosque-reach-settlement-million-land-swap/19775661/.

[170] "Confronting Discrimination in the Post-9/11 Era: Challenges and Opportunities Ten Years Later." p. 6, *Justice.gov* (19 Oct. 2011), https://www.justice.gov/sites/default/files/crt/legacy/2012/04/16/post911summit_report_2012-04.pdf.

appropriate, and, where the facts and the law warranted federal action, prosecuting those acts.[171]

When Attorney General Loretta Lynch spoke for the Muslim Advocates organization in December of 2015, she referenced mosque opposition and tied "backlash-motivated' forces to the "bending and twisting" of law to defeat mosque projects like in Murfreesboro, Tennessee: "That shows how strong the backlash can be; how strong is backlash to me."[172]

Since 9/11, agencies have reported increases in alleged hate incidents against Muslims and these statistics have resulted in energetic governmental inquiries. In 2001, the FBI reported more than a tenfold increase in religious bias crimes against Muslims. And, for the thirteen years following 9/11, the FBI's Uniform Crime Reports program indicated that annual hate crimes against Muslims have averaged at about five times higher than the pre-9/11 rate.[173]

If one accepts these data points at face value,[174] the FBI 2014 report on "anti-religious" hate crimes shows that anti-*Jewish* bias motivated 56.8 percent hate crimes, compared with 16.1 percent anti-Islamic (Muslim) bias crimes.[175] The Jewish population in the United States is estimated to be about twice that of Muslims living in America.[176]

A hate crime is a criminal offense that is classified according to the offender's motivational bias ("preformed negative opinion"). [177] The motivational element of the crime is determined when "sufficient" facts

---

[171] *Id.*

[172] "Attorney General Loretta Lynch at Muslim Advocates Dinner." *C-SPAN.org* (3 Dec. 2105); select the Loretta E. Lynch "speaker button" at: http://www.c-span.org/video/?401446-1/attorney-general-loretta-lynch-remarks-muslim-advocates.

[173] Ingraham, Christopher. "Anti-Muslim Hate Crimes Are Still Five Times More Common Today Than Before 9/11." *Washington Post* (11 Feb. 2015), https://www.washingtonpost.com/news/wonk/wp/2015/02/11/anti-muslim-hate-crimes-are-still-five-times-more-common-today-than-before-911/

[174] "Religious Bias Crimes 2000-2009: Muslim, Jewish and Christian Victims – Debunking the Myth of a Growing Trend in Muslim Victimization," *Center for Security Policy* (20 Aug. 2013) ("The Center for Security Policy (CSP) used official annual data published by the Federal Bureau of Investigation (FBI) to debunk the common fallacy spread by 'Islamophobia' proponents that Muslims have been the target of an increasing wave of "hate crimes" in the years following the attacks of 11 September 2001.")

[175] "Hate Crime Statistics for 2014." *Federal Bureau of Investigation,* (2014). https://www.fbi.gov/about-us/cjis/ucr/hate-crime/2014/topic-pages/victims_final.

[176] Pew Research Fact Tank, "A New Estimate of the U.S. Muslim Population," *Pew Research Center* (6 Jan. 2016) http://www.pewresearch.org/fact-tank/2016/01/06/a-new-estimate-of-the-u-s-muslim-population/.

[177] "Uniform Crime Report 2001 Hate Crime." *Federal Bureau of Investigation* (2002), https://www.fbi.gov/about-us/cjis/ucr/hate-crime/2001.

would lead "a reasonable and prudent person" to conclude that the offender's actions were motivated (even partially) by bias against a target group. [178] Hate violations are categorized as crimes against persons, property, and/or offenses against society in general. The crime listings are reported to the FBI via templates that record eleven offense categories from the local level. These compilations include crimes like murder, rape, robbery, and vandalism, and they also provide data on the more subjective complaints like "simple assault" (FBI definition: "assaults and attempted assaults where no weapon was used or no serious or aggravated injury resulted to the victim, including stalking, intimidation, coercion, and hazing." [179]) and "intimidation" (standard legal definition: "to intentionally say or do something which would cause a person of ordinary sensibilities to be fearful of bodily harm" although "it is not necessary to prove that the victim was actually frightened, and neither is it necessary to prove that the behavior of the person was so violent that it was likely to cause terror, panic or hysteria."[180]).[181]

In 2001, the FBI's Hate Crime Data Collection Program coded intimidation as the most frequently reported hate crime at 37.9% of the annual total.[182] This trend continued through 2015 when the FBI reported "[t]he majority of the 4,048 reported crimes against persons involved intimidation (43.1 percent) and simple assault (37.4 percent).[183] Note the potential overlap in the 2015 data where "simple assault" numbers may also include "intimidation" according to the FBI's own categorical definitions.

The FBI's Civil Rights program calls the investigation of hate crimes its number one priority. According to the website, the agency finds primary fault with the "groups that preach hatred and intolerance [that] plant the seeds of terrorism here in our country."[184] Even though the FBI profiles these groups that preach hatred, the agency notes that hate itself is not a

---

[178] *Id.* at 1,3.

[179] "Crime in the United States: Offense Definitions." *Federal Bureau of Investigation,* (Sept. 2010). https://www2.fbi.gov/ucr/cius2009/about/offense_definitions.html#top

[180] The 'Lectric Law Library, *available at:* http://www.lectlaw.com/def/i064.htm: "to intentionally say or do something which would cause a person of ordinary sensibilities to be fearful of bodily harm. It is not necessary to prove that the victim was actually frightened, and neither is it necessary to prove that the behavior of the person was so violent that it was likely to cause terror, panic or hysteria." (Adam block indent?)

[181] Crime in the United States, *supra* at note 176.

[182] *Id.* at 5.

[183] "Latest Hate Crime Statistics." *Federal Bureau of Investigation* (Nov. 2015), https://www.fbi.gov/news/stories/2015/november/latest-hate-crime-statistics-available/latest-hate-crime-statistics-available.

[184] "Hate Crimes-Overview." *Federal Bureau of Investigation* (2016), https://www.fbi.gov/about-us/investigate/civilrights/hate_crimes/overview.

crime and the FBI includes the protection of speech and civil liberties as part of its mission.[185]

As the Justice Department also investigates hate crimes, employment discrimination, and mosque opposition under the rubric of anti-Muslim bias, the data sets for any of the areas of complaint serve to buttress causes of action for the other categories. A mosque land use case amicus curiae brief on behalf of "Muslim Advocates" in the Third Circuit Court of Appeals cited Civil Rights Division Special Counsel Eric Treene who reported in 2012 that the Justice Department had "opened twenty-seven RLUIPA matters involving mosques and Muslim schools since RLUIPA passed. Of these, *seventeen have been opened since May of 2010.*" (Emphasis in original.)[186]

The Muslim Advocates brief then concluded that "expressions of bigotry have a ripple effect, extending beyond the headlines in the next day's newspaper...." The lawyers supported this contention with expressions like this from Rep. Joe Walsh of Illinois: "There is a radical strain of Islam in this country – it's not just over there – trying to kill Americans every week. It is a real threat, and it is a threat that is much more at home now than it was after 9/11." [187] The brief claimed that such examples demonstrated "allegations of naked animus" against Muslim communities that aspired to build new mosques.[188]

This "regrettable increase in anti-Muslim sentiment" is what former Assistant Attorney General Thomas Perez told the U.S. Senate is likely the reason for "the increase in RLUIPA cases involving mosques...."[189] The DOJ's Treene has also written that anecdotal complaints from (Muslim) community groups, trends in press reports, and case studies engaged by the Justice Department are consistent with reports that show "[r]esistance to mosque proposals over the last decade was tame by comparison to what we see today." Treene referenced a strategy article written for mosque applicants to show that "Muslim American applicants [in the past] had the opportunity to respond to accusations and counter speculation with facts.

---

[185] *Id.*

[186] *Al-Falah Center vs. The Township of Bridgewater*, No. 13-4267 (3rd Cir. 2014), Muslim Advocates Amicus Brief, p.6. *available at:*
http://d3n8a8pro7vhmx.cloudfront.net/muslimadvocates/pages/216/attachments/original/1393544536/Amici_Brief_Al_Falah.pdf?1393544536.

[187] *Id.* at 23.

[188] *Id.* at 5.

[189] Eric W. Treene. "Zoning and Mosques: Understanding the Impact of the Religious Land Use and Institutionalized Persons." p.4 *The Public Lawyer* (Winter 2015), *available at:*
http://www.americanbar.org/content/dam/aba/administrative/state_local_government/zoningandmosques.authcheckdam.pdf.

Now, however, a vocal and organized opposition is in the streets with placards and bullhorns."[190]

There are obvious problems with a law enforcement policy that is devoted to searching for "backlash" conditions and tangentially connecting manifestations of anti-Islamic bias. The very mission statement relies upon finding retaliatory expressions to justify the theories behind the task force's existence. Not only is this task force effort geared to the real or perceived grievances of a named victim group, but in this case, the radicalized element of the group in question is a subset (at least by religious affiliation) of an aggressive and hegemonic force. There is a fine line between societal push-back that is appropriate and retaliation that is a criminal offense. This is especially true when a complaint like intimidation is perception-based, rather than being subject to forensic evidentiary standards.

Then, there are documented (some of the encounters were recorded on neighbors' cell phones and police reports are on record) hateful crimes that have originated *from Muslim groups*. Some crime is Muslim-on-Muslim, and some like the Somali gang episodes near Minneapolis are apparently Muslim on middle class white Americans. Although little noted in the media, when a Minnesota neighborhood was terrorized by marauding young (locally described) Somali men, speeding and driving cars over curbs and sidewalks over several days, and issuing detailed threats like that directed at a woman to kidnap and rape her, American citizens have every reason to challenge the source of the lawlessness. The woman who was the subject of the direct rape threat said in a television interview that she refused to be intimated and would not allow "them" to win. When the subject of the rape threat reportedly called police three times that day, it allegedly took police some three hours to arrive, and then one minor traffic ticket was issued.[191] Police were said to be continuing the investigation at the time the news interview aired.[192]

Unless and until the Muslims that disapprove of the range of Islamist affronts to American civil society say so – in no uncertain terms – Americans will, and should, continue to challenge the leadership at large. Muslim leaders should be held accountable to name names, and to identify

---

[190] *Id.* quoting Kathleen E. Foley. "'Not in Our Neighborhood': Managing Opposition to Mosque Construction." Pp. 8-9, *Inst. For Soc. Pol'y & Understanding* (Oct. 2010), *available at*: http://www.ispu.org/wp-content/uploads/2016/08/ISPU_Not_In_Our_Neighborhood_Kathleen_Foley-3.pdf .

[191] Hohmann, Leo. "Woman Gives Chilling, 1st-Hand Account of Muslim Rape Threat." Worldnet Daily (6 Jul. 2016), http://www.wnd.com/2016/07/woman-gives-chilling-1st-hand-account-of-muslim-rape-threat/.

[192] Hoffland, Brett. "Minneapolis Police Investigate 'Terroristic Threats' Made Near Lake Calhoun." *ABC Eyewitness News* (30 Jun. 2016), http://kstp.com/news/minneapolis-police-investigate-alleged-terroristic-threats-calhoun-parkway/4186341/.

errant doctrine. As Muslim reform leader Dr. Zuhdi Jasser has said, "If we stay silent, we give Islamists a pass to suffocate critical thinking inside Muslim communities." He urges a tough-love approach, saying, "There is nothing more American, more pro-Islam, and more pro-Muslim than taking a stand against the extremist and anti-Semitic hate spewed by Islamist individuals."193

Within the unique setting of city hall, officials are required to screen comments that are based in anti-Muslim bias to only consider the resident testimony that is responsive to civic hearing inquiries. When voicing concern regarding reports from other communities on unexpected intensity of use, violations of permit terms, and abuse of ambiguity in land use law, residents should apply the examples to the specific application under consideration by focusing on ways to inspect the details of planned use and the procedures to best insure compliance.

Finally, rather than accepting the "backlash" narrative as evidence of underlying motive for everything from actual hard crimes to intimidation and mosque opposition, an inquiring media and the general citizenry should review the reports independently. Indeed, some of the highest profile "hate incidents" (in categories with more definition than the hard-to-investigate "intimidation") have proven to be false. Some of those crimes have even proven to be incidents perpetrated by Muslims. While these individuals may not have designed a hoax, they did do damage to mosques. These reports often are not corrected until some time after the initial hate-crime headlines are generated.

Other so-called hate crimes have been so generic in nature that Muslims were not named as their targets by law enforcement. Some reported crimes do not meet the standards of a police investigation, so they remain as a filed complaint. The range of challenged examples below demonstrate why it is so critical to hold the narrators who rush to affirm hate agendas to an honest account:

Newport Beach, California: CAIR issued a press release on unconfirmed reports by a Muslim taxi driver who claimed that he was "assaulted after being questioned [repeatedly] about his religion." Facts later revealed that the brawl was between two cab drivers fighting over a fare. The CAIR statement profiled a former Marine cigar storeowner as the likely perpetrator when, later accounts revealed, the businessman was not involved in the melee and that instead he claimed to have rendered aid.194

193 Jasser, Zuhdi. "It's Not 'Islamophobic' to Protest a Pro-Hamas Speaker." *National Review Online* (6 Apr. 2016), http://www.mzuhdijasser.com/18728/sheikh-monzer-taleb.

194 Hall, Sarah, "Muslim Group Says Cabbie Assault is Hate Crime," *Newport Beach Indy* (1 Apr. 2010), http://www.newportbeachindy.com/muslim-group-says-cabbie-assault-is-hate-

Houston, Texas: A homeless man set a fire at the Quba Islamic Center and burned down one building in 2015. He admitted to setting the fire, but said he just wanted to get warm.[195]

Houston, Texas: Also, in 2015, Gary Nathaniel Moore was arrested for setting fire to a mosque. Moore claimed that he was a regular attendee at the mosque.[196]

Bloomington, Minnesota: Edward Zahi Moses Saad was arrested for breaking into the Umatul Islam Center in 2016 and vandalizing the mosque. Police stated that the crime was one "of opportunity" and that there was no indication Saad had "targeted any specific group."[197]

Fresno, California: Asif Mohammad Khan vandalized the Islamic Cultural Center on Christmas Day in 2014. He desecrated the American flag while destroying property at the mosque. Khan told police detectives that his crime was "not meant to be hateful" since he had attended programs at the Islamic center.[198]

El Cajon, California: Kassim Alhimidi was convicted in 2014 of the brutal murder (also called an honor killing) of his wife. Alhimidi had left a note at

crime/; Mickadeit, Frank, "Cigar Vendor: "I was Aiding'" Hate Accuser" *Orange County Register*, (21 Aug. 2010) http://www.ocregister.com/articles/uria-294358-cabbie-one.html; Coker, Matt, "UPDATED With CAIR Backing Off Allegations Against Lounge Owner Muslim Cab Driver's Beating in Newport Beach Spurs Call for Hate-Crime Probe," *Orange County Weekly* (31 March, 2011); *also see:* http://www.ocweekly.com/news/updated-with-cair-backing-off-allegations-against-lounge-owner-muslim-cab-drivers-beating-in-newport-beach-spurs-call-for-hate-crime-probe-6456710; (CAIR statement: "Our general procedure is that when the issue involves an alleged crime, we do not contact the alleged perpetrators in order to avoid complicating the situation or being accused of threatening or influencing a witness. Investigation is the job of law enforcement, and this is often their request. Our primary role in these cases is to assist the complainant/victim in presenting their allegations to law enforcement, and to encourage law enforcement to investigate the incident as a hate crime.")

[195] Aufdenspring, Matt & Bauer, Jennifer. "Homeless Man Arrested In Arson Fire of Islamic Center." *NBC KPRC, Houston* (15 Feb. 2015), http://www.click2houston.com/news/hfd-homeless-man-arrested-in-arson-fire-at-islamic-center

[196] Christian, Carol & Binkovitz, Leah. "Man Charged With Setting Houston Mosque Fire Says He Was A Devout Attendee." *Houston Chronicle* (30 Dec. 2015), http://www.chron.com/houston/article/Federal-officials-arrest-man-in-connection-with-6727623.php

[197] Davis, Angela. "Police Arrest Man Suspected In Burglaries, Mosque Vandalism." *CBS WCCO* (2 Mar. 2016), http://minnesota.cbslocal.com/2016/03/02/police-arrest-man-suspected-in-burglaries-mosque-vandalism/

[198] Lopez, Pablo. "Clovis Man Who Vandalized Mosque Gets Court Program for Mental Illness." *The Fresno Bee* (18 Sep. 2015), http://www.fresnobee.com/news/local/crime/article35757534.html.

the crime scene that said, "This is my country. Go back to yours, terrorist." Original, and pervasive, early reports called the killing a "hate crime."[199]

Chapel Hill, North Carolina: The 2015 murders of three Muslims are often a centerpiece of the hate crimes complaints. Yet the suspect, Craig Hicks, publicly disparaged all religions and there had been an ongoing parking dispute between the parties.[200] At one time, Hicks apparently wrote: "Knowing several dozen Muslims...I'd prefer them to most Christians."[201]

Middle East scholar Daniel Pipes analyzed a CAIR hate crime report from 2004 and "discovered a pattern of sloppiness, exaggeration, and distortion":

1. CAIR cites the July 9, 2004 case of apparent arson at a Muslim-owned grocery store in Everett, Washington. But investigators quickly determined that Mirza Akram, the store's operator, staged the arson to avoid meeting his scheduled payments and to collect on an insurance policy. Although Akram's antics were long ago exposed as a fraud, CAIR continues to list this case as an anti-Muslim hate crime.

2. CAIR also states that "a Muslim-owned market was burned down in Texas" on August 6, 2004. But already a month later, the owner was arrested for having set fire to his own business. Why does CAIR include this incident in its report?

3. CAIR lists the March 2005 lawsuit filed by the Salmi family for the firebombing of their family van as one example of a hate crime report it received in 2004. However, the crime named in the lawsuit occurred in March 2003, was already reported by CAIR in 2003, and should not have been tabulated again in the 2004 report.

4. CAIR reports that "a home-made bomb exploded outside of the Champions Mosque in the Houston suburb of Spring, Texas," staking its claim on eyewitness reports that on July 4, 2004, "two white males" were seen placing the bomb. We inquired about the incident and found that Spring's sheriff department could not locate any police files about an explosion. Further inquiries to the

---

[199] Phillips, Sandra. "Courtroom Erupts After Iraqi Man Found Guilty of Killing Wife." *Fox 5 San Diego* (18 Apr. 2014), http://fox5sandiego.com/2014/04/17/verdict-reached-in-brutal-murder-of-iraqi-mother/.

[200] Casarez, Jean & Soichet, Catherine. "Chapel Hill Shooter Suspect Indicted." *CNN: Cable News Network* (17 Feb. 2015). http://www.cnn.com/2015/02/16/us/chapel-hill-shooting/.

[201] Mack, David. "Everything We Know So Far About The Alleged Chapel Hill Shooter." *Buzzfeed.com* (12 Feb. 2015), http://www.buzzfeed.com/davidmack/everything-we-know-so-far-about-the-alleged-chapel-hill-shoo#.cpOrgLpLd.

mosque and an e-mail to CAIR both went unanswered. There is scant evidence that any crime even occurred.

5. CAIR notes that "investigators in Massachusetts are still investigating a potential hate-motivated arson against the Al-Baqi Islamic Center in Springfield." However the case was long ago ruled a simple robbery, news that even CAIR's own website has posted. The Associated Press reported on January 21, 2005, that prosecutors determined the fire was set by teen-age boys "who broke into the Al-Baqi mosque to steal money and candy, then set the fire to cover their tracks." The boys, they clarified, "weren't motivated by hatred toward Muslims."

6. CAIR describes what happened to a Muslim family in Tucson, Arizona: "bullet shots pierced their home as they ate dinner in October 2004" and two months later their truck was smashed and vandalized. But the only evidence that either incident was motivated by hate of Muslims is the Dehdashti family itself, not the police. Detective Frank Rovi of Pima County Sheriff's Department, who handled the shooting investigation, said that according to the neighbors, the desert area by the Dehdashti house was often used for target practice. Neither incident was classified as a hate crime and both cases were closed by February 2005, long before the CAIR report went to press.

Of twenty "anti-Muslim hate crimes" in 2004 that CAIR describes, at least six are invalid – and further research could likely find problems with the other fourteen instances. (Hyperlinks in original omitted.)[202]

An exemplary case of media-ready Muslim bias complaints was that of seven young women who claimed that they were asked to leave Urth Caffe, a popular Laguna Beach (CA) coffee shop, in April 2016. Their attorney was quoted as saying that the women were "targeted as a way of cleansing [the predominantly white Laguna Beach] location of women that appeared to be Muslim to appease the 'Islamaphobia'."[203]

However, the married owners (one is a Muslim) of the Urth Caffe have explained that the women refused to honor the outdoor seating time limits. The owners replied with a civil suit against the Muslim women, countering that the lawsuit against Urth Caffe was fraudulent and that the Muslim women were trespassing after being asked to leave. The countersuit also

---

[202] Pipes, Daniel & Chadha, Sharon. "CAIR's Hate Crime Nonsense." *Frontpagemagazine.com* (18 May, 2005), http://www.danielpipes.org/2627/cairs-hate-crimes-nonsense.

[203] Ritchie, Erika. "Urth Caffe of Laguna Beach Counter-Sues Against Muslim Discrimination Claim. *Orange County Register* (23 Jun. 2016), http://www.ocregister.com/articles/women-720256-muslim-urth.html.

alleged that the Muslims planned a "defamatory social media and public relations campaign."[204]

Some of the items listed above have been used to suggest that "Islamophobia" is the motivation for an "unprecedented string of hate crimes [that] has swarmed not only Muslims, but other minorities" and that there is an "epidemic of anti-Muslim sentiment" that is responsible for the "rash of attacks."[205] Such inflammatory accounts are just as irresponsible as generalized hostility toward Muslims. Furthermore, as these activists predict retaliatory incidents to follow any jihadist attack, important attention should be paid to standards of verification and analytical consideration of whether Islamist operatives are merely trying to divert focus.

Ironically, when Islamophobia and anticipatory "backlash" smokescreens are used to assert Muslim victimization, it may be Muslims themselves who are most harmed. When Islamic activists are afforded public platforms to accuse Americans of unfounded hate conduct, the audience includes Muslims who are not aggrieved and isolated, as well as the American media and population at large.

Many Westerners are not aware that ISIS and the Muslim Brotherhood are intent on ushering in the "caliphate" have a declared strategy[206] to label Muslims who may choose to embrace Western standards as apostates who then may be ostracized and targeted for punishment. While reformist Muslims work to encourage fidelity to Western Enlightenment standards, extremists leverage broad-brushed indictments of all Muslims to alienate and radicalize moderate "gray zone" Muslims. ISIS is known to employ these aims "to foster a deep resentment which can be exploited by smooth-tongued cult leaders" and finally to "make it simply impossible to be a Muslim in the West."[207]

There is, therefore, moral hazard when local government authorities and the media characterize the words and actions of some thoughtless residents as a mass community mindset. If many concerns – from inviting constructive engagement with Muslims to calling for accountable debate to

---

[204] Editorial Staff. "Urth Caffe in Laguna Countersues Muslims." *The Indy* (23 Jun. 2016), http://www.lagunabeachindy.com/urth-caffe-countersues-muslim-patrons.

[205] Siddiqi, Imraan. "7 Anti-Muslim Incidents That Have Happened Since the Chapel Hill Murders." *Alternet.com* (20 Feb. 2015). http://www.alternet.org/news-amp-politics/7-anti-muslim-incidents-happened-chapel-hill-murders.

[206] Francois-Cherrah, Myriam. "Islamic State Wants To Divide The World Into Jihadists and Crusaders." *Telegraph Newspaper* (18 Nov. 2015), http://www.telegraph.co.uk/news/worldnews/islamic-state/12002726/The-grey-zone-How-Isis-wants-to-divide-the-world-into-Muslims-and-crusaders.html

[207] *Id.*

identifying radicalization elements – are characterized as attacks, there will be little room for establishing the foundations upon which common ground may be found. In acceding to the Islamic supremacists' demands that everyone critical of their agenda be condemned as racists and bigots, a much-needed national debate about that agenda is suppressed. This is an unforced error that the West need not commit as long as public debates are had on the basis of practices and defining principles, rather than groups and labels.

9. ISLAM IS DEFINED AS A RELIGION FOR CONSTITUTIONAL AND RLUIPA PROTECTIONS

Islam is understood, for American legal and constitutional purposes, to be a religion. The fact that Sharia codes [208] are promulgated in preference to American law in some mosque settings is simply not a matter for local politicians at the city and county level to adjudicate.

At present, Supreme Court rulings in religion cases mean that courts may not inquire into what extent a "religion" is more a political regime than it is a belief system. This generally works to insulate from legal inquiry the Islamists who esteem clerical rulings more highly than civil authority, dispute the rule of secular law, and who deny the separate roles of mosque and state. If socio-religious systems and leaders engage in legally-defined conspiracies to subvert American law or institutions, there are potential legal responses although caselaw in this area is complex and dated.

At present, essentially the only line of questioning that government and the courts may pursue when querying a religious group is whether the beliefs embraced are "sincerely held."[209] Government is not authorized to consider whether beliefs are "valid" or if tenets meet some civil religious test. Some "faith" groups have stretched this allowance for purposes of RLUIPA protection to strain credibility like the Jedi believers[210] in Washington State. Yes, this is an extreme example, but it shows how far government may reach to embrace non-mainstream manifestations of "belief."

Even if legally permitted, it is not the American constitutional tradition to empower city officials to separate the Sharia adherents that follow Islamic clerical dictates over American law from those that practice Islam as a

---

[208] Sharia is Islamic orthodoxy that follows cleric-interpreted (often in the form of a *fatwa*) Koranic-based prescriptions and allows little, if any, authority for civil law or representative rule. Many Muslims who adhere to the idea that Sharia law is supreme believe that they are allowed to submit to the law in a host society only until they have imposed Sharia law by increments or have accomplished domination by other means. The Reliance of the Traveler manual, widely available in book form, is considered by many Islamic scholars to be the official Sharia guide. Andrew McCarthy, successful prosecutor of the Blind Sheikh, articulates the conflict between Sharia law and Western societal principles here: McCarthy, Andrew. "Don't Blame the Charlie Hebdo Mass Murder on 'Extremism.'" *National Review* (7 Jan. 2015), http://www.newcriterion.com/articles.cfm/If-you-see-something--say-nothing-7654.

[209] *United States v. Seeger*, 380 U.S. 163 (1965) ("The test of religious belief . . . is whether it is a sincere and meaningful belief occupying in the life of its possessor a place parallel to that filled by the God of those admittedly qualified for the exemption.")

[210] Seeman, Evan, Chaffee, Karla and Merriam, Dwight , "Star Wars Church Opens in Spokane, Washington," (1, Mar. 2016), https://www.rluipa-defense.com/2016/03/star-wars-church-opens-in-spokane-washington/. Yet the Jedi "faith" statement disavows any official doctrine or scripture (http://www.jedichurch.org/jedi-doctrine.html).

religion. As time and conditions provide the urgency for establishing this dichotomy, federal law may be re-invigorated to address legally-qualified subversive activity. But zoning boards do not have the authority to do this, nor are they authorized to consider anything beyond issues related to the zoning concerns.

Fundamentally, American government officials have not been given this authority under the Constitution. According to First Amendment interpretation, any government regulation of religion must be neutral and generally applied so as not to target religion generally or a specific religious expression. There may be no government analysis of doctrine. The Supreme Court said in *United States v. Ballard* that:

> Freedom of thought, which includes freedom of religious belief, is basic in a society of free men. (citation omitted) It embraces the right to maintain theories of life and of death and of the hereafter which are rank heresy to followers of the orthodox faiths. Heresy trials are foreign to our Constitution. Men may believe what they cannot prove. They may not be put to the proof of their religious doctrines or beliefs.[211]

Since Sharia-based Islam encompasses all aspects of a subscribing Muslim's life leaving little legitimacy to civil authority, some argue that Islam should be considered as an antithetical socio-political regime. Muslims for Reform has adopted a platform plank implicitly identifying Sharia as incompatible with democratically organized society: "We oppose institutionalized Sharia. Sharia is man-made."[212]

While cultural and assimilation concerns certainly underlie these arguments, the task of unraveling Sharia-based radicalism from the modernized and societally compatible approach to Islam certainly does not fall to land use planners and their elected overseers. Land use hearings are for the simple purpose of applying zoning code and determining whether an applied for use of land is appropriate given conditions that planning staff require.

Also, the First Amendment protects much of what is said and done in a religious facility. Between freedom of speech and the free exercise of religion, there is much room for what many Americans could consider objectionable – yet protected – speech. Consider that the some appellate courts recognize First Amendment religious freedom as "first and foremost, the right to believe and profess whatever religious doctrine one desires,

---

[211] *United States v. Ballard*, 322 U.S. 78 (1944); *available at*:
http://supreme.justia.com/cases/federal/us/322/78/case.html
[212] Muslims for Reform Declaration. Section C(1), *available at*:
http://muslimreformmovement.org/declaration.

98

[and] courts are not permitted to inquire into the centrality of a professed belief to the adherent's religion or to question its validity in determining whether a religious practice exists."[213]

Therefore, although some mosque activity may be culturally objectionable, it is a matter for law enforcement and not local civic officials to establish how much of what is said or planned in some mosques can be *legally* challenged. It is not within the purview of city planners to inquire about passages in the Koran, advocacy of Sharia, the source of mosque development money, distribution of hateful or anti-American materials, attitudes on freedom of speech (Sharia blasphemy code) and tolerance for those who choose a religion other than Islam (Sharia apostasy code) for purpose of land use decisions. It is left to law enforcement to determine when lines are crossed into criminal and conspiracy actions that violate the law.

This does not mean that communities have nothing to say about these cultural conflicts, many of which do indicate tendency to extremism. Far from it. Neighborhoods where mosques are sited have an array of free speech tools with which to monitor and confront counter-cultural activity. It is possible for residents, responsive to community relations overtures from mosque officials during hearings, to state that there will be community monitoring of extremist speakers and oversight of other radicalization activity at the mosque. Communities may invite vigorous debate and engagement. Invite this while promises of openness and local participation are on the table. Quite simply, the best way to counter the radicalizing speech inside a mosque is free speech outside of the mosque.

Whether website tracking, blog commentary, op-eds in local press, or group rallies to protest radicalization activity, the community may express alarm and may say "not in this town" to anti-Semitic, anti-American, violence-promoting, and other speakers that pitch radicalization.

There are also constructive political efforts to begin the legislative inquiry into when so-called religious activity may violate equal protection and civil rights provisions. It is vital that legislators and courts tread carefully here, but Great Britain is demonstrating serious intent to regulate Sharia courts (often called arbitration systems) where clerical rulings violate women's rights and other British legal principles. As the author of the bill, One Law for All, Baroness Carol Cox has explained: "I have cried with those Muslim women. They are suffering in this country and I cannot sit on those red benches and know that they are suffering out there in those closed communities. We are in a situation where we are at risk of having a parallel

---

[213] *Fifth Ave. Presbyterian Church v. City of New York*, 293 F.3d 570 (2d Cir. 2002), *available at*: https://bulk.resource.org/courts.gov/c/F3/293/293.F3d.570.02-7073.html

legal system – on the 800th anniversary of the Magna Carta. That is unacceptable,"[214]

Federal, or state-based, initiatives in the United States that promote similar equality ultimatums as Lady Cox's exemplary Act, would help to frame the discussion in communities. American Law for American Courts (ALAC),[215] provides the basis for American states to declare to all comers that anyone presenting a foreign law-based dispute to courts in that state will receive constitutional and legal protections. This leaves little room for confusion.

It is important to understand that ALAC does not directly confront operational Sharia tribunals in America, nor does the statute address Islamists that openly advocate criminal and unconstitutional practices. An example of a speaker that should shock any community is Bloomington-area (Minnesota), Dr. Hatem Ahaj,[216] formerly a Mayo Clinic pediatrician, and a current member of the Assembly of Muslims Jurists of America's fatwa committee, as well as dean of the Sharia Academy of America. He is also listed as the president of a social services organization that sponsors speakers to various Islamic groups called The Building Blocks of Islam. His position at the Mayo Clinic was terminated in 2012, after he published a paper in Arabic on female genital mutilation (FGM).[217] He has taught classes at Bloomington's AFYFC and has given at least this one recorded public lecture on the suggested health and sexual "benefits" of FGM for the woman ("minimal" cutting to reduce "excessive sexual excitement.").[218] He also speaks on the advantages of polygamy: including ongoing services for the husband when one wife is ill, as well as options for the husband whose biological and emotional needs are not met with just one wife, as long as he is willing to take on the burdens and responsibilities of additional wives.[219]

---

[214] Crowcroft, Orlando. "Sharia law UK: Baroness Cox – 'The Suffragettes will be turning in their graves.'" International Business Times (25 Jan. 2016), http://www.ibtimes.co.uk/sharia-law-uk-baroness-cox-suffragettes-will-be-turning-their-graves-1539577

[215] "Why American Laws for American Courts." http://americanlawsforamericancourts.com/. ("The goal of the American Laws for American Courts Act is a clear and unequivocal application of what should be the goal of all state courts: No U.S. citizen or resident should be denied the liberties, rights, and privileges guaranteed in our constitutional republic.")

[216] "Dr. Hatem Ahaj", Assembly of Muslim Jurists of America, http://www.amjaonline.org/en/about-us/our-scholars-fatwa-committee.

[217] Engstrom, Timothy, "May Clinic-Dr. Ali Part ways," (18, May. 2012), http://www.albertleatribune.com/2012/05/mayo-clinic-dr-ali-part-ways/.

[218] al Haj, Hatem, "Women in Islam – Female Circumcision", The Building Blocks of Islam Vimeo.com Page, (21 Apr. 2010). https://vimeo.com/album/168165/video/11916062; http://mosquesinamerica.org/wp-content/uploads/215_Women%20in%20Islam%20-%20Female%20Circumcision.mp4

[219] al Haj, Hatem, "Women in Islam - Hijab and Polygamy." The Building Blocks of Islam Vimeo.com (17 Mar. 2010), http://vimeo.com/album/168165/video/10417505.;

Both practices are illegal in the United States; performing FGM is a federal crime and it is felony offense in many states. The practice is considered "gender-based violence" by the State Department.

There was much news coverage of inflammatory exhortations given by Sheikh Farrokh Sekaleshfar (a British-born medical doctor), who spoke in the Orlando area just two months prior to the Pulse nightclub massacre. The imam's pronouncements against gays in 2013 included the declarations that "death is the sentence [for homosexuals]", and "[o]ut of compassion, let's get rid of them now."[220] Residents correctly raised concerns about the imam's Orlando engagement to the point that local news coverage detailed the 2013 remarks and interviewed residents who opposed his April 2016 appearance in Orlando.[221] After the Pulse nightclub attack, Sekaleshfar countered that his remarks had been taken out of context.

These examples demonstrate the opportunities that local citizens have to engage a cultural and political debate. But when a city hall hearing is in process there is an important dividing line between what is the public and legal role of land use officials and what is the private and moral role of citizens to state that evidence of radicalization will be spotlighted and challenged in the public square.

The scheduling of a permit hearing provides opportunity for the community to gain assurances from mosque leadership as to a concrete plan to combat radicalization. Notice of a public hearing schedule also suggests the timely announcement of a community accountability committee. This is where the record should start with mosque leadership unequivocally committing to support American constitutional principles and identifying a plan to counter radicalization – or publicly demurring, or even outright declining, to do so.

It is then up to law enforcement to learn where dangerous radicalization is indeed occurring and to apprehend those involved.

Most importantly, communities have a vital role in assuring that Muslim organizations are not treated preferentially when applying for permits to build and expand. Waivers from planning codes and exceptions should not be granted due to intimidation or a rush to demonstrate inclusiveness. The

---

http://mosquesinamerica.org/wp-content/uploads/216_Women%20in%20Islam%20-%20Hijab%20and%20Polygamy.mp4

[220] Stephens, Chase. "Imam Who Spoke At Orlando Mosque In April Says Gays Must Die." *DailyWire.com* (14 Jun. 2016), http://www.dailywire.com/news/6521/imam-who-spoke-orlando-mosque-april-says-gays-must-chase-stephens.

[221] Stephens, Chase. "Imam Who Spoke At Orlando Mosque In April Says Gays Must Die." *Daily Wire* (14 Jun. 2016), http://www.dailywire.com/news/6521/imam-who-spoke-orlando-mosque-april-says-gays-must-chase-stephens.

purpose of zoning laws is to uphold the express goals of peaceful enjoyment of property and to provide for safe and compatible use of property within the parameters of planning authority.

Citizens must hold elected officials accountable to exercise their regulatory responsibilities even-handedly. The land use process allows for much discretionary decision-making and politicians may respond to pressure to appear inclusive. But inclusiveness does not mean giving a group that is willing to use multicultural leverage special allowances. Constitutional equal protection and religious freedom requirements protect individual and group rights but also provide for equal treatment of all applicants.

Public discussions that prompt scrutiny of Islamic supremacist tenets are vitally important to Western cultures when conducted outside of city hall. The right to have these debates must be protected. Yet, use of the few minutes that speakers have to address city planners for the purpose of arguing about Islamic practices is counterproductive. These hearings are convened for the exclusive purpose of considering the regulatory land use implications of a religious application. Presentations that deviate too far from this focus will be ignored and may be repudiated by planners.

It is important to remember that many Muslims who fled oppressive Sharia chauvinism are supportive of American constitutional freedoms. Some even work to counter Islamism, and they should be encouraged in every way possible. A city or county will proceed on the presumption that U.S. Muslims are here to participate in American culture and respect American laws. If there is a documented record to the contrary, that relates specifically to the organizational practice of the applicant at a former site – or a sponsor's site -- the community may publish factual exhibits of failure to comply with regulations. These data points, if properly documented, may suggest important use limitations and enforcement mechanisms if there is basis to approve the use permit.

Recognition of reformist and compatible Muslims, while making a formal request for a mosque-centric plan to target radicalization, will serve both the congenial Muslim community and local peace and safety concerns. This is where strong expression of community will is critical. Residents not only have an opportunity to speak to concerns about community order but have an obligation to ask for Islamic commitment to American ideals. While mostly symbolic at the time of a public hearing, proactive statements from the community will encourage the moderate Muslim community as well as put Islamic leadership on notice that residents are paying attention and, furthermore, will speak up when either zoning regulations or civil rights standards are not followed.

10. Mosque Building Permits: What to Expect From City Hall?

A popular personal development guru recommends "beginning a project with the end in mind." When preparing to organize an inquiry into a mosque application hearing, it is vital to consider what can be accomplished within the context of the process. There are defining questions that should be asked before organizing an effective mosque monitoring accountability group and these should be selected according to the facts of each case, and the rules that govern the granting of a use permit.

At this point, a very important underlying premise should be established: Mosque land use applications should receive equal treatment as compared to any other religious land use application. In the cases that the mosques appear to have received favorable treatment or infractions have resulted in less consistent enforcement (see, for example, the questions surrounding the neighborhood experience with AFYFC as detailed in this monograph), why has this occurred? What may prevent or deter localities from granting exceptional concessions? What questions should officials ask, and what tests are important? And, finally, what was missed in the cases where results have been incompatible with surrounding establishments and an unanticipated burden on that community?

While RLUIPA presents a high bar for outright denial of a religious, and therefore a mosque, land use application, it is critical to understand that there are vital roles for concerned citizens at the hearings. Free speech rights afford citizens ample ability to make relevant comments on radicalization issues and to express community will on accountability measures outside of the civic, quasi-judicial hearing process. Note again: this is not a suggestion that speakers scrutinize Islamic beliefs, complain about the practice of Sharia law, or lecture on interpretations of the Koran. What is a matter of a vital community concern, in light of radicalization and home-grown terror trends,[222] is to learn from mosque officials whether there are clear and accountable policies on extremist speakers, materials, and activities.

While political officials may not offer the procedural permit hearing venue for presentation of these concerns, articulate and compelling presentations that weave in the need for community reassurance may establish foundational interest in mosque accountability. Community input during

---

[222] Barber, Ellison, "Counterterrorism Expert: Threat of Homegrown Terror Has Escalated," *Free Beacon* (16 Aug. 2013), http://freebeacon.com/counterterrorism-expert-threat-of-homegrown-terror-has-escalated/?goback=.gde_64725_member_267055434%23!.

the process must be based on oversight of the technical aspects of the application deliberations, but good faith interest in proactive strategies to prevent radicalization may be reasonable and constructive.

It all starts with a strong foundation based upon facts. Good faith and good relationships must begin with basic respect and honesty. When mosque leadership misrepresents the number of attendees, frequency of activities, and need for parking, resentment is a natural result. If municipal officials are not prepared to press for facts and then enforce final terms, local citizens have every right to challenge while assuring that the full range of questions has been covered.

What will be the range of activities?

> Depending on the level of detail described in the permit application, compare the indicated range of offerings to other Islamic institutions. If there is no published prospectus for the organization, ask about intentions for number of prayer services and planned attendance, day care facilities, women's programs, burial preparations, the entire array of all education programs, food service, family festivals, athletic programs, recreational sports, Ramadan/Eid observances, and frequency of regional events like seminars and family festivals. It is important to establish a record of direct answers to these questions as vague and generalized categorical "plans" leave much room for interpretation.

When are the PEAK-level activities scheduled?

> The highest attendance mosque meetings are typically not on Sunday but on Friday. It is critical to know the actual expected attendance and to judge how the traffic and parking will impact other neighborhood community assembly or school release patterns.

What have been the activity levels in the past?

> If the group is expanding or relocating, what has been the pattern of attendance, rates of high traffic, and trajectory of expansion? Has the group complied with city code and permit limits at current facility? If there is a sister or parent institution, what has the record of compliance been at this facility? The answers to these questions may not be determinative but they will suggest potential permit structure.

Who is authorized to speak for the mosque project?

In some cases, organizational filings for contracts or deeds of trust do not match the names of property owners that are provided to local officials on the permit application. This may be an issue as ownership or legal title to use the property is a threshold requirement for filing a land use application in most jurisdictions. And, in a quasi-judicial hearing setting, the spokesperson is providing *testimony* and must understand that he or she is assuming the role of authorized fact provider. In some cases, accountability and enforcement have been complicated when mosque officials who were presented as designated spokespersons at the hearing have subsequently claimed not to have had authorization.

Is there a sponsor organization?

Some Islamic groups are part of a larger confederation and the organizational website will usually detail the mission statement as well as indicate expected activity levels for the mosques involved in the network. Sponsorship by, and close ties to, a few organizations like NAIT and ISNA, often indicate Muslim Brotherhood connections.[223] This is background information that informs the community as to likely orientation of materials and speakers, although it is not a direct local government zoning consideration.

Has the imam or mosque leadership made statements that are contrary to constitutional law in the areas of women's rights, criminalization of speech that is critical of Islam or Sharia law, and what are the organization's views on religious or racial tolerance?

Imams and invited speakers enjoy free speech rights, but these kinds of statements tend to reflect a slavish adherence to Sharia law and the community may be made aware outside of civic sessions of patterns of anti-constitutional public statements. The activist imams who refuse to endorse the Muslim reformist-promulgated American standards of free speech, separation of mosque and state, and religious freedom – including the right to leave Islam without penalty – indicate fidelity to Sharia rules over American customs and legal norms.

---

[223] Mauro, Ryan. "Senate HS Chair Endorses Bill to Name MB as Terrorists." *The Clarion Project* (11 Feb. 2016), http://www.clarionproject.org/news/senate-hs-chair-endorses-bill-name-mb-terrorists. ("The legislation explicitly identifies the Council on American-Islamic Relations (CAIR), the Islamic Society of North America (ISNA) and the North American Islamic Trust (NAIT) as U.S. Muslim Brotherhood entities and includes evidence tying them to a Hamas support network.")

Has this congregation associated with radical speakers or Muslim Brotherhood operatives?

> Again, this is not commentary for the formal proceedings inside city hall, but these associations are of interest to the community. A community may put mosque leadership on notice that they will watch for invitations to host featured guests and may elect to notify the community of this activity as well as make fact-based public announcements via blogposts or work to generate media comment about the radical nature of hateful or anti-American Islamist individuals present in the community. Some communities have chosen to demonstrate or hold rallies to spotlight objectionable extremists.

There is a line to be drawn between general anti-Islamic comments and expressions of intent to hold mosque leaders to anti-radicalization promises. As long as concerns are expressed as constructive notice to work with mosque officials to target radicalization and the structure of these efforts is organized outside of the hearing sessions, this activity should not complicate the hearing setting. Some city councils may complain that such inspection is not relevant, even outside the official process, but with some prominent imams calling for the criminalization of speech, distributing violent materials, inviting radicalized speakers, condoning illicit marriages and divorces, acknowledging polygamy, and providing counter-constitutional legal arbitration services, the community is right to reinforce American civil rights traditions and to declare no tolerance for radicalization efforts.

It must be underscored that these expressive activities are not a zoning or local government function and the challenges to radicalization activities, or answers to these questions, will not come from planning officials – especially in light of RLUIPA's generous treatment of facilities categorized as religious. But, private citizens may, and should, still demand to know clear intentions of mosque leadership and express intent to monitor, publicize, and challenge extremist Islamist operators. Free speech must work both ways.

11. THE MOSQUE PERMIT HEARING PROCESS

I
t is of fundamental importance to any examination of the land use permitting process to consider the foregoing sections as they applied to the AFYFC mosque and the Resurrection Power Church applications in Bloomington, Minnesota. It is one thing to consider the structured process as provided on land planning websites, but quite another to understand – based upon the actual experience of applicants, land use officials, and the impacted neighborhoods – how that process may lead to very disappointing results.

City hall, as the center of local bureaucracy, is not typically known for bypassing red tape but, in these cases, there are questions officials may not know to ask. Or, they may feel pressure to demonstrate that the community will welcome an Islamic mosque or center. Whatever the reasons, success or failure in assuring full inspection of all aspects of the intended use may be up to those determined to press for accountability, accuracy, and a careful record of all answers.

When assessing a government process, one begins with the structure. Planning authority is described on the municipal website. The website will also provide the details of the overall Comprehensive or General Plan and the more localized zoned areas will be articulated in the District Plans.

As Muslim groups file applications for zoning exceptions, variances, and conditional use permits, they often characterize the facility as a cultural center or community center. Prayer space is often mentioned incidentally, if at all. A resident in Hamtramck, Michigan complained that mosque organizers "never said [the center] would serve as a mosque." But, Sakrul Islam, from the Islamic center reportedly replied, "no one ever said it would not be a mosque, and also saying an Islamic center "covers everything.'"[224]

There are likely several reasons for making application as a cultural center, or other secular-sounding purpose, but most significant may be that the application receives both religious worship protection while also public relations consideration for a use that is described many times as offering social and community services. This does not mean that additional merit points are given, but the hearings often reveal favorable comments and approving attitudes from officials who likely factor this "bonus" into their final decisions.

---

[224] Sercombe, Charles, "Residents Complain." *The Review* (10 Nov. 2016), http://www.thehamtramckreview.com/residents-complain-that-call-to-prayer-is-too-loud/. (Resident "warned" that if she continued claiming she was lied to, a defamation lawsuit would be filed.)

Mosque officials or their building plan expeditors may meet with city staff in advance of the permit application to discuss the plans, assure decision makers of good faith, and to allege benefits to the city of recreation programs or social services.[225] Therefore, much may already have been discussed and conclusions drawn by the time that there is first public notice of plans to site a mosque in a community.[226]

Some mosque congregations may be substantially involved in community activity and charity beyond symbolic "interfaith" appearances, but those that may be cloistered facilities should not be given extra credit on permit applications when actual community offerings are unknown and unlikely probabilities.

Quite simply, if the application notes worship space or prayer space, it should be categorized as a straightforward religious land use, not a community center with incidental religious activity that, conveniently, also links to RLUIPA benefits.

For practicing Muslims generally, social and familial activity is centered in the mosque. Since Islamic practices involve individuals and families in a range of activities, these Muslims will naturally be very involved in mosque activities. Newer immigrants, used to the mosque-based communal life, will favor the familiarity of the Islamic centers that organize doctrinal segregated prayers, separate sports activities, halal food service, and unique dress codes.

Land use planners have often failed to realize the implications of the communal nature of mosque operations. They may under-anticipate the level of overall activity when the mosque is central to all aspects of Islamic life. In practical terms, city planners should expect that an application that mentions prayer space is one indicating comprehensive use including possible multiple prayer sessions, sermons, and seminars as well as a base for full familial and the range of recreational and social interaction. Queries into all of these possibilities should be considered as well as whether some activities will be planned during very late night hours.

This does not mean that there should be a template for processing mosque applications that assigns different formulas based upon unique use. For localities to adopt an Islamic-directed policy would be to implicate several laws against discrimination. But, it does mean that questions should be asked of all religious applicants to derive accurate descriptions, documents.

---

[225] Foley, Kathleen. "Building Mosques in America: Strategies for Securing Municipal Approvals." *Institute for Social Policy*, p.33-41 (Oct. 2010 October).
http://web.archive.org/web/20160114122511/http://ispu.org/files/PDFs/ISPU_-_Building_Mosques_Report_-_Kathleen_Foley.pdf

[226] *Id.* at 33.

and statements. All exhibits and responses are, indeed, testimony provided for the purpose of a formal hearing. In the case of Islamic applications, the questions might be based upon the patterns, habits, and customs of established Muslim institutions already operating in the United States.

City planning commissions may be learning to proceed more methodically in light of unique use issues posed by Islamic communities. A St. Cloud, Minnesota planning session video shows a commissioner, who is a self-described immigrant to the U.S. from a Muslim country, challenging an Islamic group to provide more honest numbers. He noted that Islam – and by extension mosque-centric life – is "the totality of all [Muslims] are." He used an example of a six-hundred member mosque organization (based upon the subject application) to say that the participation level would likely be three times that amount, or in the neighborhood of eighteen hundred. He then said that he expected that the religious education facilities, school schedule, and other concurrent activities would be "going on all the time." And he said that with those just "hanging out," it will mean that the Islamic center will be "very busy every day of the week." He instructed mosque organizers "to be realistic about number you will be serving."[227] The planning commission took the action of tabling the matter until more research and due diligence could be done.

At the start, planners should recognize that mention of Friday prayers means that the hearing process will address a defined mosque application. A recent faith-based cooperative endorsed by many Muslim scholars as an accurate depiction of the Muslim community in America today says that "a mosque is defined as a Muslim organization that holds Jum'ah Prayers (Friday Prayers), conducts other Islamic activities and controls the space in which activities are held."[228]

An attendee at the mosque in Kennesaw, Georgia, affirmed that daily prayers arc observed at the closest mosque and that compliant Muslims try to participate several times a day: "If you are close enough — five, ten minutes' drive — you can go there early in the morning prayers, in the

[227] "City of St. Cloud Planning Commission Meeting." See discussion at approximately 2:21 marker. (13 Aug. 2013), available at:
http://stcloudmn.granicus.com/MediaPlayer.php?view_id=2&clip_id=482.
http://mosquesinamerica.org/wp-content/uploads/224_stcloudmn_planning_13Aug2013.mp4

[228] Bagby Ihsan. "The American Mosque 2011." p.2 (Jan. 2012), available at:
https://www.cair.com/images/pdf/The-American-Mosque-2011-part-1.pdf.

evening prayers at least." Then, he added that this is how*"you build up the community."*[229]

Organized prayer observance, including the main Friday session, and teaching meetings will be conducted as integral to mosque functions while various family activities, and seminars are offered during the week. Cities are often challenged when quantifying occupancy since Islamic prayer space requirements are not the same as the pew space of other houses of worship. Fire codes, parking, traffic, environmental impact (especially where cemetery use is planned), and utility services must all be considered according to actual use rather than vague descriptions of numbers that may sound appropriate for purpose of the hearing audience.

Also, workers located near a mosque facility are likely to come to the facility for Friday prayers but not be part of a residential census that would be expected to attend the mosque. Since Muslims will often go to the facility that is most convenient to observe prayer rituals, this will likely entail a greater number of taxi drivers, bus, and delivery drivers. This also contributes to higher demand on Fridays for single attendee parking and so the usual ratios of building occupant per car may not reflect expected norms.[230] The courts have not ruled on whether a different standard for unique Islamic solo driver patterns is unlawfully discriminatory but some municipalities are beginning to look at whether the trend is sufficient to sustain this line of questioning. At the very least, the pattern should be considered for anticipating the totality of the use when providing conditional terms and enforcement parameters in the final permit.

Some Islamic centers have addressed the parking concerns by offering two, three, and more prayer sessions on Fridays. While this tactic may relieve parking concerns, for regular Friday observances, the in-and-out activity adds to traffic and "trip counts" over the course of the day and evening may create intolerable stress for a residential area.

Municipalities have begun to think prophylactically and some are creating easier paths to conditional approval in zones that are compatible with worship activity and assembly. If there is ample provision for religious use elsewhere, localities may offer limited opportunity within sensitive residential areas by erecting higher bars to entry. An example of this is the application of trip count limits to restrict the numbers of cars that may exit

---

[229] Brangham, William. "Freedom of Religion? Mosque Debate in Georgia Town Reveals Sharp Divide." *PBS Newshour* (20 Dec. 2014), http://www.pbs.org/newshour/bb/freedom-religion-mosque-debate-georgia-town-reveals-sharp-divide/

[230] Sadlouskos, Linda. "Mosque Traffic Expert Presents Case for Fewer Spaces." *Patch.com* (13 Feb. 2013), http://patch.com/new-jersey/baskingridge/mosque-traffic-expert-presents-case-for-fewer-spaces.

and enter a given curb cut during a period of time, whether within a period of hours or a day.

Another example would be the requirement that potentially burdensome assembly uses must be sited near, or on, arterial streets that can accommodate left-turn traffic and heavier periodic flows. The comprehensive plans and district plans undergo periodic reviews and this is a good time for planning staff to restrict conditional use availability in highly sensitive areas. At the same time, in consideration of RLUIPA expectations, an alternate zone should be made less restrictive to religious use. These adjustments may not be contemplated while a religious land use application is in process as the adoption of new rules could result in discrimination complaints.

Equal protection RLUIPA provisions will require that mosques are given the same treatment as other religious and similarly situated assembly uses. But, the community should have fair notice as to the daily activity – compounded on Friday – the traffic, noise, and burden on infrastructure concerns. Preparing for realistic use and providing enforceable limits is the key to evaluating a conditional use. If an honest assessment of the activity demonstrates that the burden on the neighboring occupants will be too great, or conditions too dangerous with no available remedy, a locality may still comply with RLUIPA by making a good faith effort to suggest suitable alternative sites.

Absolute maximum occupancy will be calculated according to fire code. Municipalities also routinely regulate parking and maximum numbers of trips according to formulas provide found in the zoning code. These formulas are structured to quantify the number cars and occupants per general tolerances. There are also additional concerns, however, if the surrounding area is sensitive to noise levels, lighting, traffic, frequent activity, and late-night usage of the property. Neighboring residents and businesses deserve to know what is the real intensity of use planned for the site and the hours that the facility will be operational. It is not unusual nor is it unreasonable for a municipality to limit a religious applicants' hours of use as well as intensity, according to generally applicable zoning provisions.

12. Holding the Planning Department Accountable

It really is all in the details. Municipal planning is based upon what are the rules and how the rules are applied. When conditional or special uses – or even variances – are the objective of applications, the details may be reviewed with a high degree of discretion as the standing rules are adjusted when certain expectations are agreed upon and codified.

It is hard to know why it seems that Islamic permit applications may meet with lower hurdles and fewer questions. To be sure, the pendulum has swung the other way and some localities seem determined to decline the applications, under any conditions. But the times that the path to approval appears easier than for others and the conditions less restrictive, is it because officials seek to prove tolerance or because they are afraid of the potential for controversy? Or is it a combination of both?

THE STAFF REPORT PHASE

Whether the application process is headed to either outcome, there is a role for citizen oversight of the entire process. That said, some parts of the process are opaque and not easily inspected. An especially determinative phase, and one that is conducted internally, is that of the planning staff research and report. This process involves staff findings on whether the intended use can meet compatibility expectations with input from other relevant agencies like police and fire.

The staff report presents a recitation of limitations on the use that will bring it into reasonable conformity with the character of the established host zone. This report is the product of extensive research into an array of technical concerns and it attempts to resolve all applicable concerns. If the property use is not deemed suitable at this point, staff recommends denial. If the applicants agree to meet an achievable range of standards, approval is recommended. The final report will be based upon the rationale for how the objectives of the Comprehensive and District Plans may still be met if this exceptional use is tailored to exist within allowable tolerances.

Most political commissions will essentially rubber stamp the staff findings as they are relied upon for accuracy and compliance with the District Plan and City Code provisions. Some would say that the "fix is in" at this point, but it is logical to acknowledge that staff planners are specially trained to process applications and analyze the appropriateness of the requests for conditional or special use. However, residents should understand that the final decision rests with the elected officials whose duty it is to thoroughly review and properly evaluate the staff report.

Many times the community will not even know that an application is pending until the staff report is finalized and the first public hearing is calendared. This is when the division of volunteers into committees or teams will allow for greater coverage of the oversight tasks. It will be important to inspect the staff report immediately for compliance with standards on environmental reports, traffic studies, attendance to parking ratios, sewer and water, setbacks, hours of operations, specificity as to type and frequency of activities, potential for overlapping events, and parking. Municipal planners must devote the same level of scrutiny to all religious and assembly applications and these are questions that should be answered in all cases.

The structured rules that govern zoned areas are all available on the municipal website as are the listed requirements for special or conditional use. It is useful to keep in mind that the rationale for conditional uses intends that they are regulated to provide general *compatibility* with the prevailing zone design. Residents who are overseeing the permitting process should keep this premise in mind. They may use the language of the Comprehensive and District Plans to keep this objective at the forefront of discussions.

THE QUASI-JUDICIAL HEARING PROCESS

The municipal websites are organized so that inquirers start with links to the planning department or building permits. Then, it will be necessary to know the zoning for the area in which the permit is sought. If, for example, the zone is R-1 (typically single family residences), there will likely be a list of uses that are conditionally *allowed* if requirements are met. Check to see what are the requirements for religious assembly. This is where research may be done to learn what the expectations are of a religious assembly applicant seeking conditional or special approval.

This is also the part of the process that caused Congress to pass RLUIPA. Much political discretion, pressure, or potential favoritism may enter the equation at the point that staff and local political officers have the ability to tweak the guidelines. Post-RLUIPA, religious uses are not as likely to be disadvantaged. But, some planning staff have set RLUIPA provisions aside and others have relied upon them more to the advantage of some groups than others.

At this juncture it is very important to review past approved or denied religious and assembly applications for the zone. The past approvals should show similar application of code provisions from requirements for setbacks, buffer zones, sewer, left turn lanes, parking, trip counts, steeple or minaret height, waivers, hours of use, and any other test. If there are discrepancies, contact the point person for the prior-approved or prior-denied use and ask if they will testify at the hearing.

Good examples of studious resident oversight are found in the Disneyworld area of Florida. The Orange County Board of Zoning Adjustment denied a mosque application for a special exemption in the Bay Hill community, and the mosque backers then appealed to the Orange County Commissioners. In August 2014, the County Commission denied the application unanimously.[231] News coverage cited the rural nature of the property, along with limited-access residential streets, as overriding concerns. Residents report that citizen oversight of applicable regulations played an important role.

Two years later, the Orange County Board of Zoning Adjustment unanimously denied another mosque application in August, 2016. In this case, the mosque needed a special exemption to be built in an R-CE zone. Although the 6,900 square foot mosque plans only showed 30 trips over local roads for afternoon prayer and 44 parking spaces, residents were adamant on enforcement of proper notice requirements for hearings, as well as regard for official designations that marked wetlands and protected habitat areas.[232]

A case in Sterling Heights, Michigan, also represents diligent community involvement and city staff adherence to zoning code. As the commissioners rejected the project, the city planner noted that "the 20,500-square-foot mosque on 4 1/2 acres of largely undeveloped property was too tall, too large and not harmonious with neighboring properties." Parking was an unresolved concern. And, even after adjustments, the minarets would still have been 27 feet taller than allowed by city regulations. Finally, the 65-foot dome would "far exceed the height of other structures."[233] The applicant is challenging the Sterling Heights' denial in court and the DOJ has announced an investigation.

Most important for residents is a complete understanding of the foregoing profiles describing the very different City of Bloomington processes and results that controlled the AFYFC and the Resurrection Power Church permit applications. These examples provide the highly discretionary practices that planners may use to defend opposite decisions when considering religious land use applications.

---

[231] Fox, Greg. "Orange Commissioners Unanimously Vote No on Proposed Bay Hill Mosque." *WESH News.com* (19 Aug. 2014), http://www.wesh.com/news/orange-county-commissioners-hear-debate-on-proposed-bay-bill-mosque/27617032.

[232] Hendrix, Danielle. "More Details on Proposed Windermere Religious Center Emerge." *Windermere Observer* (27 Jul. 2016), http://www.orangeobserver.com/article/more-details-proposed-windermere-religious-center-emerge

[233] Chambers, Jennifer. "Feds Target Religious Bias in Zoning Fights." *Detroit News* (25 May, 2016), http://www.detroitnews.com/story/news/local/michigan/2016/05/24/feds-target-religious-bias-zoning-fights/84881958/.

These profiles also reveal inconsistent rationale provided by the City to defend the opposite determinations: i.e., the AFYFC applicant was not held accountable for representations made regarding volume, level and kind of activity expected whereas the City relied upon the Resurrection Power Church's commitments and then added the planners' own "worst case scenario" speculation. AFYFC received a CUP conditioned upon "proof of [additional] parking," if needed, but the church was denied potential alternative parking arrangements or parking lot modifications. The City of Bloomington did not review AFYFC's application in light of how future occupants would use the property but the Pastor Udeh of Resurrection Power was held to this standard. The AFYFC CUP supplied a condition restricting concurrent use of certain buildings to control parking but the City never offered similar considerations to the church when the City expressed reservations as to whether warehouse space *would ever be used* for assembly (Pastor Udeh had "eliminated" the warehouse space).

It is always advisable to consult anyone who has had experience with city hall to review documents and decisions and to advise oversight committees. Former or current building contractors or permit expeditors have had many encounters with city planners on related issues. Commercial builders and expeditors know how to read the code requirements and some have navigated the process many times. Land use attorneys may also be very helpful and may answer questions for a flat fee.

The public hearing session will provide an opportunity for comment and questions but research must be done in advance. There may be a short window between the issuance of the staff report and the city vote to act on the staff recommendations. The meeting agenda may also be the first time that the community is made aware of a pending land use application. Public notice of the hearing is issued typically after the staff report is published and it may be in the form of newspaper item, website entry, and/or letters to nearby residents. Municipal code on this varies according to state law that governs public notice requirements.

One of an accountability committee's interests is to assure that all worship groups follow the same rules. Islamic groups should not receive preferential treatment as compared to other religious groups. Comparing prior permit authorizations for the applicable zone with any attached conditions is the best way to do this. Per RLUIPA, applications for religious and general assembly permits must be treated equally. Generally this means that if a variance for a higher steeple is granted one organization, then the same amount of variance may be considered for minarets. But if the answer to one applicant for a special request is no, then planners may negatively consider similar requests in the future.

Typically, city and county websites offer a link to the Planning Department. Then it is a matter of selecting the Zoning or City Planning section. Then, locate the area where zoning sectors are described: light industrial, office, commercial, and residential are examples (these will be coded for variations of use with letter-number codes like residential "R-1"). Religious applicants will usually seek a Conditional Use Permit (CUP) since little land remains where religious use is designated as a right. The criteria for the permit may be found under the listing for "allowed" uses. If not an allowable use, then the applicants may be seeking an outright variance from the code.

It is possible to review the minutes from prior hearings since the documents are usually linked on the city website. Recorded minutes vary in accuracy and level of detail according to city practice and local rules. Cities are required to archive video recordings and minutes after the postings expire. The time parameters vary by municipality but all records not available by website should be provided upon written request.

Additionally, desk clerks will have access to prior permit approvals with listed conditions available for copying. Clerks will often answer questions about the various processes and may provide copies of official documents although sometimes there is a nominal printing fee.

Outright variances from the zoning code typically will be even more difficult for an applicant to obtain since they represent a deviation from the rules, rather than an effort to create compatibility through conformity with the rules. If the application is for an outright variance, the oversight process is the same. Residents should learn the procedures the govern variance policy and compare to the record of past decisions.

A request for rezoning, or re-characterization of the site to allow deviation from the District Plan is even more burdensome. This process involves exempting much of the project from the prevailing area zoning rules and detaching the project from the definitions that control the surrounding area.

If city planners are to consider sidelining staff recommendations, either in pursuit of more information or to challenge a staff finding, they generally will have to be persuaded by very compelling information. This is the reason why resident presentations must be supported with professional studies, credible sources, and historical records. Residents are able to review all of the applicant documents to compare submissions with public testimony for consistency and accuracy (including even artist's renderings). This exercise should consider whether the intended use is aligned with city code, as well as past treatment of similarly situated assembly and religious applicants. Any discrepancies should be noted and questioned according to accuracy standards, transparency expectation, and compliance with law.

When the City of Bloomington realized that AFYFC was using the property to a much greater extent than stated on the application and at the hearing, the city attorney said, "We have learned not to rely on statements in the application for the conditions." She admitted that "in the past, when [other institutions] said 'this is all we are going to do,' we expected them to honor that."[234] Localities that are on the pre-approval side of the hearing process have opportunity to ask the detailed questions, inspect the answers for conformity with zoning code, and build in enforceable conditions where future developments will foreseeably stretch limits. Assuring that this process is performed according to regulations, and consistent with treatment of similar past applicants — and with all attention to detail — is where accountability overseers are most useful.

---

[234] City of Bloomington City Council Meeting Video, Sep. 23, 2013, *supra* at note 84; approximately 4:31 on the marker,
http://bloomingtonmn.granicus.com/MediaPlayer.php?publish_id=deed4eb7-7681-1031-bf4f-32d5966f69c1.

13. UNIQUE CONCERNS WHEN RESIDENTIAL HOMES ARE CONVERTED TO MOSQUES

When a residence purchased by private individuals is converted to a mosque, the neighbors living in the surrounding area will usually not expect this development. Although this change in the residential designation typically involves a variance from zoning code, the notice to the neighborhood will likely only be what is required to meet the hearing requirements. Many will first notice it as a matter of an agenda item listed for consideration at the next city or county planning session. Planning staff may already have prepared a full report.

Since city staff reports take months to process, the hearings to formalize staff recommendations will take place after much of the fact-finding is done. Yet, it is very important for residents to be involved in this process at the earliest phases. If a permit for religious use is approved in a residential area, residents should have input into all of the various concerns over activity levels and impact, but especially the requirements for traffic and parking management, whether a parking lot may be created on a residential lot, limitation on street parking, reasonable provisions for off-site parking, and enforcement mechanisms. Since typical residential quiet hours are from 10 p.m. to 7 a.m., activities should not be scheduled as a matter of routine during residential zone's quiet time.

If there is confusion regarding the difference between a home that may host a weekly meeting like a Bible study for a small group of people (usually less than 50) and a mosque, Bible study meetings have been treated in the courts on the same basis as other home gatherings like football game viewings.[235] By definition, a mosque facility is a full-fledged worship site and it likely encompasses many weekly functions and full participation – plus observant Muslims who work in the area – for prayer attendance on Fridays and other days, in some cases.

---

[235] "San Juan Capistrano Adopts Changes to Shield Home Bible Studies." *CBS KCAL, Los Angeles* (21 Jun. 2012), http://losangeles.cbslocal.com/2012/06/21/san-juan-capistrano-adopts-changes-to-shield-home-bible-studies/

14. TESTING CONDITIONAL MOSQUE PERMITTING IN PHASES

Some religious applications for non-conforming, but allowable, uses are granted permits in stages. The applicants receive the permit to operate in terms of years: two, five, ten, etc. Terms as low as two years do not give institutions sufficient time to amortize the investment in improvements, or to do even intermediate planning. But terms as long as five, seven, and certainly ten years provide predictability and opportunity to establish good relationships with the surrounding zone occupants.

The reason for limited conditional use is to provide officials opportunity to review the compatibility of the use after a period of time. If the religious organization has not exceeded the permitted limits and the operations at the site have not been detrimental to the prevailing establishments or residents, the use will be extended.

When contemplating a termed CUP, officials should know that courts in many jurisdictions have determined that there is an actual property interest in renewal or transfer of a CUP. Thus, there is a rebuttable presumption that the CUP should continue unless the local officials can demonstrate that the user or the use is simply not a good fit for the area in which it is situated. In the case of an outright denial of a religious CUP term extension or transfer, the reasons should be based upon a record that will show the locality's legal compelling interest to overcome the institution's assertion of a substantial burden.

Even so, in the case of a CUP holder like AFYFC that refuses to follow the rules and a city that enables the abuses, much comfort would be available to the community and the councilmembers who would use the leverage of a comprehensive future review.

In fact, the prior Lutheran occupant at the AFYFC facilities was granted a limited-term five-year CUP. It is hard to know why the City of Bloomington deviated from this policy for AFYFC rather than continuing to issue the permit with a review and conditional re-issue date. In 2016, Bloomington issued a two-year CUP to religious applicant, The Father's House. This short a term likely would not survive judicial review if challenged, and the organization certainly had RLUIPA equal terms and non-discrimination claims based upon the generous AFYFC grants, but the City clearly was willing to treat other religious applicants on an earned trust basis.

The phased permit approach works well in conjunction with legally-described safe harbor methods that assure a degree of predictability and later recourse in the event of overuse or abuse of permit limits. The termed

CUP may be especially useful when municipalities are unsure about the veracity of projections and commitments made during the application process.

15. PERMIT HEARINGS AND PUBLIC COMMENT STRATEGY

When government processes implicate property interests there must be safeguards that protect private ownership. Part of the process that is due to property owners is notice of government deliberations regarding policies that potentially impact the value, use and peaceful enjoyment of property. Local zoning regulations will specify the kind of notice required and will describe the geographical area that will be notified of pending applications for exceptional uses.

Another part of due process concerns is the requirement that governments conduct a hearing to allow public questions and input. The hearing process for zoning decisions includes allotted time for questions or comments from interested citizens. Speakers during these sessions are typically given three minutes to speak from a podium. In most hearing rooms, the podium is equipped with a light system that indicates time expired when light turns from green to yellow to red. Each speaker is expected to fill out a form (or some method of registration), usually prior to the public comment session for the purpose of providing name and subject matter that the speaker wishes to address.

Many planning authorities will accept printed material from speakers at the podium. In some cases, there may be an overhead projector for speaker use in presentation of documents and studies at the podium. If there is *relevant* study material or a printed presentation of useful resources to underscore remarks, make enough copies for council members or planners with a few extra for staff. Any handouts are usually accepted by a clerk and then distributed to the officials. Use this opportunity wisely to provide useful documentation that supports remarks.

An accountability group should decide well in advance of public sessions who will speak for the group. Speakers should address regulatory concerns like environmental and traffic studies (as discussed elsewhere in detail) with a focus on accountability. After studying similar religious and assembly hearings and the conditional use code provisions, speakers should hold officials to exacting standards. At this point, readers should review again the chapter on the AFYFC experience in Bloomington, MN, to consider how attention to every detail with subsequent enforcement provisions in mind is important. Again the vote whether to approve, and what conditions will apply, should also be considered in light of comparable treatment of other religious or assembly applications.

Overall, the tone of speakers is critically important. Speakers must stay on point and speak to issues that the decision makers are authorized to address. Speakers should organize material so that each has a topic and an area of expertise. It is also helpful to structure the presentations so that there is as little repetition as possible. Not every interested resident needs to have a speaking role for the level of interest to be noted. The larger the supportive group in attendance, the more emphasis that speaker points will be given. It should be noted that this is not the time for outbursts or applause.

The most important instruction to remember when making a presentation at a public hearing is to speak in a thoughtful and credible way. If remarks are dismissed as hysterical or rant-like, the comments only serve to discredit the entire effort. This is the reason that the 3-minute allotment of podium time should not be used to discuss the dangers of Sharia, civilizational jihad, or violent passages from the Koran. This is likely to be counterproductive as these issues have no place in a local government hearing. In fact, over the top religiously animated remarks may prompt city officials who are working to apply the zoning standards in a deliberative manner to disregard even the potentially credible points that these speakers, and those they represent, hope to make.

As one will observe in the footnoted video segment, the impact on Temecula city planning commissioners, after over eight hours of 3-minute comments, was not what was intended.[236] During the endless hours of short comments, only a handful of speakers attempted to address relevant issues like traffic, parking, and measurable impact on the surrounding residential zone.

It should go without saying that lecturing officials in public is not an effective method of persuasion. There is a difference between matter-of-factly explaining a concern or questioning the rationale behind a regulatory procedure, and scolding or ranting. The decision makers were popularly elected and they have strong political instincts. Many desire to be elected again and some intend to run for higher office. Some are very uncomfortable with this kind of controversy and they feel tremendous pressure to find the fastest route to negotiated compromise. The best rule of thumb is to stick to matters of substance relating to the hearing business and to clearly articulate the interests of the community.

In the event that an elected representative has betrayed the public trust or conducted himself in a manner that is negligent or irresponsible, these are political matters and a response may be organized away from the hearing procedures.

---

[236] "Temecula Planning Commission Vote on Mosque." *YouTube* (9 Aug. 2012). https://www.youtube.com/watch?v=Z6DEeyBKyiE; *also see*: "Temecula Approves Mosque After Contentious 8-Hour Hearing." *Los Angeles Times* (26 Jan. 2011), http://latimesblogs.latimes.com/lanow/2011/01/temecula-approves-mosque-after-contentious-8-hour-hearing.html

Furthermore, it may be a good idea to ask an attorney who is familiar with zoning law to give a prepared summary of legitimate concerns and to offer to answer questions that the council or planners may have. Many city attorneys have been to seminars on the religious land-use protections covered under RLUIPA, but may not be as familiar with current rulings on the statute as an attorney that specializes in the field.

As has been noted elsewhere, commercial contractors may also have invaluable insight as they know the system and they have learned how to make effective presentations to planning committees and support staff.

From a legal and ethical perspective, city officials are required to make a statement distinguishing their objective duty to apply the rules equally from commenters that sound religiously or racially biased. Many cities will open the public comment period with a disclaimer saying that comments do not reflect the views of city planners and they will remind speakers to address only matters relevant to the application review process. If city officials do not stay above the fray while carefully executing civil duties, litigants may attempt to impute the hostility of vocal opposition speakers to the decision-makers.

Take, for example, the case of the Al Madany Islamic Center that settled in 2014 with the City of Norwalk, Connecticut, for $1.8 million and an agreement that the city would locate a suitable alternative site for the Islamic organization. Interestingly, in light of the parking concerns at AFYFC as related previously, the proposed settlement shows that careful parking management plans to avoid on-street parking were included.[237]

The Al Madany legal complaint was based, in part, upon discrimination charges. In an unusual move, the lawyers included private comments from outside the hearing hall that were entered into a community blog: "Yay, just what the USA needs, another house where they teach to kill those that disagree with their ideology; Why don't the locals just defile the ground with pork products; Let 'em build it. Then we burn it."[238] According to news coverage, officials did ask speakers who attended the hearing to refrain from comments about "religion" and to limit remarks to zoning issues.

---

[237] Chapman, Nancy. Al Madany Plans to Make Union Park Church into a Mosque." *NancyonNorwalk.com* (12 Nov. 2015), http://www.nancyonnorwalk.com/2015/11/al-madany-plans-to-make-union-park-church-into-a-mosque/; copy of proposed settlement *available at*: http://www.nancyonnorwalk.com/wp-content/uploads/2014/08/Settlement-Terms.pdf.

[238] Seeman, Evan. "Can the Publics Discriminatory Comments Play a Role in RLUIPA Claims?" *Rluipa-defense.com* (11 Sep. 2012), https://www.rluipa-defense.com/2012/09/can-the-publics-discriminatory-comments-play-a-role-in-rluipa-claims/. ("When such statements are made in a public forum, local officials may wish to take corrective action, such as having the chairperson immediately renounce any discriminatory statements. ...")

There was no record of official discriminatory remarks. This case involved a protracted settlement process and no final judicial ruling that referenced the extra-hearing comments.

As in the Al Madany case, even though there may be no direct link between local hostility and official action, some attorneys have asked judges to consider whether a denial in the presence of hostility constitutes circumstantial evidence of bias. As mentioned previously, the DOJ is planning to build cases on the legal theory that adverse impact, or disproportionate outcome, is the same as legally-defined discrimination.

If these attempts to shift more authority from local government officials to federal overseers succeed over time, it will be even more difficult to draw proper lines between hostility or animus, and residents who are seeking straight answers and work to ensure predictable levels of use. Resident comments should be evaluated for proper and thoughtful lines of questioning in search of reliable facts and proper limits. There must always be a valid and vital role for the community to play in oversight of the many planning department procedural requirements. Residents have every right to speak to the enforceable limits that should accompany a special, or conditional, use.

The determined attempts by Islamic civil rights groups and the DOJ to link adverse decisions and delays directly to discrimination are ominous. And, the attempts to connect critical comments, issued outside of civic hearings, to official animus serve to chill First Amendment protected speech. This disregards the Supreme Court's highest level of protection covering robust debate on matters of public concern. Even so, the line between public domain and formal civic speech must be carefully considered. It bears repeating that prudent elected officials should clearly distinguish their deliberative roles from surrounding commentary in the public arena, or inappropriate opinion expressed in the hearing hall.

There have been clear examples of decision makers crossing the animus line and courts do correct these displays of direct discrimination. In an example involving a church application, a lawsuit resulted after a religious application met with such fierce official resistance to "another church" that a councilwoman's instructions to the planners were to "kill" the project. In this case, the court ruled that this "open hostility" contributed to a violation of RLUIPA protections.[239]

---

[239] *Fortress Bible Church,* 694 F.3d 208, *supra* at note 137. ("Karaman (planning board member) asked what he could do to move the process along, and Feiner responded that the Church could agree to make yearly financial contributions to the fire department. Another Board member suggested to Russo on multiple occasions that he should 'stop' or 'kill' the project.")

While there are important presentation protocols for formal hearing sessions, individual free speech interests in the issue generally must be protected. When residents in Pittsfield Township, Michigan, organized to petition against an Islamic school and community center mosque based upon traffic and infrastructure concerns, the permit application was denied. In response, in 2012, the Ann Arbor chapter of CAIR sued for civil rights violations and subpoenaed records including emails from the citizen activists. After the American Freedom Law Center responded on behalf of seven community members, the judge ordered CAIR to pay attorneys fees and the "harassing" subpoenas were quashed.[240]

But this judicial reprimand did not deter an Islamic group in Basking Ridge (Bernards Township), New Jersey, from also issuing subpoenas to residents who opposed a mosque application. In 2016, the township of Basking Ridge denied a mosque land use application, after several years of hearings, determining that essential questions regarding parking and activity levels had not been answered in sufficient detail. The Islamic Society of Basking Ridge complained to the DOJ and filed a lawsuit. Part of the litigation included subpoena "commands" for residents to produce communications and documents, including social media posts, that, for example, referenced "Muslims, Islam, mosques, the Quran (also known as the 'Koran'), Muslim worship or prayer services, wudu, imams, burkas, hijabs, Sharia (also known as 'Shari'ah'), jihad, or anything else associated with or related to Muslims or Islam."[241]

At the time of this writing the federal judge had not ruled as to whether constitutional First Amendment protections would prevail, and whether potential overbreadth or vagueness concerns would defeat these "commands."

Some local politicians forget at times that their authority is law-based and that discretionary decisions must be squared with the law. Even though they are popularly elected, they cannot just make up new rules and "because we said so" is not a sufficient answer. It may even be a matter for the courts when the exercise of discretionary political power exceeds constitutional boundaries or legal parameters. However, citizens do

---

[240] "Federal Court Orders CAIR to Pay AFLC $9,000 in Legal Fees." *americanfreedomlawcenter.org* (28 Aug. 2015), http://www.americanfreedomlawcenter.org/press-release/federal-court-orders-cair-to-pay-aflc-9000-in-legal-fees/.

[241] Perry, W. Jacob. "Mosque Subpoenas Stir Anger in Bernards Township." *The Bernardsville News* (16 May, 2016), http://www.newjerseyhills.com/bernardsville_news/news/mosque-subpoenas-stir-anger-in-bernards-township/article_79cc47d4-6015-51d9-a680-ccbd1d59d914.html; *also see,* Islamic Society of Basking Ridge (ISBR) subpoena, *see* http://mosquesinamerica.org/wp-content/uploads/2016/10/238_mosque-subpoenas-stir-anger-in-bernards-townsh.pdf

perform an important oversight role when they have studied the law governing the process and then when they question officials for assurance that zoning codes are applied accurately and even-handedly.

16. SCALING STONEWALLS: PUBLIC RECORD REQUESTS AND OPEN MEETING ACTS

PUBLIC RECORD REQUESTS

Most Americans have heard of the federal Freedom of Information Act (FOIA). State laws govern similar mechanisms that apply to local government proceedings and these are usually called something like "public record act requests." An internet search will provide references to state laws that govern the format of the requests. It may also be possible to find several sample presentations.[242] These requests can be a very powerful tool for obtaining documents, inter-agency communications, and study results that are not routinely made available to the public.

State data requests may also be used to access original records of municipal meetings. Most localities are required to archive these complete records. In the event of heavily-summarized minutes, old, or missing videos, an original transcript usually must be retained and offered to the public for inspection upon request. There are resources that provide insight into the various "state records act requests" as they also offer insight into the respective procedures.[243] When utilizing any guides or handbooks, it is always advisable to check city codes for any updates or revisions.

The records request tool does something to level the playing field where it provides resident access to copies of submitted documents, tests, emails, notes, and other records. When the proceedings are scheduled to run quickly and much seems to have been already decided, submit the records requests early. There is a municipal code to regulate the number of days allowed for responsive documents but it may take the full allotment to receive the requested items.

Some localities do allow documents that are "under consideration" to be withheld for a time. This may mean that they are legally sensitive under attorney-client privilege rules or that the items are still the subject of a decision under consideration by the body, but not yet finalized.

Such requests require that parties follow the protocol as recorded in the state statute and often further defined in local procedural code. It may be best to have an attorney or legal practitioner write or review these requests

---

[242] Sample Public Records Act Request (California) letter sample: https://firstamendmentcoalition.org/public-records-2/sample-cpra-request-letter/; New Jersey form: http://www.nj.gov/grc/public/request/.

[243] A useful guide provided here: "Open Records Law: A State by State Report." http://www.naco.org/sites/default/files/documents/Open%20Records%20Laws%20A%20S tate%20by%20State%20Report.pdf

since compliance and responsiveness often hinge on how closely specific requirements are followed.

Some localities charge a minimal amount to make copies of the requested documents, so residents should be prepared to provide the required funds when a public records act request is made. Alternatively, residents may use a room provided for the purpose of reviewing and copying the documents on site. Whether photographing items with a cell phone or scanning pages digitally, it is possible that the session will take some time as municipal employees do not always sort documents.

The "public records act" request is a very important mechanism for local residents to employ when there is concern about transparency and consistency in the land use permitting process, but the relevant procedures must be followed closely.

State "open meeting" acts govern local government proceedings, and they serve to impose the methodical and transparent process that is foundational to the rule of law. Many of these regulations also provide definitions for the legislative and quasi-judicial responsibilities assigned to local representatives. For example, the CUP *formal* hearing process, involving *testimony* and *findings of fact,* is a quasi-judicial act. [244] Just because applicants are not sworn in by raising the right hand does not mean that they may mislead the panel of official fact-finders in order to then violate the agreed upon CUP limits with impunity.

Many states will require local municipalities to keep detailed records and follow specific procedures when officials perform legislative quasi-judicial functions. Open meeting acts often provide the framework for local rules regarding notice, video recordings of public meetings, agendas, and minutes. These local regulations are essential tools for use in obtaining *accurate records* of past proceedings and the keeping track of ongoing deliberations. These records must be published and presented per specific procedures, and back-up data produced according to local deadlines.

Open meetings acts also define what is a quorum and they enunciate rules prohibiting private council-member conversations on matters that will be voted upon by the local government body. These rules protect citizens from private deliberations on matters that will become local government pronouncements. These acts vary state-by-state and it is very important to find the law in each respective state and to hold local officials to the letter of this law.

---

[244] Example: "Minnesota Open Meeting Law." *Minnesota Department of Administration*; available at: http://www.ipad.state.mn.us/docs/omlnotice.html,

PUBLIC OFFICIALS MAY NOT HOLD SUB-GROUP PRIVATE DISCUSSIONS

Most states have "open meeting" laws enacted to assure that discussions regarding the people's business is conducted in an open, accountable, and transparent fashion. These laws typically announce that government and quasi-government meetings must be open to the public and written notice must issue of the subject of each meeting held. Posted minutes that record the details of the meeting are also usually required.

A meeting is usually defined as the consideration of any official business between a majority, or quorum, of the members. The "meeting" may occur in person, by email, or telephone. Many municipalities have established a best practices policy of not discussing any matter that could be construed as "business" at an informal gathering, or on the phone, or by e-mail, or via the Internet.

If, during a permit application process it appears that officials have come to conclusions that were not deliberated during a public session, it is time to remind officials that citizens are aware of the open meeting law provisions and expect adherence to the rules.

Also, if Islamic organizers have had meetings with planners before the permit application was filed or anytime during the staff investigations and hearing procedures, "open meeting" regulations may apply, and sessions may only be allowed with one council member at a time. The local Open Meeting Act code sections will provide all regulatory terms.

Some issues may be considered during a closed session but the posted regulations must be followed for this alternative to a public session. Most municipalities require posting of the closed session subject matter and provide that notice of the executive session be posted in advance by a specified number of days.

Also, there are rules that govern local executive sessions. These closed sessions may only be used for specific deliberations. It is very important for residents to know how these procedures apply so that proper challenges may be registered if the rules are not followed.

17. WITHDRAWAL OF UNREASONABLE MOSQUE APPLICATIONS

In 2013, concerned residents in St. Cloud, Minnesota were alarmed when the township used the procedural vehicle of an amendment to consider whether to allow a mosque with attendant facilities and housing in a residential area. The special application was for a parcel situated in a single-family residential area and the mosque complex would have included a religious school, two two-unit residential dwellings, a community building with a gymnasium, offices, and retail and restaurant space. Residents complained that this kind of dramatic departure from residential use required a full variance process.

Local citizens formed committees to study the regulations that governed the utilization of the amendment process to achieve zoning modifications and they reviewed examples of how the amendment process had been used in the past. They decided that this application really represented what amounted to something like "re-zoning" and they formed a citizen action committee around a "No Re-Zone" theme.

Residents then organized a multi-fronted challenge to the township's decision to call the process for permitting the mosque complex an "amendment to the Planned Use Development (P.U.D)." Local residents saw this exceptional use as a re-characterization of the residential neighborhood zoning designation.

These residents developed a website[245] for stating the issues and posting updates, printed posters, car signs, yard signs, bought radio air time and newspaper space, organized press communications, and prepared questions for public hearings. Organized neighbors held press conferences, monitored press coverage, and wrote letters to the editor when the coverage was not complete.

The focus of the resident group was restricted to only regulatory issues including impact, compliance with zoning regulations, original intent of zoning, and infrastructure burdens. When the St. Cloud planning commissioners and the City Council expressed grave concerns about the re-zoning proposal, even in light of a modified application for fewer buildings, mosque officials withdrew the application. The applicants ultimately

---

[245] "St. Cloud Citizens for Reasonable Zoning. St. Cloud. MN City Council: Deny the Application to Amend Paradise Park." *Change.org* (24 Jul. 2013), avail: https://www.change.org/p/st-cloud-mn-city-council-deny-the-application-to-amend-paradise-park-pud-dated-7-24-2013 (The organizational website is no longer available but the link shows what could be called the group's mission statement): http://mosquesinamerica.org/wp-content/uploads/2016/10/242_Deny_application_Paradise_Park.pdf

decided that they would consider other sites or might submit a revised application for the original site.[246]

An Islamic Center in Fredricksburg, Virginia, offered to sell a proposed mosque site to a builder for a housing project, pending county re-zoning, after encountering opposition from the community based in parking and activity concerns.[247]

Another exhibit in the category of withdrawn mosque applications is one in Brentwood, Tennessee, where neighbors united to voice concerns about traffic and flooding (most of the proposed site was on a flood plain and there had been recent storms).[248]

[246] Collins, Jon. "St. Cloud Islamic Center Withdraws Mosque Proposal Before Final City Council Vote." MPR News (8 Oct. 2013), http://www.mprnews.org/story/2013/10/08/religion/st-cloud-islamic-center

[247] Branscome, Jeff. "Islamic Center May Stay At Its Current Location If Residents Agree To A Compromise." The Free Lance-Star (31 Jul. 2016), http://www.dailyprogress.com/starexponent/news/islamic-center-may-stay-at-its-current-location-if-residents/article_7d911b40-dca3-530f-8b4c-a29d1b41076f.html

[248] Smietana, Bob. "Brentwood, TN: Mosque Not Alone in Defeat." Virtueonline.org, from The Tennessean (23 May, 2010), http://www.virtueonline.org/brentwood-tn-mosque-not-alone-defeat.

18. ANTICIPATING ENFORCEMENT: WHEN GOVERNMENT FAILS TO UPHOLD THE LAW

When law enforcement prioritizes keeping the political peace above upholding the law, the officer becomes a seeker of the path of least resistance. Conflict avoidance is a disastrous policy when Islamists design to replace the American rule of law with a counter cultural mindset and Sharia-based practices. As police step back, even when the infractions seem to be of little consequence, they telegraph weak commitment to consistent application of the laws. Political managers may intend this approach to speak tolerance and welcome, but the special treatment is understood by Islamists to be symptomatic of a lack of conviction and moral resolve.

Recall the AFYFC case: What were the Islamic leaders of that mosque in Bloomington to think when the City altered the ordinance that prohibited double-parking, and when police consistently declined to ticket attendees for unsafe parking in lanes needed for access and emergency vehicles? Would Class III vehicles be allowed in other residentially coded parking lots? What about when the City decided that the only occupancy limit was the fire code rating for the buildings, contrary to attendance limitations in the CUP? And, how would the decision to ignore wildly low applicant activity level testimony that committed to maximum attendance of two hundred persons be interpreted? And, what of the finally updated Joint Use Agreement that allowed for periodic "permitted" all-night activity? And, why did that agreement create a series of negotiation phases rather than penalties? Worst, what comes next when various widely advertised activities and programs are advertised as running concurrently and/or consecutively, although not authorized by the CUP?

None of the apparent individual singular concessions granted AFYFC may seem shocking, but when considered in their totality, it would not be surprising if the AFYFC mosque's leaders expected to continue to obtain exemptions from rules that apply to everyone else. What could be called a sense of entitlement only grows when government is increasingly reluctant to enforce the law evenhandedly.

When law enforcement is reduced to walking a delicate public relations line between hostile mosque-goers and disturbed homeowners, the rule of law becomes a mediation negotiation. As law enforcement practices something more like containment policy – keeping the aggressive party from further encroaching on the turf of complaining party – than hewing to a commitment to the rule of law, the encroaching party has nothing to lose by continuing to push the limits. Respect for rules cannot help but be undermined when officials give *de facto* assent by ignoring infractions. Ultimately, it becomes very difficult to draw the line when enforcement should begin.

Is it just an early stage in "no-go" zone development when local government essentially decides to look the other way? What likely happens next when police and local authorities do not recognize baselines from which rules will be upheld? What is at the core of European zones that reject accountability to the host society? It all has to start with pockets of isolation that refuse to recognize civil authority and the legitimacy of consensual government.

Andrew McCarthy, the successful prosecutor of the Blind Sheikh and estimable author on issues of Islamist hegemony finds that America's unique demographic, geographical, and historic experience with immigrants has deterred the development of the balkanized zoned areas. He warns, however, that America's better assimilation success rate is the only real insurance against Islamic separatism. McCarthy expects that the "voluntary apartheid" conditions – what he calls "the strategy by which Muslims of the fundamentalist bent integrate but quite intentionally resist assimilation" – found in Europe will embed in the United States if historic assimilation expectations fail.[249] As McCarthy perceptively urges, "It is very difficult to assimilate a subpopulation that comes to a host country with the specific intention of changing the country, rather than becoming part of that country's culture."[250]

As a warning of what may repeat if American communities fail to erect bulwarks against Islamist separatism, McCarthy provided an example of the rapid transition experienced by a suburb of Chicago called Bridgeview:

> In 1981, the Muslim Brotherhood enjoyed a middle American coup, using the [North American Islamic Trust – a Brotherhood organization that buys up American real estate for the establishment of mosques and Islamic community centers] to wrest the Bridgeview Mosque in Chicago from its moderate founders. The mosque became an anchor for the Brotherhood's voluntary apartheid strategy.

> As the Chicago Tribune reported in 2004, the mosque's leaders "are men who have condemned Western culture, praised Palestinian suicide bombers and encouraged members to view society in stark terms: Muslims against the world." Those leaders drove out moderates, they enforced Islamic dress codes and strict

---

[249] McCarthy, Andrew C. "European-Style Islamic Enclaves in the United States?" *PJ Media* (31 Mar. 2016), https://pjmedia.com/andrewmccarthy/2016/03/31/european-style-islamic-enclaves-in-the-united-states/?singlepage=true

[250] *Id.*

separation of the sexes, and they imported Salafist clerics, whose salaries were paid by Saudi Arabia. [Salafism is a fundamentalist form of Sunni Islam.]

The mosque's communiqués reeked of Brotherhood's doctrine: one brochure, for example, warned that Chicago Muslims were at risk of "melting in the American society, culture and lifestyle"; a plea to a Saudi charity sought funding "before it becomes too late and we may lose our children because they are living in an un-Islamic society."

A whole new community sprang up. The area became an upscale enclave, featuring new houses with Arabic script over the doors and sparkling chandeliers. Mosque leaders built two schools and started a youth center for basketball and religious classes. New clothing stores, groceries and restaurants opened in Bridgeview. A floor-covering store turned into a Middle Eastern restaurant. A music store became an Islamic hair salon. Men who attended the mosque grew their beards and traded their T-shirts for long tunics. Women draped themselves in loose, ankle-length robes. Cook County was fast becoming home to more Palestinians than any other part of the nation. And the mosque was now one of the area's largest Islamic centers....

Most non-Muslims moved away from the mosque neighborhood, frustrated by traffic jams on Fridays and the call to prayer that rang out over mosque loudspeakers. Muslims were happy to take their places. ...[251]

Europe may have difficulty defining a no-go zone, but such areas are generally considered those where police are not confident that they will be respected. While there is not a physical barricade to the point of a moat and drawbridge to bar police entry, police only dare enter with full back-up and, even then, they may be swarmed as mob assemblies converge on them.

Middle East scholar Daniel Pipes has concluded that European local governments when allowing "partial" no-go zones are "shirking responsibility" and are acceding to a "Muslim drive for exclusion and domination." He observed that these zones are declared for a particular purpose:

[T]hey are no-go zones in the sense that representatives of the state — police especially, but also firefighters, meter-readers, ambulance attendants and social workers — can only enter with massed power for temporary periods of time. If they disobey this

---

[251] *Id.*

basic rule (as I learned first-hand in Marseille), they are likely to be swarmed, insulted, threatened and even attacked.[252]

Soeren Kern, an investigative reporter known for in-depth analysis of Islamization in Europe, researched the question of no-go zones in Europe in 2015 and presented his findings in two articles. These reports are replete with links to interviews, academic studies, news exposes, and governmental assessments concerning the "Muslim dominated neighborhoods" that were "de facto off-limits to non-Muslims due to a number of factors, including the lawlessness, insecurity or religious intimidation that often pervades these areas."[253]

If America is to avoid the ominous trajectory and possible final fate of Europe, the early signs of separatism here must be confronted. Local authorities should assure enforcement of the constitutional rule of law by providing clear requirements that they are prepared to consistently enforce. It should be a routine matter when zoning code violations occur that they will first trigger a notice of warning with subsequent infractions entailing either a fine or other penalty for non-compliance. Ultimately, cities should be prepared to call the very permit to use into question if the conditional terms are violated and corrective process has not been followed.

It is true in Europe that government and law enforcement officials have stepped back while Islamic demands for accommodation have been stepped up. There are ample illustrations from European countries that are experiencing an incremental transfer of power in Islamic districts to provide lessons on the "culturally sensitive zones" that have become increasingly assertive in their refusal to submit to civil authority.

Whether it is taxi drivers in New York that park in stacked up fashion during prayer sessions, or it is a mosque administration that is allowed to re-interpret a conditional use permit, relaxation of the rules will be expected, if not respected, and it will become the new status quo.[254] It should be understood that, when a segment of society esteems an alternate

---

[252] Pipes, Daniel. "The Danger of Partial No-Go Zones." The Washington Times. (28 Dec. 2015), http://www.washingtontimes.com/news/2015/dec/28/daniel-pipes-the-danger-of-partial-no-go-zones/

[253] Kern, Soeren. "European 'No-Go' Zones: Fact or Fiction? Part 1: France" *Gatestone Institute* (20 Jan. 2015), http://www.gatestoneinstitute.org/5128/france-no-go-zones; *also see*: Kern, Soeren. "European 'No-Go' Zones: Fact or Fiction? Part II: Britain" *Gatestone Institute* (3 Feb. 2015), http://www.gatestoneinstitute.org/5177/no-go-zones-britain; *also see*: Kern, Soeren. "European No-Go Zones Proliferating" *Gatestone Institute* (2011), http://www.gatestoneinstitute.org/2367/european-muslim-no-go-zones.

[254] "Upper West Side Parking Dispute Breaks Out Between Muslim Cab Drivers, Residents." *CBS WCBS, New York* (9 Dec. 2011), http://newyork.cbslocal.com/2011/12/09/upper-west-side-parking-dispute-breaks-out-between-muslim-cab-drivers-residents/; (strong language warning for second video): "NYC Parking Cop- 'We Do Not Ticket If Wurshepin.'" *Liveleak.com* (6 Sep. 2013), http://www.liveleak.com/view?i=b16_1378500208.

system of law as transcendent, any success that it enjoys in undermining local law will be seen as a significant symbolic accomplishment.

19. RADICALIZATION DETECTION IS A LEGITIMATE COMMUNITY CAUSE

According to state authority, local officials are charged with the administration of general health, safety, and welfare matters. Communities then delegate to law enforcement the duties of surveillance, detection, and apprehension of those planning to commit violent or unlawful acts.[255] Law enforcement oversight is separate from zoning decisions and it is triggered by activities that meet legally measured probable cause patterns. Thus, it is important to understand the separate functions of these agencies and to recognize their prescribed roles. The land use hearing must follow published procedures and must satisfy zoning checklists. Under existing law, it is not within local land planning responsibilities to make forays into religious organizational beliefs, project funding sponsorship, or leadership bona fides.

Thus, states authorize cities, according to their constitutional police power mission, to apply zoning power for the safe enjoyment and use of property. It is not the role of municipalities to adjudicate an understanding between the community and the mosque directors on the leadership role that officials will assume if and when the mosque is established.

There are some who may find the term "radicalization" lacking specificity as it generally is used to convey alarm on the full spectrum from failure to assimilate to joining jihad campaigns. It is sufficient for the purposes here that it is the term used to communicate a cultural threat level sufficient to merit local concern. It is the term used in the public square and the media. It is a term that is defined by the context of the particular crisis.

Consider the tragic 2009 radicalization case of Carlos Bledsoe (a.k.a. Muhammad) who shot two Army privates, killing one, at a military recruiting center in Arkansas. His father, Melvin Bledsoe, testified before Congress, and also gave interviews to media outlets, to describe the "evildoers" who "brainwashed his son." He warned, "If it can happen to my son, it can happen to anyone's son."[256]

Melvin Bledsoe chronicled the brainwashing process that resulted in observable "personality changes" like his son changing his name and removing a picture of Dr. Martin Luther King from his bedroom wall, and

---

[255] "NYPD Designates Certain Mosques as Terrorist Enterprises." *The Clarion Project* (1 Sep. 2013), http://www.clarionproject.org/news/nypd-designates-certain-mosques-terrorist-enterprises.

[256] Dao, James. "A Muslim Son, A Murder Trial, and Many Questions." *New York Times* (16 Feb. 2010), http://www.nytimes.com/2010/02/17/us/17convert.html?_r=0.

turning his dog loose in the woods (because Muslims consider dogs to be dirty creatures).[257] This is exemplary of the radicalization process and it begins with alienation from Western democratic norms. It ends, if the process is completed, with allegiance to contrary Islamist dictates. This is the radicalization that threatens European and American communities.

Even though there is no direct municipal role, in light of known radicalization trends[258] that have produced disturbing levels of anti-Americanism and "homegrown" Islamist terror agents, municipalities should understand that residents may engage in constructive efforts outside of the hearing process to articulate the means of identifying situations that promote radicalization and hold imams accountable to help. It is reasonable for concerned citizens to ask imams for assurance that radicalization centers will not develop in their neighborhoods. This overture should be an affirmative one and should not be stated in or around a city forum as accusatory.

The request for a concrete and public commitment to a clear plan to foster assimilation and disrupt radicalization may be taken to the Islamic organization's office, a local church, or even a coffee shop. When respectfully submitted outside of city hall, commitments to confront radicalization and declarations of intent to uphold human rights are proper concerns of citizens in light of some glib public pronouncements made by American imams that serve the interest of getting zoning approval, but may be abandoned once the mosque is established. This is just a simple matter of setting a baseline expectation that community values will be upheld. And, it is a matter of establishing a record for future review.

In the context of asking any religious group for a broad policy statement, it is useful to consider that various mainstream faiths hold doctrinal positions on abortion, homosexuality, and other matters of conscience that may not be aligned with American statutory or constitutional provisions at any given time. The important distinction here is that Americans agree to submit to civil authority as they consent to live in accord with a society of free individuals organized according to a system of popularly adopted law.

Presumably, nearly half of American Muslims would be relieved to have a community-wide focus on extremism in mosques as forty-eight percent say that "Muslim leaders in the United States have not done enough to speak

---

[257] Hearings Before The Committee on Homeland Security, House of Representatives. "Compilation of Hearings on Islamist Radicalization, Vol. 1." , p.58 (10 Mar., 15 Jun., and 27 Jul. 2011), *available at*: https://www.gpo.gov/fdsys/pkg/CHRG-112hhrg72541/pdf/CHRG-112hhrg72541.pdf.

[258] Kassam, Raheem. "Young Muslims in the West: A Ticking Time Bomb?" *Middle East Forum* (22 Mar. 2016), http://www.meforum.org/5917/young-muslims-ticking-timebomb.

out against Islamic extremists." According to this Pew survey, only thirty-four percent say that Muslim leaders have done enough.[259]

American Muslim reform leader, Dr. Zuhdi Jasser, is very concerned about the influence on his own children of anti-Western imams and wonders what will be the stronger influence on them: American patriotism or hardline Islamism that rejects reason in favor of radicalism. His words are worth quoting to public officials that see any attempt to mention radicalization as generally anti-Muslim:

> We cannot ignore the fact that radicalization occurs within our faith communities. We also cannot ignore the fact that this radicalization does not occur in a vacuum. Nidal Hasan did not wake up one morning and decide to be a radical. He over time was exposed to an ideology that led him down the path to radicalization. There is a continuum that begins with a non-violent separatist, Islamist narrative and ends with an adherence to a violent militant ideology that believes in the supremacy of the Islamic faith.

> That does not mean that every Muslim travels the full continuum, but it does mean that a narrative that is commonplace in Muslim communities is the starting point. That narrative preaches a victim mindset and a separation of Muslims from American society. It is a narrative that is preached by supposed moderates and radicals alike. It is a narrative that as a Muslim father I do not want to ensnare my children....

> But the foundations of the Islamist narrative are being laid each time my children come to pray at our Mosque. Soon they will be of an age where this Imam and those that follow will have impact on the way my children identify themselves as Muslims and as Americans....

> The only way to change the damage that is being done to the Muslim community, and particularly to our youth, is to demand transparency and accountability, and to have an open, honest debate over what is preached at American mosques and what exactly is the real ideology, self-identity, and agenda of Muslim speakers and leaders.[260]

---

[259] "Muslim Americans: No Sign of Growth in Alienation or Support for Extremism" p.7, *Pew Research Center*, (30, Aug, 2011) http://www.people-press.org/2011/08/30/section-6-terrorism-concerns-about-extremism-foreign-policy/.

[260] Jasser, M Zudhi. "AIFD Analysis: The Power of the Pulpit: An American Muslim's Struggle to Define Faith In An American Perspective For His Children." *American Islamic Forum for*

Many non-Muslims are reluctant to believe that isolationism and radicalization can happen when American Muslim populations are not organized in colonies, as they are in Europe and the UK. But the Islamic separatist mentality may still be prevalent in the mosque and the defiant mindset it cultivates may prove to be just as toxic here as it is in the geographical enclaves in Europe.

The city of Bloomington, Minnesota, is an American story that exemplifies this Islamic isolationism, although it also includes a strong element of Somali tribalism. When a reporter for Fox News visited the Minneapolis/St. Paul suburb, it was difficult to find a Somali resident who could converse in English and a local Muslim community organizer described the mindset of first generation immigrants as increasingly isolated and separate.[261]

Europeans and Americans are also learning another hard lesson about the Muslim attitudes and it is that younger Muslims are much more likely to be culturally defiant and radicalized. Even back in 2007, a comprehensive study of Muslim opinions in the UK revealed that 37% of 16-24 year-olds would prefer to live under Sharia law than British law compared to just 17% of 55+ year-olds. The interviews also showed that 36% of 16-24 year olds believe if a Muslim converts to another religion they should be punished by death, compared to 19% of 55+ year-olds. While 74% of 16-24 year-old respondents would prefer Muslim women to choose to wear the veil, only 28% of 55+ year-olds favored the veil.[262]

Young Muslims also expressed alarming support for violent jihad in 2013: sixteen percent in Belgium believed that state terrorism is "acceptable," while 12 percent in Britain said that suicide attacks against civilians in Britain can be justified.[263]

Two more recent studies coming out of France led former career journalist for *Le Monde*, Yves Mamou to draw this conclusion: "One out of every two

---

Democracy (27 Sep. 2011), http://aifdemocracy.org/aifd-analysis-the-power-of-the-pulpit-an-american-muslims-struggle-to-define-faith-in-an-american-perspective-for-his-children/.

[261] Fox&Friends. "How Terrorists Recruit in "Little Somalia": Interview with Pete Hegseth." *Fox News Channel* (6, May 2016), http://video.foxnews.com/v/4881244287001/how-terrorists-recruit-in-little-mogadishu-of-minneapolis/?#sp=show-clips; http://mosquesinamerica.org/wp-content/uploads/2016/10/258_Little_Somalia_Fox.mp4

[262] Munira, Mirza, Senthilkumaran, & Ja'Far, Zein. "Living Apart Together: British Muslims and the Paradox of multiculturalism." *Policyexchange.org* (2007), http://www.policyexchange.org.uk/images/publications/living%20apart%20together%20-%20jan%202007.pdf.

[263] Kassam, Raheem "Young Muslims in the West Are a Ticking Time Bomb, Increasingly Sympathising with Radicals, Terror," *Breitbart.com* (22 Mar, 2016) http://www.breitbart.com/london/2016/03/22/polling-muslims-in-the-west-increasingly-sympathise-with-extremism-terror/.

young French Muslims is a Salafist of the most radical type, even if he does not belong to a mosque." [264]

Former UK Equalities and Human Rights Chief, Trevor Phillips, used to think that the most difficult issue facing Muslims and Westerners was anti-Muslim hostility. He was commissioner on a "British Muslims and Islamophobia" task force project in 1997 known as the "Runnymede Report."[265] This study was largely responsible for introducing both the concept and the word "Islamophobia" into common parlance.[266]

But by 2016, Phillips confessed that the report was wrong on the main issues and he admitted that "there is a widening gap in society with many Muslims segregating themselves." Observing the alarming hostile tendencies of younger Muslims, he noted that "the gaps between Muslim and non-Muslim youngsters are nearly as large as those between their elders." Phillips referenced a recent poll that confirmed a hardening of Muslim mindsets on "issues such as marriage, relations between men and women, schooling, freedom of expression and even the validity of violence in defense of religion."[267]

The West is losing this socio-religious war of attitudes and allegiances and it starts at the mosque. Local officials and media rarely have a clear understanding of the unique role of the mosque and imam in the Sharia-adherent Muslim's family and civic life. Not only is the mosque the hub around which all aspects of life revolve, they sometimes function as city hall and family law legal centers, as well.

Many may remember press coverage of Rifqa Bary's story, but her book[268] fills in disturbing details of official insistence to interpret attitudes and practices of hardline Islamists through an American mindset. Time and time again, officials refused to believe that Rifqa left home as a vulnerable teenager to run across state lines in an attempt to escape what she was convinced would be her "honor" killing for converting to Christianity. It is

---

[264] Mamou, Yves. "France: The Ticking Time Bomb of Islamization." Gatestone Institute (3 Oct. 2016) https://www.gatestoneinstitute.org/9058/france-islamization.

[265] ."Islamophobia: A Challenge For All Of Us." *Runnymede Trust* (1996), http://www.runnymedetrust.org/uploads/publications/pdfs/islamophobia.pdf.

[266] Bikhu Parekh. "Report Introduction." *Runnymede Trust* (2016), http://www.runnymedetrust.org/reportIntroduction.html.

[267] Kassam, Raheem. "UK Equalities Chief Who Popularised The Term 'Islamophobia' Admits: 'I Thought Muslims Would Blend into Britain... I Should Have Known Better.'" *Breitbart London* (10 Apr. 2016), http://www.breitbart.com/london/2016/04/10/thought-europes-muslims-gradually-blend-britains-diverse-landscape-known-better/

[268] Barry, Rifqa. *Hiding In The Light: Why I Risked Everything To Leave Islam And Follow Jesus.* *Available at: Amazon.com* (May 2015). http://www.amazon.com/Rifqa-Bary/e/B00NW9PD6C/.

145

not hard to understand that Americans simply have no frame of reference for this behavior and prefer wishfully to think that only ISIS or tribal Mid-Eastern attitudes have remained so ossified. But there is ample evidence that these practices have been condoned in America, too, and even protected, and encouraged, in some mosques.[269]

There is an acronym used when citizens declare a particular land use to be objectionable and it is "NIMBY," or not-in-my-backyard. The NIMBY mindset reflects popular will regarding proposed land uses and it works well to indicate neighborhood attitudes on radicalization. In the course of allowing Islamic religious practice on the same basis as any other religious belief system, private citizen Americans may and should still say "no go" to radicalization efforts in their communities. So, in the event of known radicalization efforts in mosques, communities should emphatically say, "Not in This Town!"

It is difficult for unsuspecting "interfaith" groups and busy local officials to understand that the Islamists' narrative is designed to enroll those blindly seeking ways to "get along." Therefore, the speeches at mosque hearings often include promises of appealing openness, community involvement, and neighborhood recreational programs that rarely materialize.

Despite commitments to feed the hungry, clothe the homeless, and offer a range of after- school activities to area young people at public hearings, mosques like the ones in Bloomington, Minnesota; [270] Falls Church, Virginia;[271] the sister mosques in Boston, Massachusetts;[272] as well as others suggested in this list compiled by The Clarion Project,[273] have radicalized fighters and militant agents. Representatives for these mosques undoubtedly worked to achieve a benign and compliant profile at the time of application for a permit to establish a mosque facility.

---

[269] Stutzman, Rene. "Rifqa Bary: Attorney for Muslim-Christian Teen Runaway: Columbus Mosque a threat." Orlando Sentinel (7 Jul. 2016), http://www.orlandosentinel.com/news/breaking-news/orl-bk-rifqa-teen-convert-mosque-083109-story.html. ("Rifqa ran away, Stemberger said, after other mosque members contacted the girl's father and pressured him 'to deal with this matter immediately.' That 'matter' was Rifqa's conversion to Christianity.")

[270] Yuen, Laura. "Suspicions, Speculation Grow as FBI's Minn. Terror Probe Churns." MPR News (13 Nov. 2014), http://www.mprnews.org/story/2014/11/13/mn-fbi-terror-probe.

[271] "Why is Virginia a Haven for Would-be Jihadists?" The Investigative Project (18 Jul. 2016), http://www.investigativeproject.org/5512/why-is-virginia-a-haven-for-would-be-jihadists.

[272] Mauro, Ryan. "Boston Bomber's Mosque Has Muslim Brotherhood Ties." The Clarion Project (20 Apr. 2013), http://www.clarionproject.org/analysis/boston-bombers-mosque-has-muslim-brotherhood-ties.

[273] Mauro, Ryan. "Radical Mosques in America." The Clarion Project (26 Nov. 2015), http://www.clarionproject.org/analysis/radical-mosques-america-there-one-near-you.

The role of an accountability group at a permit hearing is to anticipate the "clothe- the-homeless-feed-the-hungry" social service emphasis in presentations at city hall. They are routine in the number of times the same words have been repeated before city planners across the nation. But, instead of getting swept up in the rhetoric, vigilant citizens should instead press for a firm commitment outside of city hall that mosque officials will repudiate counter-cultural, and radicalization activity. One of the most effective methods to accomplish this is presentation of the Constitution-affirming Muslims for Reform declaration mentioned throughout this work. Residents should also put mosque officials on notice that they expect transparency and will hold them accountable.

City governments should understand that communities will want to define constructively the standards for good-neighbor practices, while expressing interest in affirmative plans for integration into the local culture and larger American civil society. This will involve defining assimilation according to full embrace of American law and constitutional principles, as also expressed by the four corners of Muslim Reform Manifesto.

These challenges must be issued in clear distinction to lectures on fine points of Sharia law and speculation about terrorism. Muslims have the same freedom of speech and religious belief rights as all Americans, even when there are areas of deep cultural or political disagreement. Unless mosques are being used to hide the actual practice of Sharia law in violation of American constitutional and state or federal law (e.g., polygamous or underage marriage, referrals for female genital mutilation (FGM)[274], unequal marital property distribution, marital contracts that disregard wife's informed consent, arbitration proceedings without sufficient due process, or forms of sedition including *legally defined* conspiracy to subvert the Constitution or to defy lawful authority), their pietistic practices are protected under the First Amendment. In the event there *is* reason to believe such mosques are tied to terrorism and jihad the responsibility for responding lies with law enforcement authorities, not land use or zoning officials.

A great example of appropriate community activism is the alert issued by Kansas Rep. Pompeo when a known Hamas-supporting Islamist speaker

---

[274] Westcot, Lucy. "Female Genital Mutilation On The Rise In The U.S." Newsweek (6 Feb. 2015), http://www.newsweek.com/fgm-rates-have-doubled-us-2004-304773; *also see*: United States Government Accountability Office. "Female Genital Mutilation/Cutting: Existing Federa Efforts to Increase Awareness Should Be Improved." (Jun. 2016), http://www.gao.gov/assets/680/678098.pdf. (The Centers for Disease Control and Prevention (CDC) estimated that 513,000 women and girls in the United States were at risk of or had been subjected to female genital mutilation/cutting (FGM/C) in 2012, a threefold increase from its 1990 estimate. CDC attributes this change primarily to increased immigration from countries where FGM/C is practiced ...)

was scheduled for a fundraiser at the Islamic Society of Wichita. Rep. Pompeo provided documentation of Monzer Taleb's open support for Hamas – a designated terrorist organization – and challenged the Islamic Society of Wichita to disinvite Taleb. Local citizens joined the campaign and Taleb's invitation was canceled.

Whether such events are sited on public land (expressive rights may be regulated by public safety, or "time, place or manner" concerns) or private property (constitutional protections of expressive rights may be limited), residents and community leaders have the right and, even a duty, to issue an alert as to the known profiles of Muslim Brotherhood operatives. Concerned citizens have used the vehicles of blogs, commentaries, talk radio, civic group e-mail lists, and organized demonstrations to inform the community as to this kind of radicalization agent.

On this occasion, former Assistant U.S. Attorney Andrew McCarthy penned an op-ed which the *Wichita Eagle* declined to publish (although the paper did accept a column written by former Rep. Pete Hoekstra[275] several days later) but it ran in the *National Review Online.* McCarthy endorsed Rep. Pompeo's action and explained why America's supportive Muslims have the most to lose when radical agents come to town:

> Radical Islam poses a serious threat to America and the West, very much including a threat against American Muslims, our fellow citizens who reject radical Islam's authoritarianism and savagery. While terrorists and their atrocities grab the headlines, much of the real battle takes place in Muslim communities.
>
> A key to winning that battle and protecting our security involves distinguishing our radical Islamic enemies from our patriotic Muslim allies. The Muslim Brotherhood and its Palestinian branch, Hamas, which is a terrorist organization and has been formally recognized as such under American law for some 20 years, are on the wrong side of that divide.
>
> Recent events in Paris and Brussels underscore that violent jihadism thrives in safe-haven communities that sympathize with the terrorists' aims, or where people who might object are intimidated into silence. It is therefore essential to our national security, and to the ability of pro-American Muslims to practice their faith free from Islamist intimidation, that we identify,

---

marginalize, and reject terrorist sympathizers. Representative Pompeo did just that.[276]

At the very least, imams should be asked to set an Open Mosque Day and visitors should plan to pose pointed questions in response to presentations on religious tolerance and fidelity to American values. If all this is true, then mosque leaders should be very willing to make emphatic and unequivocal statements denouncing civil rights abuses at home and abroad in the name of Islam. This is not the time to settle for a generalized platitude that all cultures could do more to protect human rights or work harder to get along.

This author's visits to mosques on Open Mosque Day have not been encouraging, as mosque leadership responded to questions regarding concerns about radicalization with blame for lack of American efforts to provide better immigrant welfare benefits. Questions regarding free speech prompted the vehement answer from a mosque official that there should be criminal penalties equal to that of burning a mosque for those that publicly challenge Islamism. This is the kind of information that should be publicized in the communities hosting these mosques. Imams and Islamic leaders are free to hold anti-constitutional beliefs and to agitate for constitutional changes. American citizens are obligated to join this debate and defend the constitutional order as foundational to America's survival and even continued success.

The core tenets of *Islamist supremacist* groups are rooted in a disdain for America's secularly organized systems. The Sharia supremacist agenda that would impose a transcendent and comprehensive doctrinal order on both Muslims and the society at large is not compatible with American notions of civil law, individual liberty, and due process.

Communities should seek agreement with Islamic institutions that profess good faith citizenship and full participation in civil society by asking for public production of explicit and concrete efforts to confront Islamist advocates and their schemes. The evidence of these challenges to Islamist campaigns must prove to be serious endeavors beyond mere lip service. It is this unequivocal public request for – and formal response to – documented challenges to Islamism that provides a baseline for any potential expectations of good faith and future cooperation.

---

[276] McCarthy, Andrew C. "Islamophobia Is Still Not The Problem: In Kansas, Another Case Study." *The National Review* (11 Apr. 2016), http://www.nationalreview.com/article/433918/mike-pompeo-right-criticize-wichita-mosques-invitation-hamas-sympathizer.

20. AMERICA'S 'DOMINANT TRADITIONS' ARE NOT FOR BARTER

America's national identity, as it relies upon a core sense of shared principles and is based in a deep respect for individual liberty, depends upon respect for underlying history and traditions. Impulses to deny this philosophical identity can become an existential threat and they will ultimately compromise the nation's ability to assimilate newcomers. In short, America's soul is in its historical heritage – what some are calling our "dominant traditions." And once vital precepts are undermined, the European model warns that mosque-based Islamic supremacism is geared to push into the void as America's traditions, ideals, and national identity are hollowed out.

As France especially has learned, the withdrawal of identity-fortifying religious heritage and shared tradition, while making an effort to accommodate activists who intend to supplant those traditions, leads to cultural suicide.

If Americans are willing to concede their Judeo-Christian precepts, their claim to exceptionalism, their public traditions, and their shared holiday observances, what remains of any core identity for immigrants to join? As Supreme Court cases have affirmed, the philosophical recognition of foundational religious underpinnings is not a First Amendment violation and it is an essential part of American constitutionalism. If assimilation is expected, there must be a dominant culture to join.

The English-Scottish Enlightenment principles that inspired America's founders can be rationally defended. These compelling ideals earned recognition from even liberal Supreme Court Justice William O. Douglas who wrote in *Zorach v. Clauson* of American institutional references to "the Almighty" and declared that "We are a religious people whose institutions presuppose a Supreme Being...."[277] Yes, there is room to acknowledge philosophic traditions that are the reasons for America's celebrated freedoms and virtues. While contemporary Supreme Court rulings demand balance and avoid governmental sectarian endorsements of religion, many long-held and originally religiously-based traditions may still be embraced as venerated cultural practices.

From the days of America's founding, "common schools," or public schools were expected to play a strong role in the assimilation of immigrants. "The schools were actively involved in promoting the values and beliefs that

---

[277] *Zorach v. Clauson*, 343 U.S. 306 (1952).

were considered part and parcel of the American experience."[278] The role of public schools has been radically altered with emphasis now on encouraging loyalty to original country and culture identities.

As more migrants arrive, bringing practices that are, to them, familiar and often ancestral, it is incumbent upon communities to announce American societal norms. Tribally-based attitudes can be very difficult to overcome. But practices that disadvantage women and assert clerical rule over civic law cannot happily co-exist with constitutional self-determinism and individual expression.

Americans are now more inclined to rearrange their lives and reorder their priorities on demand from groups with contrary agendas than they are to defend the principles of life, liberty, and property that the Founders envisioned.

It is one thing to have a tussle over cultural practices. But when Americans simply cave and offer up time-honored traditions, national holidays, and even "school fun days," this sends an unambiguous message about how little Americans even care about keeping the cultural core.

It is hard to believe, yet it is true: Americans are apologizing for honoring long-held traditions, customs, and rituals, often giving them up with little or no fight. A case in point is the New York schools that agreed to excuse attendance for a small minority of Muslim students on religious holidays. Then, when that was not enough, Islamists demanded that schools close on those days so that Muslim students did not miss class instruction.[279] The next phase was to insist that "dominant culture" holidays like Thanksgiving, Christmas, and Valentine's Day (who knew that Valentine's Day was especially objectionable to hardline Muslims?[280]) had to be removed from the school calendar.[281]

---

[278] DeForrest, Mark Edward. "Locke v. Davey: The Connection between the Federal Blaine Amendment and Article I, 11 of the Washington State Constitution." p.5, *Tulsa Law Review, Vol. 40* (2004), *available at:*
http://digitalcommons.law.utulsa.edu/cgi/viewcontent.cgi?article=2476&context=tlr,

[279] Mangla, Ismat Sarah. "Eid Al-Adha 2015: NYC Muslim Students Celebrate Victory As Public Schools Observe Religious Holiday For The First Time." *International Business Times* (23 Sep. 2015), http://www.ibtimes.com/eid-al-adha-2015-nyc-muslim-students-celebrate-victory-public-schools-observe-2110623. ("It's been a long seven years, but on Thursday, Bucaram's daughter, now in eighth grade, will have the day off from school – alongside some 1.1 million other public school students in New York City's 1,800 schools. It's the first time the school system will be closed for Eid al-Adha.")

[280] "Why Do We Muslims Not Celebrate Valentine's Day?" *Islamweb.net* (2 Dec. 2015), https://www.islamweb.net/en/article/142698/why-do-we-muslims-not-celebrate-valentines-day. ("Because Valentine's Day goes back to Roman times, not Islamic times, this means that it is something which belongs exclusively to the Christians, not to Islam, and the Muslims have no share and no part in it. If the Christians have a festival and the Jews have a

Not only do concessions like these deny time-honored American traditions, but the progression of accommodations usually ends with a de facto promotion of *Muslim* practices. That is also the case with educational revisionism in classroom assignments and textbooks. The process starts with complaints of too much emphasis on "dominant culture" or Western exceptionalism. Then, as accounts of Western successes, innovations, and reforms are pushed out of textbooks by leftist apologists and Islamists, historically dubious claims of historic Islamic superiority have been introduced.[282]

Indeed, such diminutions of core American values are vital to any agenda that demands that we co-exist with Sharia and related practices wholly at odds with our Constitution and norms. The Islamists that would introduce Sharia-based rules as favorable or transcendent, are present in many city halls and public schools. They urge that minor episodes of Western error are fatal to claims of moral exceptionalism, while Islamic history is selectively presented and not questioned.

Just the idea that Western ideals are exceptional must bring attacks from Islamists. Where secular republican government, foundational equal rights, and a reasoned approach to self-determination are vindicated, there is no room for clerical rule that imposes arbitrary life codes and punitive religious mandates.

So, when an American public school system hosts an Islamist program that denigrates American practices, disparages Christianity, and promotes a selective rendering of Islam, there should be outrage. But when, for example, Kennedy High School in Bloomington, Minnesota, hosted such a presentation called "One Nation, Many Beliefs," there was no challenge from the audience.

This event was hosted by a public high school and held on taxpayer funded middle school property. Reports show that teachers were offered credit for attending and students were included in the audience. Local officials and

---

festival, which belongs exclusively to them, then no Muslim should join in with them, just as he does not share their religion or their direction of prayer.")

[281] Walsh, Paul. "St. Paul School Kiss Valentine's Day, Other 'Dominant Holidays' Goodbye." *Minneapolis Star Tribune* (2016 Jan. 29), http://www.startribune.com/st-paul-school-pulls-plug-on-celebrating-dominant-holidays/366834081/.

[282] "Islam And The Text Books: A Report Of The American Text Book Council." *Middle East Quarterly* p.69-78 (Summer 2003), http://www.meforum.org/3182/history-muslim-conquests; Ibrahim, Raymond. "The Historic Concept Of Muslim Conquests." *Middle East Forum* (1 Mar. 2012), http://www.meforum.org/3182/history-muslim-conquests; and, "ACT For American Education. Education or Indoctrination? The Treatment of Islam in 6th Through 12th Grade American Text Books." *ACT For America* (2011), http://www.actforamerica.org/downloads/education/Full_Report_version_7.31.12.pdf.

members of law enforcement also attended. The program was covered by at least one news columnist who gave it a positive review.[283]

The presentation was promoted[284] as important because school children in that community were so tormented by "Islamophobia" that they were afraid to attend school. This forum, advertised to "widen cultural understandings," was a straightforward propaganda session for Islam. During the discussion, an imam and a sympathetic pastor touted such themes as: Christians were the exemplars of killing in the name of religion (based on the Crusades); Americans use carpet bombs in response to .1% of Muslims that cause havoc; Islam came to the Arabian Peninsula and brought full rights to educational opportunity and economic prosperity for women; jihad is simply doing what is good for you; Christians failed to stop the Holocaust; women currently have full rights under Islam (contrary practices are cultural); and, the Crusades brutally interrupted an Islamic period of respect and honor for Jews and Christians.

Now, many of these are complex issues that may provide framework for university level debates. But a public high school setting requires a balanced presentation. Instead, these bizarre assertions were served up in a manner that lacked historical proportion, standards for accuracy, sourcing, logic, and any attempt at critical reasoning. An open question and answer segment might have allowed for at least some inspection of the emphatic statements, but all the questions were pre-screened.

In fact, forms on audience tables suggested the format for the "Facilitated Question Session," and they featured this shockingly biased and condemnatory example:

"There is a desperate attempt out there to create hatred, divide Muslims and mainstream Americans, and incite young people into joining militant terror groups. How can we prevent this from happening in our school/community?"[285]

When a concerned citizen who attended the forum registered a complaint with the school district, a district representative agreed to an appointment. The citizen consulted an attorney who recognized the likely violations of First Amendment Free Speech and Establishment Clause provisions. The two attended the meeting with the district representative together. At this

---

[283] Heinzman, Don. "Opinion: Community Forums Can Foster Interfaith Relationships." Sun Current Newspaper, (26 Feb. 2016), https://sailor.mnsun.com/2016/02/26/opinion-community-forums-can-foster-interfaith-relationships/.

[284] "One Nation, Many Beliefs" notice. See http://mosquesinamerica.org/wp-content/uploads/2016/10/281_bloomingtononenation.png

[285] "Religious Forum Agenda Questions" document. See http://mosquesinamerica.org/wp-content/uploads/2016/10/282_Religious_Forum_Agenda.pdf

meeting, school officials immediately agreed to the following guidelines for future programs:

1. Have opposing points of view represented when debatable topics are presented.

2. School presentations will not be conclusory. Open inquiry through free dialogue will be mandatory.

3. A reasonable proportion of time will be reserved for questions from the audience. Questions will not be written and turned in for screening by anyone. No questions will be screened out, and no participants will be screened out or prevented from questioning.

4. A school representative will be present and will not allow viewpoint discrimination or other violations of existing policy.

The potential for a follow-up event with proper balance and perspective was discussed but the school waffled, saying that, there was not sufficient time on the school calendar to organize an event. More to the point, had the parent-citizen not attended and not complained, apparently the city officials, school administrators, and law enforcement representatives did not see that there were problems with this program sufficient to lodge an inquiry.

There are also examples of public school curricula and lesson plans that present tenets of Islamic doctrine, biased comparative culture exercises, and history units that are currently being challenged. Many have read of the surprising assignments like the exercise that asks students to recite the "Five Pillars of Islam."[286]

Less well known, and probably even more pernicious, is utilization of the film, "30 Days Living As A Muslim"[287] in the classroom to teach tolerance. The film depicts a young Christian man who consents to live with a Muslim couple for a month. During the course of the film, an imam mocks Christianity and Judaism while Islamic doctrine is presented favorably. By the end of the forty-minute reality show, the young Christian essentially converts to Islam by saying the Shahada and agrees to go back to his community as an emissary of Islam.[288] Presentation of this film in a public school setting calls into question a number of educational and legal-

---

[286] Jinkerson, Greg. "Maury Parents Angered Over Islamic Unit." (2015 Sep. 3), http://springhillhomepage.com/update-12-30-p-m-maury-parents-angered-over-islam-unit-mcps-to-release-statement-thursday-cms-5213.

[287] "30 Days Living As A Muslim." Vimeo.com. (2012). https://vimeo.com/35186644.

[288] "30 Days Living As A Muslim." transcript. Pp. 12 – 17. http://mosquesinamerica.org/wp-content/uploads/2016/10/285_30_Days_Living_As_a_Muslim_transcript.pdf

constitutional concerns like government preference for a religion, cultural bias, propaganda, and indoctrination.

Then, there are examples of outrageous analytic exercises where middle school students are asked to compare the treatment of Jews in the period leading to the Holocaust to "simmering Islamophobia" and "anti-Muslim hatred" in America – but this assignment was based upon one anecdotal, mostly inaccurate, and incendiary commentary written by a Muslim writer.[289]

Again, concerned parents confronted teachers and education officials with each of these issues. But how many parents understand the potential harm that may be done when teaching materials function like propaganda tools? And, how many parents who may understand the dangers are even aware that these exercises are assigned in public schools?

Another example where parents could have creatively mobilized is over the removal of pork products from student menus (but according to popular television cooking channels, Americans are in love with bacon!). If elementary schools like that in Kent, Washington state, caved to minority group pressure, it becomes easier to replicate a wider campaign for imposing Islamic dietary preferences in other places.

Sure, parents may not care so much if their children have no pork selections on the hot lunch tray, but that is not the point. There was a time when Americans did not so easily allow hegemonist groups to tell them what they could, or could not, do – or what their children could not have. If these dictates are accepted, it will be one thing after another. The lines will become harder to draw after serial concessions have been made.

This stands in contrast with past practice. Historically, Americans have fought to keep important traditions. When Jehovah's Witnesses students refused to recite the Pledge of Allegiance, the Supreme Court weighed the value of government's role in training children to be good citizens against limits on governments' coercive power. The Court decided that students may not be expelled for opting out of saluting the flag.[290] American history provides a record of respecting individual rights of conscience but it does not compel cancelation or removal of citizenship-promoting practices on the demands of small factions.

---

[289] Hameed, Mustafa. "When The Tide Of Islamophobia Reached My Hometown Mosque." *New York Times* (5 Mar. 2016), http://www.nytimes.com/2016/03/06/opinion/sunday/when-the-tide-of-islamophobia-reached-my-hometown-mosque.html?_r=1.

[290] *West Virginia State Board of Education v. Barnette*, 319 US 624 (1943). ("If there is any fixed star in our constitutional constellation, it is that no official, high or petty, can prescribe what shall be orthodox in politics, nationalism, religion, or other matters of opinion, *or force citizens to confess by word or act* their faith therein.") (Emphasis added.)

With evolving standards of agency sensitivity to small group complaints, dissenting factions have gained greater leverage. The recent introduction of federal and state "hostile environment" protocols[291] for schools, has called for administrators to develop anti-discrimination and anti-harassment policies, including redress procedures. When a platform such as this invites complaints from groups based upon "outsider" status, how much emphasis may still be afforded assimilation priorities? What has happened to Americanization elements that used to be reflected in the core school curriculum?

The Department of Education (DOE) Civil Rights Division regulates and investigates the "hostile environment" complaints, and also adjudicates settlements. This closed institutional oversight and resolution process represents a troubling trend that bypasses state authority and skirts judicial review by authorized courts. The efficacy of these "hostile environment" remedy programs may be debated elsewhere but the tendency to overcompensate should be a real concern.

An example of the pendulum swinging far enough to cause potential violations constitutional provisions occurred in the cities of St. Cloud and St. Paul, Minnesota. According to media reports, several school districts responded to Department of Education investigations by offering "multi-purpose" student prayer space (at the request of Muslims) and allowing religious-time dismissal from classes.[292] This prayer space is technically available to all faiths. In practice, though, it may be argued that this arrangement has resulted in a *de facto* institutionalization of Islamic prayer space.

Constitutional First Amendment Establishment Clause and Equal Protection considerations depend, in part, upon whether students of other faiths feel that the space is accessible, whether religious symbols are present, if schools officials dedicate time to supervision and coordination, whether the practice compromises instructional time, and whether students of all faiths have equal opportunity to address worship or prayer interests. What will happen when this practice, as established, is deemed too short, or how may a response be formulated when additional sessions are requested by these students? If the standard is defined by subjective considerations of what is a congenial academic environment, what limits will there be to institutional negotiations?

---

[291] "Protecting Students From Harassment and Hate Crime: A Guide For Schools." *United States Department of Education* (Jan. 1999),
https://www2.ed.gov/offices/OCR/archives/Harassment/policy1.html.

[292] "How One Minnesota School District Handles A Rising Immigration Population." *PBS News Hour* (23 Mar. 2016), http://netnebraska.org/node/1017935.

When the Supreme Court says that institutional Christian prayer is not allowed during the public school day[293] and once-a-week "released time" for Christian study[294] may not be organized by school officials and may not utilize school funds or occupy rooms on campus, then there are questions as to whether Islamic-driven established school prayer periods would survive court challenges.

Students and parents should be interested to learn how much total class time is compromised for prayer sessions and they could also investigate proposals of equal time for exercise of other faith practices and customs. At some point, the idea of providing equal access to school space and officially administered time to all requesting students may prove impractical and educationally indefensible.

Another example of Islamic demands occurred when Disneyland was asked to allow a themed restaurant employee to wear her hijab at work. Disney resisted and the federal court employment discrimination case was dismissed at the request of both parties (presumably reflecting a settlement with undisclosed terms). The outcome of this case may have been different if it had been tried after the 2015 Supreme Court ruling[295] in favor of a Muslim woman employed by Abercrombie and Fitch who demanded to wear her hijab on the sales floor and the subsequent passage of a California law that requires employers to "reasonably accommodate" religious dress practices.[296]

But where should individual symbolic religious expression overtake a famed corporate brand or entertainment theme, especially where a published dress code is provided at the employment interview? There generally has been a distinction made between discrete incidental religious jewelry and a prominent symbol that fundamentally alters a themed dress code.

---

[293] *Engel v. Vitale*, 370 US 421 (1962).

[294] Zorach, 343 U.S. at 308-9, *supra*, note 274. ("A student is released on written request of his parents. Those not released stay in the classrooms. The churches make weekly reports to the schools, sending a list of children who have been released from public school but who have not reported for religious instruction. This "released time" program involves neither religious instruction in public school classrooms nor the expenditure of public funds. All costs, including the application blanks, are paid by the religious organizations."); *also see*: McCollum v. Board of Education, 333 U.S. 203, 209-212 (1948). ("This utilization of the State's tax supported public school system and its machinery for compulsory public school attendance to enable sectarian groups to give religious instruction to public school pupils in public school buildings violates the First Amendment of the Constitution.")

[295] *E.E.O.C. v. Abercrombie & Fitch Stores, Inc.* No. 14–86 (2015).

[296] "Disney Worker Launches California Labor Lawsuit Alleging Religious Discrimination." *California Labor Law News* (19 Dec. 2012), https://calaborlawnews.com/legal-news/california-labor-law-lawsuit-32-18319.php?frm=b&utm_expid=102602370-11.5ULpldA8QiG55W5ky_QJhg.1&utm_referrer=https%3A%2F%2Fwww.google.com%2F.

Law is an expression of the political climate and popular will. Laws, as long as constitutionally observant, may be changed by legislative enactments or redefinition by elected or appointed judges. Activist groups that mobilize as CAIR did when backing the California labor law that addresses religious apparel demonstrate the power of a minority group to have influence on the culture.[297] The new law, among other employer restrictions, required "that 'religious belief or observance' includes religious dress and grooming practices." [298] In practice, these terms will offer broader religious accommodation than express terms of federal laws. There seemed to be no real pushback when there was a straightforward counter-argument: It is possible to protect individual religious expressive rights without imprinting them on secular institutions.

It is baffling that privileged accommodations of Islamic practice reach the point of institutionalization before significant resistance is registered. Recently, it was the ACLU that stepped up to litigate on behalf of a Christian woman in the state of Alabama when she was not allowed to wear a religious head covering for the taking of her driver's license photograph but county officials were offering an accommodation to only Muslim women.[299]

When opportunities to define and defend American culture arise, communities should take the occasion seriously. Whether the issue is curriculum or school menus, there are willing volunteers and experts who will lend useful advice and experience. To this point, some responses have been ineffective due to failure to target the agencies responsible. Records act requests are invaluable as tools to learn how policies have been developed, who was the catalyst for action, and where leverage is needed to mount a challenge. Research usually begins online to learn where there is agency accountability and how an initiative may be brought. In many cases, the tried and true committee approach, with assigned roles and shared time-commitments, works best.

---

[297] "CAIR-CA: Gov. Brown to Sign Workplace Religious Freedom Act Into Law." (8 Sep. 2012), https://www.facebook.com/notes/cair/cair-ca-gov-brown-to-sign-workplace-religious-freedom-act-into-law/10151093739329442/. ("CAIR-CA helped draft the legislation and worked with local Muslim community members and Sikh allies to mobilize support for AB 1964 during the year, beginning with the first-ever Muslim Day at the Capitol, where 50-plus California Muslims visited Sacramento and engaged their lawmakers.")

[298] Filla, Cynthia L. "California's Workplace Religious Freedom Act Lowers Bar for Employees in Religious Discrimination Cases." *JacksonLewis.com* (11 Jan. 2013), http://www.jacksonlewis.com/resources-publication/californias-workplace-religious-freedom-act-lowers-bar-employees-religious-discrimination-cases

[299] Volokh, Eugene. "Alabama ACLU Sues Government, Claiming Pro-Muslim Discrimination." *The Washington Post* (31 Aug. 2016), https://www.washingtonpost.com/news/volokh-conspiracy/wp/2016/08/31/alabama-aclu-sues-government-claiming-pro-muslim-discrimination/?utm_term=.fd42539de7f7.

A lesson that has been learned in many communities is that it is much easier and eminently more achievable to mount swift and organized opposition when the initial complaints are registered and unsupported changes are demanded.

An effective cultural campaign requires slogans that resonate and an ability to strike a chord deep within the community. Informing families as to what is at stake based upon examples from other localities is the first step.

Consider how difficult it would have been in some communities to even think about canceling a public holiday the celebrated the national patron saint. In Britain, it would have been shocking a few years ago to imagine, that in 2016, the city of Bristol would not observe St. George's Day. Yet, this national feast day – a holiday since 1415 – was simply cast aside by the city fathers as they declared the city "too multicultural" to celebrate England's patron saint.[300]

A very different response was heard from the city fathers of Owego, New York[301] when an "interfaith" group asked the town to remove the words "Islamic terrorist" from a 9/11 memorial. The town supervisor responded: "We don't whitewash things, especially here. And we just think that we've done the accurate citing of what happened."

Americans have so many opportunities to restore and share America's proud history. When one travels to Boston, it is apparent that many families are taking advantage of Boston's wonderful Freedom Trail, a brick-laid path through the city that signals stops at all of the fascinating places where the Founders and Framers spoke, rallied, argued, bled, died, and birthed our incomparable constitutional compact. The parents and grandparents who take this pilgrimage are surely the ones who provide us with young people like the teens in Heber City, Utah who organized a public demonstration around American flags in a town shopping center after a friend's flag, displayed daily as a banner from his pick up truck, was burned at school.[302]

---

[300] "Bristol "Too Multicultural" for St George's Day." *Bristol Post* (24 Apr. 2016), http://www.bristolpost.co.uk/Bristol-multicultural-St-George-s-Day/story-29167059-detail/story.html; and,

Bond, Anthony. "St George's Day 2016: What Does It Mean and Why Do We Celebrate The Patron Saint of England?" *Mirror.co.uk* (23 Apr. 2016), http://www.mirror.co.uk/news/uk-news/st-georges-day-2016-what-7739228.

[301] Interfaith Group Wants 'Islamic Terrorists' Text Removed From 9/11 Monument." *Fox News Insider* (6 Sep. 2016), http://insider.foxnews.com/2016/09/06/muslim-group-wants-islamic-terrorists-text-removed-owego-ny-911-monument.

[302] Starnes, Todd. "American Flag Burned at School - and You Won't Believe How Students React." *ToddStarnes.com* (6 Sep. 2016), http://www.toddstarnes.com/column/american-flag-burned-at-school-and-you-wont-believe-how-students-react.

Americans who do not want to find themselves in the position of trying to recover lost ground, should be vigilant *now*. Groups of British citizens saw the need to walk through areas understood as "no go" zones with signs while chanting that British law and British ways do prevail. It used to be hard to imagine this kind of wholesale cultural takeover in parts of the United States, but it is now apparent that bits of culture and tradition are easily being abandoned here, too.

21. Free Speech: Use It or Lose It

As we have discussed, free speech is essential to countering assaults on American constitutional exceptionalism. Even so, the ability to speak out on controversial issues is being undermined from many directions, including Islamist campaigns against "hate speech," or "inflammatory speech," that is considered "incitement to hate." Either Americans will confront the mounting threats to freedom of expression or they will lose the ability to engage Islamist imams and mosques that encourage and institutionalize Muslim separatism.

The fight against speech codes entails more than just refusing censorship and new "hate speech" laws. It also means fighting the even more pernicious "chilling" of speech. While speech censors work to carve away constitutional protections, they have also been creating a climate of self-censorship.

The government tells us if we "see something," we must "say something." Yet, how many times have citizens wanted to speak up or known they should report something, but they did not do so out of fear of being called "racist" or "intolerant"?

First Amendment speech rights were prominent in the minds of America's Founders for the primary reason that they protected the citizen's right to criticize government and to "petition the government for a redress of grievances." Accordingly, an almost unanimous Supreme Court recently declared controversies of "public concern" as receiving the highest levels of speech protection.[303] But some in government, local Human Relations Commissions and like quasi-government agencies, university speech minders, minority groups, and media commentators are determined to punch holes in free speech guarantees.

If speech minders are allowed even incremental success, America starts down the road to censorship by government-authorized grievance groups. As European immigration dissenters who are now subject to criminal action for critical social media posts[304] have learned, Western governments are capable of summarily shutting down inconvenient public debate.

---

[303] "Facts and Case Summary-Snyder vs. Phelps." (2016), http://www.uscourts.gov/educational-resources/educational-activities/facts-and-case-summary-snyder-v-phelps.

[304] Brooks, Libby. "Man Arrested for Facebook Posts about Syrian Refugees in Scotland." *The Guardian* (16 Feb. 2016), https://www.theguardian.com/uk-news/2016/feb/16/man-arrested-facebook-posts-syrian-refugees-scotland.

This book is not intended to engage in a full discussion on free speech developments in the United States. It is, however, very important to consider the Islamist drive to censor speech and to understand the extent to which many in the United States are already willing to concede.

That Muslims must embrace Sharia-based blasphemy restrictions is a consistent feature of the public advocacy of those like one of New Jersey's most prominent Islamists, Mohammad Qatanani. His calls "for limits and borders [on] freedom of speech," include the demand that the Department of "Homeland Security...prevent artists from producing works that are critical of Islam."

Americans should look behind the general admonitions to learn that imams like Qatanani really desire to supplant constitutional protections:

> The freedom of the American people is so different from their [Muslims'] freedoms. We believe freedoms have limits and rules, otherwise we will get people into trouble....Freedom according to Islam must be according to the Quran and Sunnah. You can do [anything] you like within the teachings of these two resources.[305]

Many remember that Chris Cuomo tweeted in response to the Pamela Geller Mohammed cartoon contest that the First Amendment doesn't cover hate.[306] Former DNC chair Howard Dean tweeted: "Free speech is good. Respecting others is better." Reflective of a generational shift, a November 2015 Pew survey revealed that "four-in-ten Millennials say the government should be able to prevent people publicly making statements that are offensive to minority groups."[307]

There is even erosion in the Supreme Court as evidenced by Justice Breyer's equivocation, writing in his *McCutcheon v. FEC* dissent, that the purpose of the First Amendment was not to prevent government abuses, but to ensure "public opinion could be channeled into effective governmental action."[308]

---

[305] Newby, Joe. "New Jersey Imam: Free Speech Critical of Islam a 'National Security Threat." *The Examiner* (20 Sep. 2012), 'http://www.examiner.com/article/new-jersey-imam-free-speech-critical-of-islam-a-national-security-threat.

[306] Carroll, Lauren. "CNN Chris Cuomo: First Amendment Doesn't Cover Hate Speech." *Politifact.com* (6 May, 2015), http://www.politifact.com/punditfact/statements/2015/may/07/chris-cuomo/cnns-chris-cuomo-first-amendment-doesnt-cover-hate/.

[307] Poushter, Jacob. "40% of Millenials Okay With Limiting Speech Offenses to Minorities." *Pew Research Center* (20 Nov. 2015), http://www.pewresearch.org/fact-tank/2015/11/20/40-of-millennials-ok-with-limiting-speech-offensive-to-minorities/.

[308] Bernstein, David. "Breyer's Dangerous Dissent in McCutcheon." Washington Post. (2 April, 2014). https://www.washingtonpost.com/news/volokh-conspiracy/wp/2014/04/02/breyers-dangerous-dissent-in-mccutcheon-the-campaign-finance-case/; and, constitutional scholar Tim Sandefur points out: "Actually, the framers

But the Constitution encourages citizens to vigorously question government and to assemble for the purpose of petitioning government representatives.

Justice Breyer also commented that burning the Koran may not be protected expression and he likened the act to shouting "fire" in a crowded theater. He said he "wasn't convinced the First Amendment would protect such an action if the case were brought to the court in the future."[309] This statement, if committed to practice, would create special status for a group that works to control both debate and political action by threatening violence. The reasoning also serves to undercut citizen engagement in constitutionally protected debate by handing complaining minorities the power to silence opponents.

Local governments tie themselves in knots trying to please constituencies that demand apologies for speech, while not admitting that they are creating speech codes. This author has appeared before many governing councils as part of various local efforts to impress upon elected officials that complying with Islamist interest group demands to declare cities "hate free zones" or to censor a councilmember's offending remark or social media posts is hazardous. In each case, we successfully reminded local governments that these issues are between voters and their elected officials. Although statements may be inartful or even crude, unless an elected official acts on discriminatory animus, personal expressions of opinion and social media posts usually should be a matter between the voters and their elected representatives.

Human Relations (or Human Rights) Commissions are also sources of unconstitutional local censorship. When partially- or fully-funded by local governments, these bodies must refrain from becoming arms of the minority grievance industry. And, when they are funded by private industry, it is up to shareholders and community members to watch for unconstitutional censorship. It is true that the organizational mission for these units centers on detecting – and responding to – discrimination. But these are advisory bodies; they are not commissioned to act on behalf of complaining groups unconstitutionally to chill speech. When only one side of a story has been presented by an offended party and a local government (or quasi-government entity) acts publicly to condemn speech, great harm may be done to constitutional due process and to First Amendment speech as well as assembly rights.

---

devised the constitutional structure to *prevent* public opinion from being channeled into effective government action." Sandefur, Tim. "Wow, Talk About Getting It Backwards." *Freespace.com* (2 Apr. 2014), http://sandefur.typepad.com/freespace/2014/04/wow-talk-about-getting-it-backwards.html.

[309] Madison, Lucy. "Stephen Breyer Questions Right to Burn Quran." *CBS News* (14 Sep. 2010), http://www.cbsnews.com/news/stephen-breyer-questions-right-to-burn-quran/.

In all such cases, government resolutions and condemnations are without official force, but they are symbolically powerful tools to the speech extortionist that demands them. These censures, city apologies, and reprimands serve to accommodate interest group speech codes, and cities who choose to begin appeasing these groups will not find a defensible place or time to stop.

Islamist groups like CAIR often come to city hall on a mission to shape policy according to Islamic Sharia speech codes. These blasphemy-based rules quite simply dictate that speech critical of Muslims or their Prophet Mohammed is not allowed. To advance this agenda in Western cultures, Islamists begin by exerting pressure on all public levers to discourage critical or philosophically confrontational speech. Europe generally has already consented to such speech bans and that is why debate on vital issues of immigration, assimilation and Islamist separatism there is near impossible.

Americans will only remain free to engage in full debate on these issues if they halt the incremental concessions. As Andrew McCarthy, the former Assistant U.S. Attorney who successfully prosecuted the Blind Sheikh and who has written extensively on the civilizational Sharia threat, puts the warning this way in his book *Islam and Free Speech*:

> Free speech does not exist in a vacuum. It is the plinth of freedom's fortress. It is the ineliminable imperative if there is to be the robust exchange of knowledge and ideas, the rule of reason, freedom of conscience, equality before the law, property rights, and equality of opportunity. That is why it must be extinguished if there is to be what al-Qaradawi calls a "place of religion" – meaning his religion. For all its arrogance and triumphalist claims, radical Islam must suppress speech because it cannot compete in a free market of conscience.[310]

So far, most American leaders have been reluctant to endorse an international push to impose Islamic-based speech codes but there is, nonetheless, a sustained effort underway. Then-Secretary of State Hillary Clinton and some on the Left have been involved with an initiative sponsored by the 57-member Organization of Islamic Cooperation and adopted by the UN Human Rights Council in 2011. This resolution, promulgated at the UN as Resolution 16/18 targets "the advocacy of religious hatred" and links it to "incitement to discrimination, hostility, or violence."

Blending advocacy and incitement with illegal discrimination and violence opens an array of constitutional issues for Americans. Further, American

---

[310] McCarthy, Andrew C. *Islam and Free Speech* 19 New York, Encounter Books (2015).

defamation law already provides an individual right to bring a complaint; this cause of action is civil and does not encompass the offended sensibilities of an entire group. These are important distinctions since the Islamic effort to criminalize defamation of religion would see government as the prosecutor of a new civil-rights-based offense.

Also, any law that bases criminal charges on "incitement" places the burden on the speaker to anticipate an unlawful response from a listener. This hands to the listener tremendous extortion power based upon threats of violence and mayhem alone. Free speech attorney, Deborah Weiss, has written about the many conflicts this approach raises with basic American individual liberty and due process guarantees.[311]

In December 2011, Secretary Clinton hosted in Washington D.C. a three-day meeting of "the Istanbul Process" – an international effort aimed at furthering implementation of UN Human Rights Council Resolution 16/18. Prior to that session, Pakistani Ambassador to the UN and OIC spokesperson, Zamir Akram spoke to the core Islamist agenda and warned that the OIC would not compromise on offensive speech described as: "anything against the Quran, anything against the Prophet, and anything against the Muslim community in terms of discrimination."[312]

The parallel UN International Covenant on Civil and Political Rights (ICCPR) Article 19 entitled, "Combating Intolerance, Negative Stereotyping and Stigmatization of, and Discrimination, Incitement to Violence and Violence Against, Persons Based on Religion or Belief"[313] provides assurances that freedom of expression will be protected and advises that blasphemy laws should be repealed.[314] It concurrently recommends, however, that member states criminalize speech-that-incites according to these vague and highly

---

[311] Weiss, Deborah, *The Organization of Islamic Cooperation's Jihad on Free Speech,* Washington, Center for Security Policy Press (2015)

[312] Lugo, Karen. "Free Speech For Me – Unless It Offends Thee." *Townhall.com* (13 Dec. 2011), http://townhall.com/columnists/karenlugo/2011/12/13/free_speech_for_me__unless_it_offe nds_thee.

[313] US Mission Geneva." United States State Department (2016): "The United States strongly supports today's resolution, which like its predecessor rejects broad prohibitions on speech, and supports actions that do not limit freedom of expression or infringe on the freedom of religion." Notably this statement rejects "broad" speech restrictions but this leaves the government room to carve out civil rights claims against speech called so insulting that it is considered "incitement." *Available at*: http://geneva.usmission.gov/tag/resolution-1618/.

[314] "Human Rights Council States Must Implement Resolution 1618 And Rabat Plan Of Action." Article 19 (28 Mar. 2014), https://www.article19.org/resources.php/resource/37505/en/human-rights-council:-states-must-implement-resolution-16-18-and-rabat-plan-of-action.

167

subjective standards: "the context of incitement to hatred, the speaker, intent, content, extent of the speech, and likelihood of causing harm."[315]

In June 2015, another Istanbul Process session took place in Saudi Arabia. Participants called for a consensual framework *universally* to "combat incitement to religious hatred and violence" while sharing "best practices used to effectively address these challenges including legal and non-legal measures...."[316]

As if at the behest of the Istanbul Process, House Democrats (one hundred co-sponsors at last count) introduced Resolution 569 in December 2015 on behalf of "the victims of anti-Muslim hate crimes and rhetoric [that] have faced physical, verbal, and emotional abuse because they were Muslim or believed to be Muslim." This House resolution also "expressed condolences for the victims of anti-Muslim hate crimes."[317] Ostensibly this legislative initiative was responsive to what sponsors called "weeks of anti-Muslim bigotry and acts of hatred"[318] in the wake of the jihadist attack in San Bernardino, California that left fourteen people dead.

In this instance, a familiar cycle ensued. First, an act of jihadist violence, then pre-emptory calls to quell an anticipated backlash against Muslims, then the backlash does not happen, and then there are spotty – and many unverified – claims of "anti-Muslim" hate reported, and finally, there are symbolic institutional overtures from media and government that acknowledge the "hate" mantra. It is astonishing during these episodes to watch the focus turn from barbaric acts of slaughter to the meme of Muslim victimization.

On the heels of introduction of House Resolution 569, Attorney General Loretta Lynch keynoted the Muslim Advocates'[319] gala dinner where she

---

[315] "Between Free Speech and Hate Speech: The Rabat Plan of Action, A Practical Tool To Combat Incitement To Hatred." Office of the High Commissioner United Nations Human Rights (21 Feb. 2013), http://www.ohchr.org/EN/NewsEvents/Pages/TheRabatPlanofAction.aspx.

[316] "From Resolution to Realization – How To Promote Effective Implementation of HRC Resolution 16/18." *Organization of Islamic Cooperation* (3-4 Jun. 2015), http://www.oic-oci.org/oicv2/subweb/istanbul_process/5/en/docs/IP_Session5_Concept%20Paper_Apr-2015.pdf.

[317] United States House of Representatives. "Condemning Violence, Bigotry, and Hateful Rhetoric Towards Muslims In The United States." (17 Dec. 2015), https://www.congress.gov/bill/114th-congress/house-resolution/569/text.

[318] "Beyer-Honda House Democrats Welcome 100th Co-Sponsor To Condemn Anti-Muslim Bigotry." *Alexandria News* (8 Jan. 2016). http://www.alexandrianews.org/2016/01/beyer-honda-house-democrats-welcome-100th-co-sponsor-to-condemn-anti-muslim-bigotry/.

[319] According to the Muslim Advocates website the group has "powerful connections in Congress and the White House" to ensure that "the concerns of American Muslims are heard by leaders at the highest levels of government." Muslim Advocates describes its role as "a watchdog of justice" using "the courts to bring to task those who threaten the rights of

described her "greatest fear" as an "incredibly disturbing rise of anti-Muslim rhetoric (accompanied by acts of violence)." She endorsed government action against those "lifting the mantle of anti-Muslim rhetoric" that "edges toward violence." Lynch noted that "over forty-five prosecutions" had arisen from hate-crime investigations that included "rhetoric" since 9-11.[320]

The Attorney General's suggestion, in principle, of criminal prosecution of speakers employing "anti-Muslim rhetoric" could indicate an institutional interest in removing such speech from protected status. Several years earlier, U.S. Attorney for the Eastern District of Tennessee Bill Killian suggested that some inflammatory material on Islam might implicate federal civil rights laws. This admonition was in response to complaints about a Tennessee politician who posted a picture of a man pointing a shotgun bearing the caption "How to wink at a Muslim." Killian was host of a townhall meeting to "educat[e] people about Muslims and their civil rights."[321]

General Lynch, and others in federal law enforcement, often characterize the type of speech that borders on being too provocative for constitutional protection as "inflammatory." This descriptor is generally used in contexts where the act of "incitement" is implied. Neither inflammatory, nor generally inciting, words are illegal unless accompanied by a legally defined threat. This conflation of terms blurs the line between unlawful and potentially offensive, yet protected, speech.

In 2016, the U.S. Attorney in Idaho, during an investigation into an alleged sexual assault of a 5-year-old girl by several juvenile Sudanese-Iraqi apparent refugees, warned that, "The spread of false information or *inflammatory* or threatening statements about the perpetrators or the crime itself reduces public safety and may violate federal law." (Emphasis added.) She chided residents on spreading falsehoods "about refugees [that] divides our communities."[322]

American Muslims." Muslim Advocates Website. *Available at*:
https://www.muslimadvocates.org/.

[320] "Attorney General Loretta Lynch at Muslim Advocates Dinner." *C-SPAN.org* (3 Dec. 2105); select the Loretta E. Lynch "speaker button" *at*: http://www.c-span.org/video/?401446-1/attorney-general-loretta-lynch-remarks-muslim-advocates.

[321] Tau, Byron. "Feds Suggest Anti-Muslim Speech Can Be Punished." *Politico* (31 May, 2013). http://www.politico.com/blogs/under-the-radar/2013/05/feds-suggest-anti-muslim-speech-can-be-punished-165163#ixzz40FJLRNvO.

[322] Volokh, Eugene. "Chief Idaho Federal Prosecutor Warns: 'The Spread of False Information or Inflammatory or Threatening Statements ... May Violate Federal Law.'" *The Washington Post* (26 Jun. 2016), https://www.washingtonpost.com/news/volokh-conspiracy/wp/2016/06/26/chief-idaho-federal-prosecutor-warns-the-spread-of-false-information-or-inflammatory-or-threatening-statements-may-violate-federal-law/.

This federal prosecutor's blanket castigation of speech on an issue of public concern, as generally protected by Supreme Court rulings, was misleading. Her ominous warning provided no definitional line between legally threatening (or libelous) speech and the otherwise robust zone of First Amendment-preserved speech rights. After criticism ensued, the federal attorney said that her statement had been misinterpreted and that she did not intend to threaten to prosecute anyone for First Amendment-protected speech.

Former CIA Director and retired four-star Army general David Patraeus joined this assault on free speech, when penning an op-ed for the *Wall Street Journal*, he declared that he has "grown increasingly concerned about inflammatory political discourse that has become far too common both at home and abroad against Muslims and Islam. He cautioned that "those who flirt with hate speech against Muslims should realize they are playing directly into the hands of al-Qaeda and the Islamic State."[323]

Social media sites, when allied with government actors, are increasingly wield censorship power. In September 2015, Facebook's Mark Zuckerberg committed to Germany's Chancellor Angela Merkel that he was working on issues like offensive posts on the refugee crisis.[324] Months later, Facebook announced the "Initiative for Civil Courage Online" to find and remove hate speech from the site.[325] Social media knows no borders, nor will any of these censorship measures. In fact, in June of 2016, many American Facebook users reported that the social media site blocked an article summarizing these anti-speech developments.[326]

With the ultimate capitulation of the social media giants that have signed on to EU hate speech codes: Facebook, YouTube, Twitter, and Microsoft, platforms for American-style robust and unfettered public policy debates

---

[323] Patraeus, David. "Anti-Muslim Bigotry Aids Islamist Terrorists." *Wall Street Journal* (13 May 2016), https://www.washingtonpost.com/opinions/david-petraeus-anti-muslim-bigotry-aids-islamist-terrorists/2016/05/12/5ab50740-16aa-11e6-924d-838753295f9a_story.html?hpid=hp_no-name_opinion-card-c%3Ahomepage%2Fstory.

[324] Chasmar, Jessica. "Angela Merkel Caught on Hot Mic Confronting Mark Zuckerberg over Racist Facebook Posts," *Washington Times*. (30, Sept 2015). http://www.washingtontimes.com/news/2015/sep/30/angela-merkel-caught-on-hot-mic-confronting-mark-z/.

[325] Griffin, Andrew. "Facebook Launches Initiative for Civil Courage Online to Delete Racist and Threatening Posts," *Independent*. (19 Jan, 2016). http://www.independent.co.uk/life-style/gadgets-and-tech/news/facebook-launches-initiative-for-civil-courage-online-to-delete-racist-and-threatening-posts-a6821581.html.

[326] Murray, Douglas. "The EU IS Coming to Close Down Your Free Speech," *Gatestone Institute*, (11, Jun, 2016), http://www.gatestoneinstitute.org/8234/eu-free-speech.

are severely jeopardized.[327] The parameters of controversial discussions in these arenas will now be controlled by those that claim offense, or feign offense to impose speech limits.

Even lawyers, the vanguards of the Bill of Rights, are under a new speech code. Once the American Bar Association passed a model rule for the purpose of state review and adoption, lawyers in compliant states when engaging in activity "related to the practice of law" will run the risk of sanction or disbarment for "harmful verbal conduct that manifest bias," among other things.[328]

These are but a few of the signs pointing to the increasingly precarious nature of American speech protections. Government officials and courts have not always upheld the First Amendment's broad guarantees. From the Alien and Sedition Act where the "sedition" component generally allowed the government to punish "malicious, false, or scandalous" expression, to the era of the so-called "bad tendency doctrine" where government was authorized to suppress speech if it was likely to cause harmful results, the nation has a somewhat checkered record on free speech. Americans should note that the "bad tendency doctrine" was applied to suppress the speech of abolitionists on the rationale that slaves *may* revolt if abolitionist activity encouraged them. Some local governments then acted on this authority to suppress speech based upon a surmised "tendency" rather than an evidentiary finding of "harmful results."

It wasn't until the 20th Century that the "clear and present danger" test asked the government for more justification before restricting speech. As judges were expected to test "whether the gravity of the 'evil', discounted by its improbability, justified such invasion of free speech as is necessary to avoid the danger,"[329] there were factual determinations required as to both the gravity of the harm and the likelihood that harm would result. Still, this was vague enough that it was hard to know where a judge might draw the line as the test involved the subjective balancing of several factors.

---

327 Hern, Alex. "Facebook, YouTube, Twitter and Microsoft Sign EU Hate Speech Code." *The Guardian* (31 May 2016), https://www.theguardian.com/technology/2016/may/31/facebook-youtube-twitter-microsoft-eu-hate-speech-code.

328 Volokh, Eugene. "A Speech Code for Lawyers, Banning Viewpoints That Express 'Bias,' Including in Law-Related Social Activities," *The Washington Post* (10 Aug. 2016), https://www.washingtonpost.com/news/volokh-conspiracy/wp/2016/08/10/a-speech-code-for-lawyers-banning-viewpoints-that-express-bias-including-in-law-related-social-activities-2/?utm_term=.2ea9ac5cf565; *also see*: Eugene Volokh's Federalist Society teleforum discussion, "Free Speech for Lawyers?" on podcast, *available at*: http://www.fed-soc.org/multimedia/detail/speech-code-for-lawyers-podcast..

329 *Dennis v. United States*, 341 U.S. 494, 510 (1951).

The rule that now determines what is controversial, but protected, speech and what is a potentially criminal utterance is based upon whether words "incite imminent lawless action including violence."[330] The speech typically called "hateful" is usually not specific in prompting imminent violence although hateful speech may be so provocative that it justifiably triggers the interest of law enforcement and suggests further investigation.

More to the point for this legal discussion, is the standing Heckler's Veto doctrine that denies coercive power to the dissenting group that threatens or does violence when offended by speech. In late 2015, the Sixth Circuit in an unusual en banc (full court) review decided one of the most dramatic Heckler's Veto cases. The fifteen-judge bench overturned the lower court, as well as a Sixth Circuit panel decision, to uphold speech protections. Very interestingly, four Republican-nominated judges voted that the speakers went too far to expect police protection.[331]

In his majority opinion, Judge Clay described the facts of the case this way:

> This case involves a group of self-described Christian [Bible Believers] evangelists preaching hate and denigration, even carrying a pig's head on a spike, to a crowd of Muslims, some of whom responded with threats of violence. The police thereafter removed, and ticketed, the evangelists to restore the peace. Bearing in mind the interspersed surges of ethnic, racial, and religious conflict that from time to time mar our national history, the constitutional lessons to be learned from the circumstances of this case are both timeless and markedly seasonable.[332]

He concluded that "[m]aintenance of the peace should not be achieved at the expense of the free speech"[333] and he said this about the efforts of hostile listeners to silence a speaker:

> The freedom to espouse sincerely held religious, political, or philosophical beliefs, especially in the face of hostile opposition, is too important to our democratic institution for it to be abridged simply due to the hostility of reactionary listeners who

---

[330] *Brandenburg v. Ohio*, 395 U.S. 444, 447 (1969) (recognizing the First Amendment rights of Ku Klux Klan members to advocate for white supremacy-based political reform achieved through violent means).

[331] Volokh, Eugene. "Sixth Circuit Rejects 'Heckler's Veto' as to Anti-Islam Speech by 'Bible Believers." *Washington Post* (28 Oct. 2015), https://www.washingtonpost.com/news/volokh-conspiracy/wp/2015/10/28/sixth-circuit-rejects-hecklers-veto-as-to-anti-islam-speech-by-bible-believers/.

[332] *Bible Believers vs. Wayne County*, United States Court of Appeals, No. 13-1635 (6th Cir. *en banc*, 2015); *available at*, http://www.ca6.uscourts.gov/opinions.pdf/15a0258p-06.pdf.

[333] *Id.*

may be offended by a speaker's message. If the mere possibility of violence were allowed to dictate whether our views, when spoken aloud, are safeguarded by the Constitution, surely the myriad views that animate our discourse would be reduced to the "standardization of ideas ... by ... [the] dominant political or community groups. Democracy cannot survive such a deplorable result. (Quotation marks and citations removed.)[334]

This clarion affirmation of the American right to robust debate, even when highly provocative, was hard won. But this result was a very close call. The prior two court renderings produced opposite results. Since an *en banc* (full federal appellate court) or Supreme Court review is not guaranteed (some cases are not appealed, appellate courts may decline an *en banc* review, and the Supreme Court does not agree to consider all cases presented) this case could easily have been finalized at the first appellate hearing where judges ruled that the speech in question was too provocative for First Amendment protection.

An important, but rarely utilized, American free speech legal doctrine is the First Amendment-based prohibition against "prior restraint." Basically, this Supreme Court-affirmed principle says that neither government nor judges may prevent most speech, and thus the remedy for unprotected expression is lawful punishment, *after the speech is uttered*, through civil lawsuits (i.e., defamation) and criminal prosecutions in the case of specific exhortation to violence. This means that government officials may not, discretionarily, create ad hoc rules to silence points of view that they do not want to hear. Legally speaking, government may not restrict speech based upon content or viewpoint.

In the context of a civic hearing, government agents may only respond to irrelevant comments to say that the input will not be considered in the application analysis. Officials then must keep an accurate and complete record of deliberations to show that such comments did not infect the objectivity of the process. To repeat a theme that runs through this book, succinct speech that addresses the civil process underway, will be the only constructively *persuasive* speech.

One controversial example of the prior restraint legal theory at work is that of Pastor Terry Jones who wanted to speak in 2011 and 2012 on issues of Islamist Sharia at a site across from the Dearborn, Michigan, mosque (at the time this mosque was called the largest in America). City and county government responded generally that the pastor's speech and demonstration may engender a violent response. The governments tried two different tactics: requiring, at one time, a "peace bond," and also, a

---

[334] *Id.*

"hold harmless agreement." By holding Jones liable for costs and fees, it seemed that government had discouraged the pastor(s) without issuing an outright denial. However, the court saw these discretionary tactics as content-based restrictions on speech and denied the constitutionality of both maneuvers.[335]

The Michigan chapter of the American Civil Liberties Union submitted an amicus brief in the "peace bond" case and called the city hall requirement "an unconstitutional 'prior restraint' on [Pastor Jones'] free speech."[336]

It bears repeating that speech related to matters of public concern receives a special level of protection and government efforts, whether the DOJ or local government, to restrict speech based upon content run counter to essential prior restraint warnings. There is no doubt though, that lawfare tactics utilizing even-failed legal methods, punish speakers by requiring a costly and traumatic legal defense. This predictably has a chilling effect on others in the community, the state, and the nation. This reality is not lost on those that would control speech rights.

And, as this historical overview demonstrates, America may be only one or two Supreme Court justices away from a return to the "bad tendency" days where speech may be proscribed for its tendency to provoke a societally difficult response. Judges who should recognize the coercive power of the Heckler's Veto, instead, try to find a category of insults that they believe to be too provocative.

Troubling free speech indicators show that robust speech protections are under societal and institutional assault. If Americans begin to self-censor and cower into the corners, the generous space afforded public debate will shrink accordingly. At the same time, Islamists will not stop complaining until they have reached their goal of censoring and criminalizing expression that scrutinizes and challenges their supremacist agenda.

When speaking or engaging in any part of this culture debate, research is critical preparation. Not all sources strive for factual information while providing sourcing that will be necessary for a credible presentation. An excellent tutorial is an Intelligence Squared debate on the proposition that

---

[335] *Stand Up American Now v. City of Dearborn*, No. 12-11471, Eastern Dist. of Michigan, *available at*:

http://www.thomasmore.org/sites/default/files/files/ORDER%20Granting%20TRO%20-%20Pastor%20Jones,%20Dearborn%20040512.pdf.

[336] *Michigan v. Terry Jones, et al*, Amicus Curiae Brief of The American Civil Liberties Union Fund of Michigan, *available at*:
http://www.aclumich.org/sites/default/files/TerryJonesACLUAmicus.pdf.

"Islam is Not a Religion of Peace."[337] Former Muslim Ayaan Hirsi Ali and British writer Douglas Murray won the debate by convincing more of the audience to support this proposition, than their opponents did to reject the statement. They were effective because Ali took a reasoned position based her comments on personal experience and philosophy. Hers was also a human story, and so powerfully compelling. Murray employed powerful logic, as well as irresistible wit. They spoke confidently; they argued their cases, and let the audience draw their own conclusions.

The following are some highly recommended information outlets. For those sites that do not offer an email subscription, it is possible to set up a search engine-generated news alert with an author's name to receive notifications of any new publications:

- The Investigative Project on Terrorism[338]

- Islamism Watch[339]

- Gatestone Institute: features highly credible investigative writers like Soeren Kern and Giulio Meotti[340]

- Andrew McCarthy, *National Review*[341]

- Center for Security Policy[342]

- Daily Roll Call: Exploring and Exposing Islam in America[343]

---

[337] Ali, Ayaan Hirsi and Douglas Murray. "Proposition: Islam Is A Religion of Peace." *intelligencesquaredus.org* (17 Apr. 2016), http://www.intelligencesquaredus.org/debates/islam-religion-peace; *also see,* Ayaan Hirsi Ali for PragerU on "Is Islam A Religion of Peace?" for a useful, incisive, 5-minute, essay on defending Western traditions by supporting the efforts of vital Muslim dissidents and reformers: https://www.facebook.com/prageru/?hc_ref=NEWSFEED&fref=nf.

[338] The Investigative Project, http://www.investigativeproject.org/.

[339] David Swindle, blogger at Middle East Forum's *Islamist Watch* says: "I want to support moderate Muslims as they make the case from within their own religion against the Islamists. - For many years I hesitated to stand with moderate Muslims because I feared theirs was a lost cause. I think the new technologies that have already emerged and that will emerge in the coming decades will effectively level the playing field, such that the Muslims whose theology reconciles with modernity will ultimately be able to triumph. They just need to be emotionally encouraged, financially supported, and their future leaders promoted in the media." http://www.islamist-watch.org/

[340] See biographies and archives for these analysts *at:* http://www.gatestoneinstitute.org/author/Soeren+Kern, *and* http://www.gatestoneinstitute.org/author/Giulio+Meotti.

[341] Andrew C. McCarthy, http://www.nationalreview.com/author/andrew-c-mccarthy.

[342] Center for Security Policy, http://www.centerforsecuritypolicy.org/

[343] Daily Roll Call. http://dailyrollcall.com/. (Much of the site's substance addresses Islam as a monolithic problem, and does not distinguish the reformist Muslims from Islamist activists,

- ACT! for America Education Reform Project[344]
- Gates of Vienna blog[345]
- Clarion Project: information consolidator
- Fousesquawk monitors UC Irvine and Southern California radicalization efforts
- Counter Jihad Coalition,[346] known for provocative stance, but exemplary of local efforts

It should always be the goal to speak artfully while understanding that even well-intentioned and informed comments will be taken out of context. This is an arena fraught with emotion and deeply held convictions. There are times that additional clarification or perspective may be needed but, if a speaker is thoughtful when making his or her case, an apology is rarely in order.

Consider the firestorm that hit Mayor Beth Van Duyne of Irving, Texas in October 2015 when the "clock boy" controversy landed in her city. This incident followed on the heels of the mayor's hotly contested opposition to an Islamic tribunal's establishment in her city and her support for the "American Laws for American Courts" state legislation. The mayor was pressured from many national sources (while receiving vulgar email threats[347]) to abandon her support for school district policies and standard police protocols.[348] Rather than back down, she repeated reasonable and rational reasons for her positions. She was calm, and confident that her decisions best served her constituency and furthered her civic duty to protect schoolchildren. Much of the community rallied around her leadership.

Another constructive example was offered when Colonial Williamsburg was attacked for referring to 9-11 and the terror attack on the Twin Towers in a February 2016 Super Bowl commercial about adversity that the nation has overcome. The city also issued this tweet: "Including WTC is powerful &

---

but the creator, Cathy Hinner, is a thoughtful former police officer who provides thought-provoking material.)

[344] "Textbook Reform Project." *Actforamerica.com* (2016), http://www.actforamerica.org/get-the-facts/our-issues/empowering-women-protecting-children/textbook-reform-project.

[345] Gates of Vienna, http://gatesofvienna.net/.

[346] Counterjihad Coalition, http://counterjihadcoalition.org/brochures/..

[347] Hope, Merrill. "Texas Mayor Target of Vile Online Attacks over 'Clock Boy' Ahmed." *Breitbart Texas* (10 Oct. 2015), http://www.breitbart.com/big-government/2015/10/10/exclusive-texas-mayor-target-vile-online-attacks-clock-boy-ahmed/.

[348] Hope, Merrill. "Texas Boy Arrested Because of Zero Tolerance Policies Not Islamophobia." *Breitbart Texas* (16 Sept. 2015), http://www.breitbart.com/texas/2015/09/16/texas-boy-arrested-because-of-zero-tolerance-policies-not-islamophobia/.

subject to debate. But Am. Hist. is full of tragedies & triumphs. It made us who we are today. We must remember." Controversy ensued, but the city did not back down or apologize. Colonial Williamsburg simply explained that America should "not shy away from these difficult moments in our history because they have made us who we are just as surely as our many triumphs."[349]

A very different process and result played out in a Washington State community when an effort to involve residents in a mosque permit hearing went off track and ended badly. Not only did the effort result in a series of apologies, but the entire episode was also used to underscore anti-Muslim "hate" and to associate such speech with crimes. This is the worst outcome for the cause of free speech, as the public often reacts with emotion and calls for a reflexive policy action.

When a mosque was planned for Mukilteo, a suburb of Seattle, a local aerospace business owner mailed out an informational postcard to local residents providing basic hearing details.[350] He intended the post cards to be anonymously mailed but, over time, businessman Steve Zieve was identified as the author and various past "anti-Islamic" email communications were revealed. The Washington State Commission on Human Rights launched an investigation into the matter and media reports revealed that the result, in part, was to require Mr. Zieve to participate in several meetings apparently designed to instruct him on tolerance, including some sessions with CAIR officials.[351] The upshot was a series of apologies and a second mass mailing, this time the post card conveyed Mr. Zieve's apology for speech that may incite others to act in a hateful manner.

Only Mr. Zieve knows all of the details involved in this process and the reasons for his final actions, but the result played directly into the meme that certain speech causes others to attack Muslims.[352]

It does take some finesse to construct an explanation that does not cross into an apology, in the cases that an apology is simply not warranted. When

---

[349] Mendoza, Jessica. "Colonial Williamsburg Ad Evokes 9/11: Tasteful Tribute or Blatant Exploitation?" *The Christian Science Monitor* (8 Feb. 2016), http://www.csmonitor.com/USA/Society/2016/0208/Colonial-Williamsburg-ad-evokes-9-11-tasteful-tribute-or-blatant-exploitation.

[350] Zieve first post card, http://mosquesinamerica.org/wp-content/uploads/2016/10/347_Zieve1.jpeg

[351] Sayler, Sharon, "Community Turns Out to Hear About Proposed Mukilteo Mosque," *The Herald* (25, May, 2016), http://www.heraldnet.com/article/20160525/NEWS01/160529444; and see the Washington Human Rights Commission Website for mission statement that relates to cases like the Mukilteo Mosque inquiries: "About Us," *Washington State Human Rights Commission*, http://www.hum.wa.gov/about-us.

[352] Zieve final post card, http://mosquesinamerica.org/wp-content/uploads/2016/10/349_Zieve2.jpg

a position is based thoughtfully upon historic and moral foundations, there is ample room to expand and explain by providing additional context. However, an unwarranted rush to an apology can be tacit participation in censorship. If speech that is offensive is censored, the offended operator learns that he can shape society by wielding veto power over selected speech. Pointed lessons from history and contemporary Europe offer ample illustration of this point and underscore the imperative of preserving free speech.

If Americans voluntarily vacate the robust protection afforded speech on matters of public concern, this surrender cannot be blamed on the courts or on government. The Constitution and the Supreme Court have limited what government and the courts may do to restrict speech. No, various surrenders on free speech are first coming from citizens who feel the chill of disapproval and decide to shrink into the corners. Free and robust speech will only continue to be protected in the public square if citizens exhibit determined interest in exercising their expressive rights.

22. Ask An Imam

I mams are the hub around which mosque activity revolves. And unlike Western religious norms, the mosque is often the center of personal, familial, and civic life. The clerics in Sharia-centric mosques seek to fulfill the roles of political and legal authorities. American Muslims report that marriages and divorces are often only filed at the mosque, bypassing civil authorities. Local residents are beginning to ask what right they have to know if the mosque on the corner is working to supplant the American societal compact.

Imams often say that they want to be accessible to the community at large, will offer programs that include locals, and that they plan to be accountable to residents. The chairman for the AFYFC mosque generously promised at the CUP hearing to maintain an open and friendly relationship with neighbors.[353] Instead, this Islamic center and many others may be described as generally closed, exclusive, and hostile to the community.[354]

These imams do seem, however, very anxious to be involved in strategically arranged interfaith public relations. In many showcase interfaith events, imams are happy to be featured if the script is closely controlled and all pastoral participants agree to present the politically palatable version of Islam and life as a Muslim.

As with leadership from any religious organization, mosque leaders in America are not exempt from challenge. Americans are not just concerned about unequivocal imam condemnations of what happens beyond our borders where unimaginable brutality is occurring in the name of Islam. It is their business, as well, to be highly concerned about whether newcomers in their neighborhoods are fully assimilating.

It starts with laying a concrete foundation. Is mosque leadership participating in public forums where they can refer to a record of lectures, op-ed commentary, or interviews that demonstrate unwavering

---

[353] City of Bloomington City Council Meeting for Review of AFYFC Application, Mar. 24, 2011, https://www.youtube.com/watch?v=wJ-9ci-gB3A&feature=youtu.be. (Sampling of pledges: "All problems will be solved. A new webpage will be constructed to help Smith Park neighbors communicate suggestions, ideas, complaints or even appreciation with the center from work or home. We will not tolerate any discomfort or inconvenience to the Smith Park neighbors and we will promote good relations with them. If the neighborhood would like to have meetings on a monthly basis to discuss neighborhood improvements, etc. that can be done as well. Our door will always be open for neighbors.")

[354] Hegseth, Pete. "How Terrorists Recruit in 'Little Mogadishu' of Minneapolis." Fox News (6 May 2016), http://video.foxnews.com/v/4881244287001/how-terrorists-recruit-in-little-mogadishu-of-minneapolis/?#sp=show-clips.

commitment to American imperatives of individual liberty and self-determination? Have they called for critical thinking and have they challenged imam control of all issues including mosque and state? Have they demanded an end to the genocide of Christians and others in the Middle East? Have they worked to expose and reform the unequal treatment of women under Sharia codes?

Some American Muslims have proven their patriotism and commitment to reform by doing all this at every opportunity. The standard that they have set is an example of how Muslims may be a powerfully positive benefit to American culture. Imams should be asked if they endorse their Muslim pledge of alignment with American constitutional standards: the important and declarative Muslim Reform Manifesto. [355]

It is not out of line for neighbors to keep a religious leader honest. Americans would have no qualms about holding leaders of other faiths to their pledges. Of course, there is no way to force transparency or interaction. But there is a way to put local imams on record – or the record becomes *avoidance of a record*. And a record of even that pattern of avoidance is important to chronicle.

There is a known Koranic instruction that Sharia adherents have used to justify the practice of making false statements with the intent of obfuscating Islamic practices and tactics that would be repugnant to Western sensibilities.[356] Whether Islamists employ this tactic known as taqiyya, or just seek to push the envelope, engagement with local mosques and leadership is the only method of knowing where there are Islamic communities that are committed to combating radicalization.

From every Open Mosque Day to all open public forums where Islamic leadership participates, the questions regarding what plan is in place for encouraging assimilation and what strategy exists to defeat radicalization should be asked. The Muslims for Reform declaration should be presented at every opportunity as it enunciates the four main constitutional conflicts that Islamists have with American cultural precepts: separation of mosque and state, free speech, freedom to choose a religion or no religion, and equality for women.[357]

Alternatively, accountability committees may present a fundamental human rights manifesto like key sections from the 1948 United Nations Declaration

---

[355] Muslim Reform Movement Facebook page:
https://www.facebook.com/MuslimReformMovement/timeline.

[356] Ibrahim, Ray. "Tawriya: Islamic Doctrine Permits 'Creative Lying.'" *Raymond Ibrahim* (28 Feb. 2012),

http://www.raymondibrahim.com/2012/02/28/tawriya-lying/.

[357] Muslims for Reform, *supra*, at note 209.

of Human Rights. Public recognition of sections like Article 18 and Article 19 demonstrate recognition of foundational rights like "freedom of thought, conscience, and religion, including the freedom to change religion or belief" and "freedom of opinion and expression."[358] These are indisputable cornerstones to Western civilizational cultures and can be presented as an affirmative endorsement of widely recognized societal norms.

If Muslims who have not committed to the reform elements are engaged in interfaith activities, public venues are an excellent time to establish clear loyalties to constitutional principles and assimilation goals. Also, pastors, priests, and rabbis should be urged to inquire as to what serious challenges these Islamic leaders have issued to the radical and extremist elements that persecute Christians, Jews, and minority faiths around the world. Non-Muslim faith leaders have no business giving public credibility to Muslim clerics who have not taken a strong stand in the media, in the mosque, and in the public square on this issue, as well as having publicly committed to the aforementioned foundational American principles.

Accountability groups may consider inviting informed pastors and rabbis to speak as counterweights to the unquestioning "interfaith" priests, pastors and rabbis that often show up to tout the virtues of Islamic practices. Unfortunately, too many Christian and Jewish leaders offer the hand of ecumenical fellowship without inspecting the record of a particular Islamic group or its affiliations. It is up to thinking faith leadership to vet interfaith representatives who claim to speak on behalf of a particular denomination or belief.

Islamist leaders may be representing an organization that not only tolerates religious persecution in other countries of all "others," but approves of it. The now systemic exclusion and barbaric punishment of religious minorities in many Islamic countries is epidemic and Muslim leaders should be aware that Americans expect Muslim leaders emphatically to both condemn it, and use their influence to counter it. Maajid Nawaz, Muslim founding chairman of the Quilliam Foundation in the United Kingdom agrees, and he urges, "We Muslims must admit there are challenging Koranic passages that require reinterpretation today. Reformers either win, and get religion-neutral politics, or lose, and get ISIL-style theocracy."[359]

This is not to say that other religious communities should shun Muslims by any means. The reality is that there is an obligation to deny credibility and

---

[358] "Universal Declaration of Human Rights." *The United Nations* (10 Dec. 1948), http://www.un.org/en/universal-declaration-human-rights/index.html.

[359] Qureshi, Nabeel. "The Quran's Deadly Role in Inspiring Belgian Slaughter:." *USA Today* (22 Mar. 2016), http://www.usatoday.com/story/opinion/2016/03/22/radicalization-isil-islam-sacred-texts-literal-interpretation-column/81808560/

support to Islamists who will then exploit the bona fides of the interfaith fraternity to insinuate themselves further into the pluralistic system with the intent to undermine it.

Also, Christians and Jews owe it to their brothers and sisters that are being cruelly persecuted elsewhere in the name of Islam to demand condemnation of these practices from American Muslim leaders. Statistics show Christians to be the most persecuted religious minorities in the world today.[360] If American Muslim leadership does not take a much more active role in criticizing these abuses and demanding reform, Americans are left to conclude that they condone it.

If past examples are any indication, Islamic leaders will likely respond that requests for such a commitment will be taken under advisement. But such deflection gives community members the opportunity to present these statements again at future public events for the purpose of holding Muslim leaders to basic American constitutional and internationally-recognized fundamental human rights conventions. If imams and Islamic authorities continue to shirk public commitment to these accepted Western precepts, a skeptical media and uninformed public will learn they cannot square the platitudes and double-speak with a refusal to adopt a very basic statement reflecting foundational values.

One distraction tactic that Islamists will often employ when asked for a commitment to indisputable and well-settled human rights is to complain of various American or Western so-called "violations" of international law norms or human rights understandings: e.g., the U.S. military's use of Predator drones and the incidence collateral damage. However, just as the land-use hearing context is simply for the purpose of considering the merits of a particular application, citizens are on solid and high moral ground when simply asking the mosque leadership, publicly and emphatically, to embrace non-controversial human rights standards.

---

[360] "Persecution Report." (2016), http://www.persecutionreport.org/; *also see*, "Subcommittee on the Middle East and North Africa: Testimony of Nina Shea, Director of the Hudson Institute's Center for Religious Freedom." U.S. House of Representatives (25 June, 2013). http://docs.house.gov/meetings/FA/FA16/20130625/101036/HHRG-113-FA16-Wstate-SheaN-20130625.pdf.

CONCLUSION AND SUMMARY

This book has laid out the challenge facing the American people from Islamists who seek to undermine Western civilization, and who have become skilled in using America's celebrated liberties to build an infrastructure for that purpose. It behooves those of us who love this country, its Constitution and the freedoms it guarantees to protect what we have inherited for future generations.

Throughout these pages, practical steps for doing that have been offered, born of first-hand experience with zoning boards, city councils, school boards, newspaper editorial committees, state legislatures and courts across the United States. To summarize, here are some of the most important take-aways:

RECOMMENDED READING

Read these books both to understand and to gain perspective on the civilizational clash with Islamism. The first grouping does not deal with history or religion; rather these selections present the insights of thoughtful individual authorities and their very personal valiant struggles to wake up citizens of the West. These are the vital accounts that tell the powerful backstories as these are what must inform the debate in the public square. Use the words of these authors to share their first-hand insights:

- Dr. Zuhdi Jasser's A Battle for the Soul of Islam: An American Muslim Patriot's Fight to Save His Faith to learn of the reformers' sincerity, courage, and commitment.

- Ayaan Hirsi Ali's *Heretic: Why Islam Needs a Reformation Now* for a former Muslim's practical and passionate pleas to Americans to defend Enlightenment ideals against Islamism.

- Dr. Qanta Ahmed's *In the Land of Invisible Women: A Female Doctor's Journey in the Saudi Kingdom* for sensitive insight into an intellectual woman's fight to identify Islamism as totalitarian and toxic to Muslims in general, and the West at large.

- Rifqa Bary's *Hiding in the Light: Why I Risked Everything to Leave Islam and Follow Jesus* to learn how badly our system treated a young Muslim girl that chose to exercise freedom to leave a religion, in this case, Islam.

- Andrew McCarthy's *The Grand Jihad: How Islam and the Left Sabotage America* for an expert and relevant tutorial on the nature of the threat.

- Mohamed Akram's *The Explanatory Memorandum on the General Strategic Goal of the Group in North America*, which was entered into evidence in the United States v. Holy Land Foundation et al. trial in 2007-2008.

MOSQUE PERMIT PROCESSING

- Organize an accountability group and create committees that will: perform research; conduct outreach to public officials; designate and prepare individuals to make public comments; and hold government officials, imams and mosques accountable.

- Get the facts regarding permit applications for community centers and mosques *early in the process*. Hold the city or county to an assessment of *actual* use, rather than idealized projections, by researching the prior activity level of the applicant organization, or its parent or sister organizations. Analyze the application for disclosure of *full range* of activities and participation compare to *similar* assembly or religious uses that have been approved. Compare conditions and restrictions placed on prior permits.

- Prepare for enforcement. Ensure that limitations on capacity, concurrent uses of buildings and parking are clearly enunciated and that triggers for enforcement and CUP review are unequivocal.

- Do thorough homework. Master the applicable zoning codes and ascertain that *all* requirements are met. Watch video recordings of other mosque land use hearings to learn how staff reports are used and what is line of questioning for applicants. This is important for the purpose of organizing focused presentations. Also, understand what is considered constructive questioning and commentary during the open public comment sessions.

- Insist upon technical accuracy and full details. The community is entitled to answers that describe the complete scope and intensity of the proposed use.

- Understand the role of RLUIPA (federal religious land use statute) and anticipate institutional awareness of the restrictions placed upon zoning officials. Also, be prepared for an official mindset that RLUIPA ties the hands of city zoning officials. In a broad sense, it does, but when attorneys or city managers oversimplify RLUIPA and impress officials with fear of lawsuits or government intervention to the point that zoning questions are not satisfied, make it clear that the application of RLUIPA protection likely has gone too far.

- Inspect the process to establish that published requirements are not waived in an exceptional fashion and that officials are not communicating outside of public hearings (in violation of state open meeting act terms). Be prepared to use the state records act request mechanism to learn of applicant to staff communications, staff to official board communications and discussion content between official voting members.

- Do *not* use the comment session at a land use public hearing to berate Muslims, lecture about Sharia, or quote the Koran. Questions about anti-radicalization strategies or discussion of applied Sharia may be legitimate subjects of debate in the public square, but a land use hearing is not the venue to introduce these issues. Stick to relevant issues that implicate zoning regulations and the concurrent community concern of the ancillary threat of radicalism to safety and security.

- Establish a fund for possible attorney consultation and preparation of potential professional traffic, parking, trip count, fire code, or infrastructure studies if needed to demonstrate likely – rather than idealized – impact of the use. Also, funds may be needed for a public records act requests or copying of archived documents.

- Keep comments brief, but elegant, accurate, and appealing. As important as it is to exercise the American right to full and free debate, it is also smart to craft compelling arguments. Consider the audience and work to persuade. Telling personal stories and citing anecdotal examples is a powerful way to establish common ground. The ability to convince the uninformed depends upon getting them to stop and listen.

POST-APPLICATION FOLLOW-UP WITH MOSQUES

- In the event of mosque application approval, prepare statements to outline zero community tolerance for radicalization activities and issue challenges to transparency and openness. Establish your community as a "no-rad zone" and demonstrate that Islamist radicalization will not be tolerated in this town. This means involving the smallest units of neighborhoods within cities and counties. Ask for public commitment (videotape where allowed) to fundamental rights by presenting mosque leadership with the cornerstone principles from Dr. Zuhdi Jasser's writing and the Muslims for Reform Manifesto: the separation of mosque and state, free speech, freedom of religion, and equal rights for women.[361] Some follow-on public forums may provide opportunities for presentation of the "Muslim Pledge for Religious Freedom and Safety from Harm for Former Muslims" statement for signature (and the aforementioned freedom of conscience and expression affirmations from the 1948 United Nations Declaration on Human Rights):

> I renounce, repudiate and oppose any physical intimidation, or worldly and corporal punishment, of apostates who leave Islam, change their religion from Islam to another religion, or express unbelief in Islam, in whatever way that punishment may be determined or carried out by myself or any other Muslim including the family of the apostate, community, Mosque leaders, Sharia court or judge, and Muslim government or regime.[362]

- Prepare to monitor mosque activities. Whether via blogs or websites, identify radical speakers and materials. Exercise the same level of free speech as Islamist operatives and counter radical events with demonstrations to expose such Islamists, using their own words.

- Monitor enforcement of permit terms to ensure there is no slippage. The city or county must be held accountable for timely enforcement of code violations or permit infractions. These matters should be brought to the attention of those who are politically responsible for maintaining the peace and public safety as soon as any violations occur. It is difficult to evade the issue if many residents present concerns at the very next public meeting of the councilmembers.

EXERCISE YOUR FREEDOMS

- Speak out, or watch speech freedoms shrink.

- Reasoned and human-interest based speech is persuasive speech.

- Above all, plant the flag and hold the ground. Every skirmish is important: For example, keep Christmas, Thanksgiving and Valentine's Day on the calendar and Islamic-biased curriculum out of the classroom.

---

[361] Muslims for Reform, *supra*, note 209.

[362] "2012 Freedom Pledge." *Former Muslims United* (4 Jul. 2012), http://formermuslimsunited.org/the-pledge/cover-letter-pledge/

- Keep interfaith dialogue to faith and not an embrace of unexamined and radical clerics.

Some mosques operate within permit allowances and have proven to be good neighbors. The mosques that have exceeded limits, misrepresented use intentions, and exploited the constitutional religious veil between church and state to radicalize, however, have created potential concerns for all communities that are anticipating mosque construction.

Radicalization trends add another layer of concern in light of current and past mosque extremist activity. Permanent accountability committees that will begin by monitoring the permit hearing process and then will continue to watch the character of speakers and content of materials can do much to hold local officials and mosque leadership to clear legal and cultural standards.

Efforts to engage the Muslim community while upholding American constitutional ideals, cultural mores, and legal guidelines will provide a strong foundation for good will and assimilation outreach.

Contrary to popular thinking, multiculturalism and tolerance should not be ends in themselves. Rather, these goals, as clearly re-defined, should be reached via commitments to exceptionally American values. Former Muslim Ayaan Hirsi Ali writes that Western preference for tolerance over fidelity to core values has left moderate Muslims without true defenders. Her experience as a translator for social services agencies in Holland has compelled her to warn America of the dangers of Islamic separatism:

> Holland's multiculturalism – its respect for Muslims' way of doing things – wasn't working. It was depriving many women and children of their rights. Holland was trying to be tolerant for the sake of consensus but the consensus was empty. The immigrants' culture was being preserved at the expense of their women and children and the detriment of the immigrants' integration into Holland. Many Muslims never learned Dutch and rejected Dutch values of tolerance and personal liberty. They married relatives from their home villages and stayed, inside Holland, in their tiny bubble of Morocco or Mogadishu.[363]

Europe's experience with segregated Muslim communities is a lesson to Americans. The most prescient warning, often attributed to the widely regarded and authoritative Muslim Brotherhood cleric, Yusuf Al-Qaradawi, illustrates the intentional migration design to exploit Western freedoms

---

[363] Ayaan Hirsi Ali, *Infidel* 246 (Free Press 2007).

while working to establish Sharia supremacy: "With your democratic laws, we will colonize you. With our Koranic laws, we will dominate you."[364]

If Muslim immigrants are to be persuaded to reject the "bubble" settlements that Ms. Ali describes, and instead, embrace Western-styled communities, the invitation best comes from modernized Muslims. Giulio Meotti, cultural editor for *Il Foglio* in Italy, heralds Muslim dissidents as heroic in the tradition of Cold Warriors like Lech Walesa and Alexander Solzhenitsyn. He urges "financial, moral and political support" for these "Friends of Western Civilization" and he faults the "elites of the West" for slandering them.

Meotti notes that these Muslim dissidents are considered "traitors" within their communities, and that they must feel they are standing "alone against all."[365] He points to, among others, the example of Paris imam Hassen Chalghoumi who preaches while wearing a bullet-proof vest and is accompanied on the streets by five police officers with semiautomatic weapons. Chalghoumi is known for backing the ban on burkas and paying tribute to the victims of Charlie Hebdo.[366] If these convicted Muslims are willing to confront the Islamic supremacists, why would we not stand with them?

Dr. Qanta Ahmed, a British-born Muslim of Pakistani origin, who practiced in Saudi-Arabia, calls herself an "anti-Islamist Muslim." She warns Westerners who refuse to identify totalitarian Islamists: "It is *nonviolent* Islamism that legitimizes Islamism's escalating jihadist terrorism. It is nonviolent Islamism that preaches virulent anti-Americanism and anti-globalization, seducing both Western academics and Islamist sympathizers." (Emphasis in original.)[367] Dr. Ahmed appears regularly on CNN and other media outlets to urge Americans to support the pluralistic Muslims who stand against Islamism and for individual liberty and rights of conscience.

When Islamic organizations appear before local government boards to promise openness, adherence to the rule of law, and support for American cultural customs, American constitutional generosity is pre-disposed to give them the benefit of the doubt.

---

[364] Usually attributed in French writing to Sheikh Yusuf Al-Qaradawi but an early version of the quote appears in an October 1999 article appearing in the French newspaper *La Croix* where it is attributed to "influential Muslim": http://www.la-croix.com/Archives/1999-10-22/Rassemblement-interreligieux-_NP_-1999-10-22-485627.

[365] Meotti, Giulio, "The West's Most Important Ally: Islam's Dissidents," *Gatestone Institute*, (12, Jun, 2016). http://www.gatestoneinstitute.org/8227/muslim-dissidents.

[366] *Id.*

[367] Ahmed, Qanta. "As Islamism Marches West, Pluralist Muslims Must Stop Its Advance." *National Review* (Apr. 2016), http://www.nationalreview.com/article/434339/islamism-marches-west-pluralist-muslims-must-stop-it.

Therefore, it is up to local citizens to monitor these commitments and prove their veracity. If Americans do not run to this opportunity in their own communities, we have only ourselves to blame when the American identity is splintered and ultimately re-defined.

ABOUT THE AUTHOR

Karen Lugo has worked at the intersection of law, politics, and culture for years. As a lawyer, constitutional law instructor, and clinical professor, she taught foundational constitutional principles and also co-authored briefs to the United States Supreme Court with some of the nation's leading constitutional scholars. These appellate briefs covered issues like expressive religious rights, material support for terrorism, First Amendment free speech, NSA surveillance, government-sponsored prayer, federalism, and separation of powers. Her father was a minister and Ms. Lugo has defended religious assembly interests under RLUIPA (federal law) provisions. She is known for her interest in building alliances with America's compatible Muslims who are seeking constitutionally sound responses to Islamism's challenges.

www.ingramcontent.com/pod-product-compliance
Lightning Source LLC
Chambersburg PA
CBHW021426170526
45164CB00001B/113